SEVEN PLAYS

£4

SEVEN PLAYS

SAM SHEPARD

Introduction by Richard Gilman

faber and faber
LONDON · BOSTON

First published in the USA and simultaneously in Canada in 1981
by Bantam Books Inc., New York
First published in Great Britain in 1985
by Faber and Faber Limited
3 Queen Square London WC1N 3AU
Reprinted 1988

Printed in Great Britain by
Redwood Burn Limited, Trowbridge, Wiltshire

ACKNOWLEDGMENTS

Lines from 'Alberto Rojas Jimenez Comes Running' from
Selected Poems of Pablo Neruda by Pablo Neruda; © Grove
Press, Inc. 1962. By permission of Grove Press Inc.
Lines from 'Red Sails in the Sunset' copyright 1935 by The
Peter Maurice Music Co., Ltd., London, England; copyright
for USA and Canada buy Shapiro, Bernstein & Co., Inc., New
York, U.S. Copyright renewed and assigned to Shapiro,
Bernstein & Co. Inc. By permisson of Shapiro, Bernstein &
Co. and EMI Music Publishing Ltd.

British Library Cataloguing in Publication Data

Shepard, Sam
Seven plays.
I. Title
812'.54   PS3569.H394

ISBN 0–571–13615–X

For my father, Sam

CONTENTS

SEVEN PLAYS

SAM SHEPARD

INTRODUCTION

by Richard Gilman

Not many critics would dispute the proposition that Sam Shepard is our most interesting and exciting American playwright.

Fewer, however, can articulate just where the interest and excitement lie. There is an extraordinarily limited and homogeneous vocabulary of critical writing about Shepard, a thin lexicon of both praise and detraction. Over and over one sees his work described as "powerful"—"brutally" or "grimly" or "oddly" powerful, but muscular beyond question. Again and again one hears him called "surrealist" or "gothic" or, a bit more infrequently, a "mythic realist" (the most colorful appellation I've seen, affixed to Shepard by our most rococo reviewer, is the "bucking bronco" of American theater). To his detractors he is always "obscure," usually "willfully" so, and always "undisciplined." But even some of his enemies acknowledge his "theatrical magic," always with that phrase, and admirers and some enemies alike point to his plays' "richness of texture," always in those words.

The same sort of ready-made language can be found in discussions of Shepard's themes or motifs. Nearly everyone is agreed that the great majority of his plays deal with one or more of these matters: the death (or betrayal) of the American dream; the decay of our national myths; the growing mechanization of our lives; the search for roots; the travail of the family. (The trouble is, this cluster of related notions would apply to a good many other American writers as well.)

Most critics find it hard clearly to extract even these ideas from Shepard's plays, many of which are in fact extraordinarily resistant to thematic exegesis. Shepard's most ardent enthusiasts have got round the problem by arguing that he isn't (or wasn't; there's been a significant change in his latest plays, which I'll take up later) talking *about* anything but rather *making* something, a familiar notion in avant-garde circles and, as far as it goes, a correct one. They point out that his genius lies not in ideas or thought but in the making of images; he speaks more to the eye, or to the ear (in terms of expressive sound, though not necessarily in terms of immediate sense), than to the mind.

I don't fully accept this argument, though I see its virtues, and I do share in some of the prevailing uncertainties. I don't mean that I'm uncertain about the value of Shepard's work, but I find the question of "themes" troubling, primarily because I detect a confusion in *him* about them. But the real difficulty I share with many critics isn't so much deciding what the work is as knowing how to write about what it is. How to wield a critical vocabulary that won't be composed of clichés and stock phrases, how devise a strategy of discourse to deal usefully with this dramatist who slips out of all the categories?

I hold Shepard before me as the subject of this essay. There he is, changing his skin as though by an annual molting; seeming, and often being, disorderly, sometimes to the point of chaos; obeying—until recently at any rate—no fixed or familiar principles of dramatic construction; borrowing, like an exultant magpie, from every source in or out of the theater; being frequently obscure, though never, I think, "willfully" so.

If there's a more nearly perfect exemplar of a cultural education gained ("absorbed" is a better word) in the fifties than Sam Shepard, I can't imagine who it might be. I first saw him at the Open Theater in 1965, a James Dean-like youth with an un-Dean-like intellectual glint in his eyes. Even after I'd overcome my initial dismay at such easy and untutored confidence, it took me awhile to see that there wasn't any reason he couldn't be a playwright or anything else. For the fifties, out of which he came, or sidled, was the era in which two things started to happen of great importance to our subsequent culture. One was that the distance between "high" and "low" in art began to be obliterated, and the other was that the itch for "expression," for hurling the self's words against anonymity and silence, began to beat down the belief in the necessity for formal training, apprenticeship and growth, that had always been held in regard to drama or any art.

Shepard is much more than the product of these developments, but they do infect or, from another judgment, animate him in profound ways. He was born in Illinois but grew up in Southern California, and that vivid, disastrous milieu has been the psychic and imaginative ground of all his plays, whatever their literal geography might be. He has said that he lived in a "car culture for the young" and that the Southern California towns held a "kind of junk magic." In a few autobiographical fragments and elliptical interviews he tells of a life resembling that in the movie *American Graffiti*, only tougher, shrewder, more seeded with intimations of catastrophe in the midst of swagger.

Shepard seems to have come out of no literary or theatrical tradition at all but precisely from the breakdown or absence—on the level of art if not of commerce—of all such traditions in America. Such a thing is never a clean, absolute stride away from the ruins; fragments of tradition, bits of history, cling to every razed site and to one's shoes. But in his case one does see a movement with very little cultural time at its back, or only the thinnest slice of the immediate past, a *willed* movement, it might be said, for one sometimes suspects Shepard of wanting to be thought *sui generis*, a self-creation. That he must, for example, have been influenced by Jack Gelber's 1959 play *The Connection*, by some of Ronald Tavel's work, by certain aspects of Pinter and, more recently, by Edward Bond, as well as by elements of what we call theatrical "absurdity," are things he has never mentioned.

What we do know is that in a sense he's a writer in spite of himself. In 1971 he said that "I don't want to be a playwright, I want to be a rock and roll star . . . I got into writing plays because I had nothing else to do. So I started writing to keep from going off the deep end." Naturally, there's much disingenuousness in this, something tactical, but it oughtn't to be disbelieved entirely. Shepard's plays sometimes do give off a whiff of reluctance to being plays, a hint of dissatisfaction with the form. And his recent incarnation as a film actor increases our sense that he's had something else, or something additional, in mind all along.

For what was true for him when he started (as it was true for the general culture in its youthful sectors), was that a mode of expression existed more compelling, more seductive and more in affinity with the outburst of the personal than writing in the old high formal sense. In light of Shepard's rock ambitions, listen to him on the genre. It made, he said (without punctuation) "movies theater books painting and art go out the window none of it stands a chance against the Who the Stones and Old Yardbirds Credence Traffic the Velvet Underground Janis and Jimi . . ."

Nevertheless Shepard did pluck drama from outside the window and became a writer. But the influence of rock is major and pervasive, if most direct in his early plays. It can be seen in the plays' songs, of course, but also, more subtly, in a new kind of stage language, contemporary in a harsh, jumpy way, edging, as both rock lyrics and rock talk do, between pseudo-professional argot and a personal tone of cocksure assertion. It is almost hermetic at times, but one can always detect a type of savage complaint and a belligerent longing. Thematically, rock, or rather the legendary status of its star performers, provided the direct subject of *Suicide in bFlat* and *The Tooth of Crime*.

But rock isn't the only musical style Shepard employs. A whole range of other genres can be found: modern jazz, blues, country and western and folk music of several kinds. Shepard has always claimed, or others have on his behalf, that these musical elements are as important to many of his plays as their speech, and that the same thing is true for his decors. Indeed it's difficult to imagine much of his work without its music, by which I mean that it's not an embellishment or a strategic device, in the manner of Brecht, to interrupt the flow of a sequential narrative, but an integral part of the plays' devising of new consciousness.

Shepard's physical materials and perspectives come largely from developments in the graphic arts and dance during his adolescence and early career. He has said that Jackson Pollock was important to him, but what seems more active in his sensibility are emanations from the "happenings" phase of painting and sculpture, collage in the manner of Johns and Rauschenberg, and the mixed-media experiments of the latter artist with John Cage and others. His sets reveal all these influences at two extremes: their occasional starkness, a bare space in which lighting is the chief or only emotive or "placing" factor, and their frequent stress on dirt, *dreck*—the kitchen of *4-H Club*, "littered with paper, cans, and various trash," or the set for *The Unseen Hand*, composed of an "old '51 Chevrolet convertible, bashed and dented, no tires . . . garbage, tin cans, cardboard boxes, Coca-Cola bottles and other junk.''

More generally, in regard to subject and reference, to iconography, we can observe a far-flung network of influences, interests and obsessions that have gone into the making of Shepard's work. The most substantial of these are the car or "road" culture of his youth, science-fiction, Hollywood Westerns and the myth of the West in general, and television in its pop or junk aspects. Besides these Shepard himself has mentioned "vaudeville, circuses . . . trance dances, faith healing ceremonials . . . medicine shows," to which we might add telepathic states, hallucinatory experiences (drug-induced or not), magic and witchcraft.

Eclectic as all this seems, something binds it together, and this is that nearly everything I've mentioned is to one degree or another an interest or engagement of the pop and counter cultures that had their beginnings in the fifties. When we reflect on what these movements or climates have left us—their presence is still felt in the form of a corpse not quite grown cold—a set of major impulses immediately emerges: a stance against authority and tradition, anti-elitism, the assertion of the untaught self in impatience and sometimes mockery.

But one sees in it all too—something most pertinent to a rumination on Shepard's plays—another and more subtle configuration: a world of discards and throwaways, of a *nostalgie de boue* appeased by landscapes filled with detritus and interiors strewn with debris, of floating images, unfinished acts, discontinuity and dissonance, abruptnesses and illogicalities; an impatience with time for proceeding instead of existing all at once, like space; and with space for having limits, fixed contours and finality.

This in large part is Shepard's theatrical world. I said that his plays emerged far more from new movements outside the theater than from within it, but what really happened can't be that clear. If he's never acknowledged any debt to the so-called Absurdists, or to any other playwrights for that matter, whether or not he learned directly from them scarcely matters. He learned alongside them, so to speak, or in their wake, in the same atmosphere of rejection of linear construction, cause and effect sequences, logical procedures, coherent or consistent characters, and the tying of language to explicit meanings that distinguished the new drama from its predecessors.

Except for its final phrases, a note to the actors preceding the text of *Angel City* might have been written by almost any avant-garde playwright of recent years, and in fact goes back in its central notion to Strindberg's revolutionary preface to *Miss Julie*. "The term 'character,' " Shepard wrote, "could be thought of in a different way when working on this play. Instead of the idea of a 'whole character' with logical motives behind his behavior which the actor submerges himself into, he should consider instead a fractured whole with bits and pieces of characters flying off the central theme. Collage construction, jazz improvisation. Music or painting in space."

What distinguished Shepard's plays from most others in the new American repertoire was their greater vivacity and elasticity, even more their far greater impurity, the presence in them of so many energies and actions not previously thought properly dramatic. More than any other American playwright of the sixties, he broke down the fixed definitions of the dramatic. But doing this brought risks. He has said he wants to create "total" theater, and this ambition is both the spur to his triumphs and the clue to his delinquencies. For total theater, where everything is present at once, can result in a canceling-out, a murk and confusion.

If the American theater was ready for Shepard's wayward gifts, it was because it was ready for anything in the emptiness in which it then existed. In the late fifties and early sixties our theater was just beginning to catch up with developments in arts like painting and dance, and with the revolutionary changes in drama that had taken place in France with Beckett and Ionesco and, more modestly, in England with the early Pinter. Albee's first plays, Gelber's *Connection* and the work of the Living Theater were all signs and artifacts of a stirring here that was to result a couple of years later in the burgeoning of off and off-off Broadway. A major aspect of this was the creation of experimental, insurrectionary groups like the Open Theater, the Performance Group and others.

Shepard's first plays to be staged were done in New York in late 1964, and it's no accident that a few months later he appeared at the door of the Open Theater, for that body of actors, directors and writers was one of the centers of the upheaval.

This isn't the place for an extended discussion of Shepard's debt to the Open Theater, nor are the intellectual transactions between them entirely clear. What can be said is that Shepard learned something important about "transformations," one of the group's main lines of exploration into both the psychology of the actor and the relationship between acting and formal texts. Briefly, a transformation exercise was an improvised scene—a birthday party, survivors in a lifeboat, etc.—in which after a while, and suddenly, the actors were asked to switch immediately to a new scene and therefore to wholly new characters. Among the aims (which were never wholly clear) were increased flexibility, insight into theatrical or acting clichés and more unified ensemble playing.

Shepard carried the idea of transformations much farther than the group had by actually writing them into his texts, in plays like *Angel City*, *Back Bog Beast Bait* and *The Tooth of Crime*, where characters become wholly different in abrupt movements within the course of the work, or speak suddenly as someone else, while the scene may remain the same. Besides this, Shepard has maintained a connection to the Open Theater's Joseph Chaikin, collaborating with him on the two theater pieces included in this book.

More than that of any important playwright I know, Shepard's work resists division into periods, stages of growth or development. The only exceptions to this, once more, are the latest plays, which do seem to constitute a rough phase. Unlike the serial way in which we arrange most writers' work in our minds, the body of Shepard's writing seems present to us all at once, lying rudely sprawled across our consciousness, connected in all its parts less by organic adhesion than by a distinctive ebb and flow of obsession. Shepard doesn't move from theme to theme or image to image in the separate plays; he doesn't conquer a dramatic territory and move on, doesn't extend his grasp or refine it. What he does from play to play is lunge forward, move sideways, double back, circle round, throw in this or that, adopt a voice then drop it, pick it up again.

Most of his plays seem like fragments, chunks of various sizes thrown out from some mother lode of urgent and heterogeneous imagination in which he has scrabbled with pick, shovel, gunbutt and hands. The reason so many of them seem incomplete is that they lack the clear boundaries as artifact, the internal order, the progress toward a denouement (of some kind: a crystallization, a summarizing image, a poise in the mind) and the consistency of tone and procedure that ordinarily characterize good drama, even most avant-garde drama of the postwar time.

Many of his plays seem partial, capricious, arbitrarily brought to an end and highly unstable. They spill over, they leak. They change, chameleon-like, in self-protection as we look at them. This is a source of the difficulty one has in writing about them, as it's also a source of their originality. Another difficulty is that we tend to look at all plays for their single "meanings" or ruling ideas but find this elusive in Shepard and find, moreover, his plays coalescing, merging into one another in our minds. Rather than always trying to keep them separate, trying by direct plunges into their respective depths to find clear meanings tucked away like kernels within gorgeous ragged husks, I think we ought to accept, at least provisionally, their volatility and interdependence; they constitute a series of facets of a single continuing act of imagination.

Beyond this, and as an aspect of it, we have to see Shepard's work as existing in an especially intricate and disorderly relationship with life outside the theater. Such a relationship obviously is true of any drama, but in Shepard's case it shows itself as a rambunctious reciprocity in which the theatrical, as a mode of behavior, takes a special wayward urgency from life, while the living—spontaneous, unorganized and unpredictable—keeps breaking into the artificial, composed world of the stage.

There is a remark of John Cage's that's especially pertinent here: "Theater exists all around us and it is the purpose of formal theater to remind us that this is so." Much of Shepard's energy and inventiveness are given (undeliberately, of course; as part of the action of being an artist) to this kind of reminder; his theater is as much about theater as about the "real" world. Above all, it's about performing, and here the relations between art and life become particularly close.

There are indeed themes in his work—sociological, political, etc.—but the plays aren't demonstrations or enactments of them; they exist as dispositions, pressures, points of inquiry. And if there's any over-riding vision it's this: our lives are theatrical, but it's a besieged, partly deracinated theater we act in. We want, as though in a theater, to be *seen* (the Greek root of "theater": a place for *seeing*), but there are great obstacles to this desire.

If it's not useful to search for the specific meanings of all Shepard's plays, then their general meaning or significance (or perhaps simply what these plays cause in our minds, what Henry James called the "thinkable" actions of drama) is something else. I want to start on the way toward that by contemplating the surfaces of this ungainly body of drama, and what more immediate data are there than Shepard's titles?

Most of his titles float, bob up and down from the plays on shorter or longer strings. They appear as aggressions, put-ons or parodies, but almost never as traditional titles in some direct or logical connection to the works. They seem crazily theatrical in themselves; they scare you or break you up before the curtain has even risen: *Dog; Killer's Head; 4-H Club; The Holy Ghostly; Cowboy Mouth; Shaved Splits; Fourteen Hundred Thousand; Back Bog Beast Bait; The Tooth of Crime; Blue Bitch; Action; The Mad Dog Blues; Angel City; Geography of a Horse Dreamer; Operation Sidewinder; Curse of the Starving Class; Forensic and the Navigators; Icarus's Mother.*

I don't know if it has been pointed out how these titles resemble the names of rock groups, or pieces of graffiti or certain writings on tee-shirts. They don't denote finished, discrete dramas as much as a continuing action, a calling of attention; they're less identifications than announcements.

This is also true of his characters' names, which are like knives, road-signs or trade-marks. There are some prosaic ones—Ed, Frank, Jill, Becky, Stu—but with these we think Shepard is playing a joke. The real names are and ought to be: Cherry and Geez and Wong; Shooter and Jeep; Shadow; Beaujo and Santee; Forensic; Galactic Jack; Dr. Vector; Tympani; Hoss and Crow; Salem and Kent; Kosmo and Yahoodi; Miss Scoons; Sloe Gin Martin and Booger Montgomery; Gris Gris; Ice; Blood; Blade; Dukie; Dude. There are very few last names, for like the titles they're less identifiers than assertions.

It's as if these characters had named themselves or gone behind the playwright's back to get named by some master of hype, some poet of the juke-box. They're like movie starlets and a type of star—Rock, Tab, Tuesday; they're like rock personalities, even bands. Their names seek to confer one or another quality on their persons, soliciting us to read them as dangerous or alluring or zany—in any case as original. This is a function of nicknames or pseudonyms at any time, but in Shepard they're the names first given; his characters start with a flight from anonymity.

Some of them smack of science fiction, others of pop sensibility. They're partly japes, sly mockeries of staid naming in theater and life. But most of them aren't just tactical but move in our minds like signals from a particular human and geographical environment, one that vibrates simultaneously with sadness and violence, eccentricity, loneliness and self-assertion, bravado and the pathos of rootless existence. The "real" place is California and the Southwest; the site in our minds is American toughness and despair, danger and isolation. I think of rodeo riders, poker dealers, motorcycle gangs, bar hostesses, gangsters' sidekicks, hotrodders and drifters, killers on the plains, electric guitarists in roadhouses. And I think of the stars who would wear such epithet-like names if they didn't have to use reasonable ones.

In laying such emphasis on these names I naturally don't mean to suggest they can bear a weight of interpretation of the plays, only that they can help us toward the dramatic center. For if something like a "quest for identity" is central to Shepard's vision, as I think it is, then names, first clues to identity or its lack, are greatly instructive.

Now "quest for identity" is a flaccid term in popular psychology and perfunctory cultural criticism, and it has of course to do with the question of "who am I?" But is this a useful or even a true question, especially in the theater? Can we ever, in life, know who we are except in a formal, abstract way, as the result, say, of a Cartesian inquiry, a religious definition or membership in a human category? Might not the true questions in putting forth the self, certainly in the theater but also in life with its theatrical hunger, be "who do I seem to be?" and "what am I taken for?" And might not the quest for identity really be the quest for a *role*?

I intend nothing pejorative by this, nothing having to do with "role-playing" as a neurotic maneuver; but rather that we either take our places in a drama and discover ourselves as we act, or we remain unknown (as some indeed choose to do). In the reciprocal glances of the actors we all are, in our cues to dialogue, the perpetual agons and denouements that we participate in with others, identities are found, discarded, altered but above all *seen*. Not to be able to act, to be turned away from the audition, is the true painful condition of anonymity. But to try to act too much, to wish to star, the culmination and hypertrophy of the common desire, is a ripeness for disaster.

I think Shepard's shamanistic or totemistic names are the initial signs of his art's fundamental impulse. The selves behind the names, the characters, are avid to be but above all to be *seen* to be. I know this can be said in one way or another of the substance of all formal theater. Jarry once said that a playwright wants to "unleash" his characters on a stage, and Robbe-Grillet said of Beckett's Didi and Gogo that they have to "ad lib for their very lives." To write plays is to invent characters to live more visibly and perilously than oneself.

But what is remarkable about Shepard's plays is the way they display the new raw unstable anguish and wit that marks the self seeking itself now, and that they display with such half-demented, half-lyrical force the things that oppose this quest, its exacerbated American circumstances, which Shepard's own new raw questing sensibility has made its scene, obsession and poetry.

I believe that all Shepard's themes or motifs can be subsumed, even if loosely and with jagged projections everywhere, by this perspective. Consider the question of "roots," so stark or shadowy in his plays. To have roots is to have continuity and so a basis on which to act (a step to a step), to act in both senses of the word. Not to have roots is to risk acting on air. This is why I think the facts of Shepard's literal and cultural background are important. He couldn't have come from the East or North or at another time. In the West rootlessness is far more widespread and for many almost the condition of life. But at the same time the West, particularly California, is the place where, most acutely, visible success, gestures of self, personality, fame are means, conscious or not, of making up for or disguising the lack of roots.

Isn't it also the place—as a metaphor beyond its kleig lights and therapies and bronzed bodies—where energy and anguish, talent and emptiness, the hope of a name and the corruption of a self are the matings from which come a special piercing sense of dismay, which may be one thing we mean by the destruction of the "American Dream"?

"Identity" and "roots" merge as themes in Shepard. For if the American Dream means anything more than its purely physical and economic implications, it means the hope and promise of identity, of a "role" in the sense I indicated before. Inseparable from this is the hope of flexibility, of suppleness in the distribution of roles—the opportunities of being seen—such as was largely absent from the more fixed and closed European world. In turn this promise, sometimes fulfilled, is met with the ironic condition of rootlessness, lack of continuity and ground. The effect of this in Shepard's theater is either to crush or literally deracinate—tear the mind from *its* roots—the seeking self or to hyperbolize it into flamboyance, violence, or the ultimate madness, the fever for what we call "stardom."

The very "rootlessness" of Shepard's theater, its springing so largely from a condition outside the continuity of the stage, is a source of the difficulty we have with it, as it is also a source of its dazzling disturbances. But inside his theater, within its own continuousness, a tragi-comic drama of names and selves unfolds. I think of the frantic efforts of so many of his characters to make themselves felt, often by violence (or cartoon violence—blows without injuries, bullets without deaths: dream or make-believe, something filmed), of the great strand in his work of the ego run wild, of the craving for altered states of being and the power to transcend physical or moral or psychic limitations—and the very alterations and transcendences of this kind carried out in the plays: the transformations, the splitting of characters, the masks, the roles within roles, the mingling of legendary figures with invented ones. And I think of the "turns," the numbers, the oratorios and arias, and especially the monologues or soliloquies that aren't simply contributions to the plot but outcries of characters craving to be known.

The monologues take many forms. One is a kind of technical disquisition, such as Jeez's on deer-skinning in *Shaved Splits* or Howard's on flying in *Icarus's Mother*. They may be prosaic or bizarre but they have the effect of claiming for the speaker an individuality based on some sort of detailed knowledge. More often the monologue is simply a "story," matter-of-fact or exotic, which may or may not contribute to the plot, but which always serves to distinguish the speaker as a voice, as someone with *something* to tell.

Occasionally such a monologue will contain within itself a

crystallization or recapitulation of the play itself and of Shepard's angle of vision. A speech of this kind is Shooter's in *Action* about the risks and necessities of acting:

. . . You go outside. The world's quiet. White. Everything resounding. Not a sound of a motor. Not a light. You see into the house. You see the candles. You watch the people. You can see what it's like inside. The candles draw you. You get a cold feeling being outside. Separated. You have an idea that being inside it's cosier. Friendlier. Warmth. People. Conversation. Everyone using a language. Then you go inside. It's a shock. It's not like how you expected. You lose what you had outside. You forget that there even is an outside. The inside is all you know. You hunt for a way of being with everyone. A way of finding how to behave. You find out what's expected of you. You act yourself out.

Another is Miss Scoons on the dream of stardom, in *Angel City*:

I look at the screen and I am the screen . . . I look at the movie and I am the movie. I am the star . . . For days I am the star and I'm not me. I'm me being the star. I look at my life when I come down . . . and I hate my life when I come down. I hate my life not being a movie. I hate my life not being a star. I hate being myself in my life which isn't a movie and never will be. I hate having to eat. Having to work. Having to sleep. Having to go to the bathroom. Having to get from one place to another with no potential. Having to live in this body which isn't a star's body and all the time knowing that stars exist . . .

The monologues are most often tight, staccato, gathering a strange cumulative eloquence. In their varied voices they reveal as nothing else does Shepard's marvelous ear, not for actual speech but for the imagined possibilities of utterance as invention, as victory over silence.

Everything I've been discussing converges in *The Tooth of Crime*, which I think is Shepard's greatest achievement, the one play which is most nearly invulnerable to charges of occlusion or arbitrary procedures, the one that rests most self-containedly, that seems whole, inevitable, *ended*. It contains his chief imaginative ideas and obsessions at their highest point of eloquence and most sinewy connection to one another. It exhibits his theatrical inventiveness at its most brilliant yet most uncapricious and coherent, and it reveals most powerfully his sense of the reciprocities of art and life. A splendid violent artifact, it broods on and wrestles with the quest not simply to be known but to be known inexhaustibly, magically, cosmically: the exaltation and tragedy of fame.

For this drama of confrontation between a rock "king" and his challenger, Shepard calls on an astonishing range of sources. The chief plot action, the eventual "shoot-out," is borrowed of course from Western movies and legends. But the play is more than its narrative; or rather, the true narrative, the tale of consciousness, is of the vivacity and anguish of the swollen name, the self propelled into a beleaguered exemplary condition in which the general need is fulfilled for some selves and names to be transfigured so that others may at least elbow into their light. The mobile levels of discourse, the amazing variety of textures serve to proffer and sustain a painful, refulgent myth, itself drawn from a public mythology, that greed for and apotheosis of *status* that began to gather intensity some years ago and rages without let-up now, so that we meet its vocabulary everywhere: "We;" "Us;" "Superstar;" "King of the Hill;" "Number One."

On a bare stage with its only prop an "evil-looking black chair," or throne, Shepard composes a drama whose main impulsions are the rage for competing, the savage jostling for the top that strangely implies there isn't enough fame to go round; and the dehumanization induced by celebrity, which converts true actions into poses, frozen stances. Hoss, the menaced king, says at one point that he'd be "O.K." if he ". . . had a self. Something to fall back on in a moment of doubt or terror or even surprise." And when Crow, his rival, who has been talking in a murderous insider's jargon, speaks normally once, Hoss says: "Why'd you slip just then? Why'd you suddenly talk like a person?"

The contest employs various "languages," some actual, others invented or mythical, to display the half-real, half-imagined ways we define ourselves by vying. The gunfighter metaphor is central, but there's also car talk, where you top through rare makes and horsepower, and a range of images from sports. Shepard brilliantly places the event in a deadly sci-fi world where computers determine rankings and an interplanetary commission guards the rules or "codes." Against this Hoss, who retains something of the older humanness, speaks of a time when "we were warriors" not incarnate appetites, and when there was a correlation between style and being. In a greatly revealing speech he indicates the new distance between authenticity and appearance: "Just help me into the style. I'll develop my own image. I'm an original man, a one and only. I just need some help."

In the play's climactic moments Hoss makes a last effort to re-establish his rule over the new soulless domain where nothing is valued except the deified name. He describes himself as a "true killer," who "can't do anything false," who's "true to his heart . . . his voice . . . pitiless, indifferent and riding a state of grace." Upon which he breaks down and cries over and over "It ain't me!" The last word is Crow's, the victor: "Didn't answer to no name but loser. All that power goin' backwards . . . Now the power shifts and sits until a bigger wind blows." The power, the force of ego turned ruthless and mechanical, will reign in a world without grace or true light; only the blinding sterile "stars" remain in their pitiless hierarchy.

In his last three plays Shepard has withdrawn noticeably from the extravagant situations, the complex wild voices and general unruliness of the earlier work. His themes, so elusive before, seem clearer now, if not pellucidly so, his vision dwells more on actual society. Physical or economic circumstances play more of a part than before.

I said before that one has to go beyond the economic implications of the "American Dream," but you do start there. Having money is both a form of and a means to identity; it lets you act. More than that, money makes itself felt in America as a chief agency of the distortion of the human theater; it forces people into roles and out of them, and by its presence or absence it dictates the chief values of our dramas. The very pursuit of it, beyond sustenance, flattens out selves, converts them into instances of success or failure, makes the play we're in single-minded and soulless. Still, as Freud once said, money isn't a primal need of the psyche, and it isn't one for Shepard's characters.

In *Curse of the Starving Class* the family is poor but not hopelessly so; their material need isn't so much the question as the instigation to enact a deeper need. They're starving but not really physically. The set is a kitchen, images of food and eating abound, but the weight isn't on physical hunger as a motif and nothing indicates this better than the incident when to a depleted larder Weston brings an enormous number of artichokes. The absurdity of this is evident, but what it reveals is the way food operates as a metaphor for a quest and not its aim.

What they're really starved for is selfhood, distinctiveness, satisfying roles. On any level they refuse to be of the starving *class*. As Emma insists, they're different from those who are starving as a function of their *status*, their definition, which is obscurity. They struggle to emerge, be seen by others, escape from being members of a class, a category.

The "curse" is the dark side of the American Dream and is manifested in its victims partly through standardization, and the quantification of values imposed by lawyers, developers, admen, and the like (the "zombies . . . they've moved in on us like a creeping disease," Wesley says) and partly by the very distortions of the craving for selfhood that results in ill-fated measures to achieve it. Apart from Wesley the members of the family come to disastrous ends or these impend; only he, the quiet, somewhat deadened, unambitious one, has the right, if uncolorful, idea. He wants to remain on the seedy place, extend such roots as there are. He will settle for that role, that tiniest of bit parts.

In *Buried Child* the family to which the son, Vincent, returns is also poor, or marginal, but this isn't their *dramatic* condition. Vincent discovers that they don't know him, that in fact they're locked together in unknowingness, in a fixity of objectless rage and spiritual lameness. A struggle ensues between what we might call principles of movement and arrest. After fleeing the maimed scene, Vincent comes back to take over: "I've got to carry on the line. I've got to see to it that things keep rolling." The father, the incarnation of discontinuity, shouts that there's no past to propel a future. In the face of a photo from his youth, he insists: "That isn't me! That never was me! This is me. This is it. The whole shootin' match . . ."

The mysterious field behind the house that everyone knows

to be arid nevertheless produces vegetables in abundance. The fantastic field is a metaphor for fecundity, of course, and at the same time works as a hope of future life against the bitter, hidden truth which emerges at the end in the form of the murdered, "buried" child. The childhood buried in the adult who has refused the connection and so the continuity? An image of the secret life of families, burying the issue of their lovelessness? I don't think the symbol or metaphor is susceptible of neat interpretation. But it remains, as does the play with all its loose ends and occasionally unconvincing events—Vincent's violent change near the end, for example—strong and echoing in the mind.

In its straightforwardness and sparseness of action *True West*, Shepard's newest play, is surely the least typical of all his works. Its protagonists, two brothers who somewhat resemble Lenny and Teddy in Pinter's *Homecoming* (as the play itself also resembles Pinter in its portentous pauses and mysterious references) clash over their respective roles. Lee, the drifter and man of the desert, envies Austin, the successful screenwriter and takes over his position by selling a producer on an "authentic" Western, one, that's to say, drawn entirely from his own matter of fact and therefore non-artistic, uninvented experience.

Austin, not an artist but a contriver of entertainment, nevertheless represents the imagination against Lee's literalness. Their battle shifts its ground until Austin, in the face of Lee's claim that his story reveals the "true" West, retorts that "there's no such thing as the West anymore. It's a dead issue!" The myths are used up. Still, his own identity has been found within his work of manipulating popular myths and he finds himself draining away under the pressure of Lee's ruthless "realism." The play ends with Austin's murderous attack on his brother, a last desperate attempt to preserve a self.

A last word on *Tongues* and *Savage/Love*, the last two works in this collection. Both are more theater pieces than plays. They're the outcome of Shepard's and Chaikin's experiments with a dramatic form stripped of accessories, of plot elements and physical action, reduced to essentials of sound and utterance. When they rise, as they sometimes do, to a point of mysterious and resilient lyricism, they reach us as reminders at least of Shepard's wide and far from exhausted gifts.

I suspect he'll astonish us again.

TRUE WEST

AUSTIN: *early thirties, light blue sports shirt, light tan cardigan sweater, clean blue jeans, white tennis shoes*

LEE: *his older brother, early forties, filthy white t-shirt, tattered brown overcoat covered with dust, dark blue baggy suit pants from the Salvation Army, pink suede belt, pointed black forties dress shoes scuffed up, holes in the soles, no socks, no hat, long pronounced sideburns, "Gene Vincent" hairdo, two days' growth of beard, bad teeth*

SAUL KIMMER: *late forties, Hollywood producer, pink and white flower print sports shirt, white sports coat with matching polyester slacks, black and white loafers*

MOM: *early sixties, mother of the brothers, small woman, conservative white skirt and matching jacket, red shoulder bag, two pieces of matching red luggage*

True West was first performed at the Magic Theatre in San Francisco on July 10, 1980. The director was Robert Woodruff, and the cast was as follows:

AUSTIN	Peter Coyote
LEE	Jim Haynie
SAUL KIMMER	Tom Dahlgren
MOM	Carol McElheney

SCENE: *All nine scenes take place on the same set; a kitchen and adjoining alcove of an older home in a Southern California suburb, about 40 miles east of Los Angeles. The kitchen takes up most of the playing area to stage left. The kitchen consists of a sink, upstage center, surrounded by counter space, a wall telephone, cupboards, and a small window just above it bordered by neat yellow curtains. Stage left of sink is a stove. Stage right, a refrigerator. The alcove adjoins the kitchen to stage right. There is no wall division or door to the alcove. It is open and easily accessible from the kitchen and defined only by the objects in it: a small round glass breakfast table mounted on white iron legs, two matching white iron chairs set across from each other. The two exterior walls of the alcove which prescribe a corner in the upstage right are composed of many small windows, beginning from a solid wall about three feet high and extending to the ceiling. The windows look out to bushes and citrus trees. The alcove is filled with all sorts of house plants in various pots, mostly Boston ferns hanging in planters at different levels. The floor of the alcove is composed of green synthetic grass.*

All entrances and exits are made stage left from the kitchen. There is no door. The actors simply go off and come onto the playing area.

NOTE ON SET AND COSTUME: *The set should be constructed realistically with no attempt to distort its dimensions, shapes, objects, or colors. No objects should be introduced which might draw special attention to themselves other than the props demanded by the script. If a stylistic "concept" is grafted onto the set design it will only serve to confuse the evolution of the characters' situation, which is the most important focus of the play.*

Likewise, the costumes should be exactly representative of who the

3

characters are and not added onto for the sake of making a point to the audience.

NOTE ON SOUND: *The Coyote of Southern California has a distinct yapping, dog-like bark, similar to a Hyena. This yapping grows more intense and maniacal as the pack grows in numbers, which is usually the case when they lure and kill pets from suburban yards. The sense of growing frenzy in the pack should be felt in the background, particularly in Scenes 7 and 8. In any case, these Coyotes never make the long, mournful, solitary howl of the Hollywood stereotype.*

The sound of Crickets can speak for itself.

These sounds should also be treated realistically even though they sometimes grow in volume and numbers.

ACT ONE

SCENE ONE

Night. Sound of crickets in dark. Candlelight appears in alcove, illuminating AUSTIN, *seated at glass table hunched over a writing notebook, pen in hand, cigarette burning in ashtray, cup of coffee, typewriter on table, stacks of paper, candle burning on table.*

Soft moonlight fills kitchen illuminating LEE, *beer in hand, six-pack on counter behind him. He's leaning against the sink, mildly drunk; takes a slug of beer.*

LEE: So, Mom took off for Alaska, huh?

AUSTIN: Yeah.

LEE: Sorta' left you in charge.

AUSTIN: Well, she knew I was coming down here so she offered me the place.

LEE: You keepin' the plants watered?

AUSTIN: Yeah.

LEE: Keepin' the sink clean? She don't like even a single tea leaf in the sink ya' know.

AUSTIN: (*trying to concentrate on writing*) Yeah, I know.

  (*pause*)

LEE: She gonna' be up there a long time?

AUSTIN: I don't know.

LEE: Kinda' nice for you, huh? Whole place to yourself.

AUSTIN: Yeah, it's great.

LEE: Ya' got crickets anyway. Tons a' crickets out there. (*looks around kitchen*) Ya' got groceries? Coffee?

AUSTIN: (*looking up from writing*) What?

LEE: You got coffee?

AUSTIN: Yeah.

5

LEE: At's good. (*short pause*) Real coffee? From the bean?

AUSTIN: Yeah. You want some?

LEE: Naw. I brought some uh— (*motions to beer*)

AUSTIN: Help yourself to whatever's— (*motions to refrigerator*)

LEE: I will. Don't worry about me. I'm not the one to worry about. I mean I can uh— (*pause*) You always work by candlelight?

AUSTIN: No—uh— Not always.

LEE: Just sometimes?

AUSTIN: (*puts pen down, rubs his eyes*) Yeah. Sometimes it's soothing.

LEE: Isn't that what the old guys did?

AUSTIN: What old guys?

LEE: The Forefathers. You know.

AUSTIN: Forefathers?

LEE: Isn't that what they did? Candlelight burning into the night? Cabins in the wilderness.

AUSTIN: (*rubs hand through his hair*) I suppose.

LEE: I'm not botherin' you am I? I mean I don't wanna break into yer uh—concentration or nothin'.

AUSTIN: No, it's all right.

LEE: That's good. I mean I realize that yer line a' work demands a lota' concentration.

AUSTIN: It's okay.

LEE: You probably think that I'm not fully able to comprehend somethin' like that, huh?

AUSTIN: Like what?

LEE: That stuff yer doin'. That art. You know. Whatever you call it.

AUSTIN: It's just a little research.

LEE: You may not know it but I did a little art myself once.

AUSTIN: You did?

LEE: Yeah! I did some a' that. I fooled around with it. No future in it.

AUSTIN: What'd you do?

LEE: Never mind what I did! Just never mind about that. (*pause*) It was ahead of its time.

(*pause*)

AUSTIN: So, you went out to see the old man, huh?

LEE: Yeah, I seen him.

AUSTIN: How's he doing?

LEE: Same. He's doin' just about the same.

AUSTIN: I was down there too, you know.

LEE: What d'ya' want, an award? You want some kinda' medal? You were down there. He told me all about you.

AUSTIN: What'd he say?

LEE: He told me. Don't worry.

(*pause*)

AUSTIN: Well—

LEE: You don't have to say nothin'.

AUSTIN: I wasn't.

LEE: Yeah, you were gonna' make somethin' up. Somethin' brilliant.

(*pause*)

AUSTIN: You going to be down here very long, Lee?

LEE: Might be. Depends on a few things.

AUSTIN: You got some friends down here?

LEE: (*laughs*) I know a few people. Yeah.

AUSTIN: Well, you can stay here as long as I'm here.

LEE: I don't need your permission do I?

AUSTIN: No.

LEE: I mean she's my mother too, right?

AUSTIN: Right.

LEE: She might've just as easily asked me to take care of her place as you.

AUSTIN: That's right.

LEE: I mean I know how to water plants.

(*long pause*)

AUSTIN: So you don't know how long you'll be staying then?

LEE: Depends mostly on houses, ya' know.

AUSTIN: Houses?

LEE: Yeah. Houses. Electric devices. Stuff like that. I gotta' make a little tour first.

(*short pause*)

AUSTIN: Lee, why don't you just try another neighborhood, all right?

LEE: (*laughs*) What'sa' matter with this neighborhood? This is a

great neighborhood. Lush. Good class a' people. Not many
dogs.

AUSTIN: Well, our uh— Our mother just happens to live here.
That's all.

LEE: Nobody's gonna' know. All they know is somethin's missing.
That's all. She'll never even hear about it. Nobody's gonna'
know.

AUSTIN: You're going to get picked up if you start walking
around here at night.

LEE: Me? I'm gonna' git picked up? What about you? You
stick out like a sore thumb. Look at you. You think yer
regular lookin'?

AUSTIN: I've got too much to deal with here to be worrying
about—

LEE: Yer not gonna' have to worry about me! I've been doin' all
right without you. I haven't been anywhere near you for five
years! Now isn't that true?

AUSTIN: Yeah.

LEE: So you don't have to worry about me. I'm a free agent.

AUSTIN: All right.

LEE: Now all I wanna' do is borrow yer car.

AUSTIN: No!

LEE: Just fer a day. One day.

AUSTIN: No!

LEE: I won't take it outside a twenty mile radius. I promise ya'.
You can check the speedometer.

AUSTIN: You're not borrowing my car! That's all there is to it.

(*pause*)

LEE: Then I'll just take the damn thing.

AUSTIN: Lee, look— I don't want any trouble, all right?

LEE: That's a dumb line. That is a dumb fuckin' line. You git
paid fer dreamin' up a line like that?

AUSTIN: Look, I can give you some money if you need money.

(LEE *suddenly lunges at* AUSTIN, *grabs him violently by the shirt and
shakes him with tremendous power*)

LEE: Don't you say that to me! Don't you ever say that to me!
(*just as suddenly he turns him loose, pushes him away and backs off*)
You may be able to git away with that with the Old Man. Git
him tanked up for a week! Buy him off with yer Hollywood

blood money, but not me! I can git my own money my own way. Big money!

AUSTIN: I was just making an offer.

LEE: Yeah, well keep it to yourself!

(*long pause*)

Those are the most monotonous fuckin' crickets I ever heard in my life.

AUSTIN: I kinda' like the sound.

LEE: Yeah. Supposed to be able to tell the temperature by the number a' pulses. You believe that?

AUSTIN: The temperature?

LEE: Yeah. The air. How hot it is.

AUSTIN: How do you do that?

LEE: I don't know. Some woman told me that. She was a Botanist. So I believed her.

AUSTIN: Where'd you meet her?

LEE: What?

AUSTIN: The woman Botanist?

LEE: I met her on the desert. I been spendin' a lota' time on the desert.

AUSTIN: What were you doing out there?

LEE: (*pause, stares in space*) I forgit. Had me a Pit Bull there for a while but I lost him.

AUSTIN: Pit Bull?

LEE: Fightin' dog. Damn I made some good money off that little dog. Real good money.

(*pause*)

AUSTIN: You could come up north with me, you know.

LEE: What's up there?

AUSTIN: My family.

LEE: Oh, that's right, you got the wife and kiddies now don't ya'. The house, the car, the whole slam. That's right.

AUSTIN: You could spend a couple days. See how you like it. I've got an extra room.

LEE: Too cold up there.

(*pause*)

AUSTIN: You want to sleep for a while?

LEE: (*pause, stares at* AUSTIN) I don't sleep.

(*lights to black*)

SCENE TWO

Morning. AUSTIN *is watering plants with a vaporizer,* LEE *sits at glass table in alcove drinking beer.*

LEE: I never realized the old lady was so security-minded.

AUSTIN: How do you mean?

LEE: Made a little tour this morning. She's got locks on everything. Locks and double-locks and chain locks and— What's she got that's so valuable?

AUSTIN: Antiques I guess. I don't know.

LEE: Antiques? Brought everything with her from the old place, huh. Just the same crap we always had around. Plates and spoons.

AUSTIN: I guess they have personal value to her.

LEE: Personal value. Yeah. Just a lota' junk. Most of it's phony anyway. Idaho decals. Now who in the hell wants to eat offa' plate with the State of Idaho starin' ya' in the face. Every time ya' take a bite ya' get to see a little bit more.

AUSTIN: Well it must mean something to her or she wouldn't save it.

LEE: Yeah, well personally I don't wann' be invaded by Idaho when I'm eatin'. When I'm eatin' I'm home. Ya' know what I'm sayin'? I'm not driftin', I'm home. I don't need my thoughts swept off to Idaho. I don't need that!

(*pause*)

AUSTIN: Did you go out last night?

LEE: Why?

AUSTIN: I thought I heard you go out.

LEE: Yeah, I went out. What about it?

AUSTIN: Just wondered.

LEE: Damn coyotes kept me awake.

AUSTIN: Oh yeah, I heard them. They must've killed somebody's dog or something.

LEE: Yappin' their fool heads off. They don't yap like that on the desert. They howl. These are city coyotes here.

AUSTIN: Well, you don't sleep anyway do you?

(*pause*, LEE *stares at him*)

LEE: You're pretty smart aren't ya?

AUSTIN: How do you mean?

LEE: I mean you never had any more on the ball than I did. But here you are gettin' invited into prominent people's houses. Sittin' around talkin' like you know somethin'.

AUSTIN: They're not so prominent.

LEE: They're a helluva' lot more prominent than the houses I get invited into.

AUSTIN: Well you invite yourself.

LEE: That's right. I do. In fact I probably got a wider range a' choices than you do, come to think of it.

AUSTIN: I wouldn't doubt it.

LEE: In fact I been inside some pretty classy places in my time. And I never even went to an Ivy League school either.

AUSTIN: You want some breakfast or something?

LEE: Breakfast?

AUSTIN: Yeah. Don't you eat breakfast?

LEE: Look, don't worry about me pal. I can take care a' myself. You just go ahead as though I wasn't even here, all right?

(AUSTIN *goes into kitchen, makes coffee*)

AUSTIN: Where'd you walk to last night?

(*pause*)

LEE: I went up in the foothills there. Up in the San Gabriels. Heat was drivin' me crazy.

AUSTIN: Well, wasn't it hot out on the desert?

LEE: Different kinda' heat. Out there it's clean. Cools off at night. There's a nice little breeze.

AUSTIN: Where were you, the Mojave?

LEE: Yeah. The Mojave. That's right.

AUSTIN: I haven't been out there in years.

LEE: Out past Needles there.

AUSTIN: Oh yeah.

LEE: Up here it's different. This country's real different.

AUSTIN: Well, it's been built up.

LEE: Built up? Wiped out is more like it. I don't even hardly recognize it.

AUSTIN: Yeah. Foothills are the same though, aren't they?

LEE: Pretty much. It's funny goin' up in there. The smells and everything. Used to catch snakes up there, remember?

AUSTIN: You caught snakes.

LEE: Yeah. And you'd pretend you were Geronimo or some damn thing. You used to go right out to lunch.

AUSTIN: I enjoyed my imagination.

LEE: That what you call it? Looks like yer still enjoyin' it.

AUSTIN: So you just wandered around up there, huh?

LEE: Yeah. With a purpose.

AUSTIN: See any houses?

(*pause*)

LEE: Couple. Couple a' real nice ones. One of 'em didn't even have a dog. Walked right up and stuck my head in the window. Not a peep. Just a sweet kinda' surburban silence.

AUSTIN: What kind of a place was it?

LEE: Like a paradise. Kinda' place that sorta' kills ya' inside. Warm yellow lights. Mexican tile all around. Copper pots hangin' over the stove. Ya' know like they got in the magazines. Blonde people movin' in and outa' the rooms, talkin' to each other. (*pause*) Kinda' place you wish you sorta' grew up in, ya' know.

AUSTIN: That's the kind of place you wish you'd grown up in?

LEE: Yeah, why not?

AUSTIN: I thought you hated that kind of stuff.

LEE: Yeah, well you never knew too much about me did ya'?

(*pause*)

AUSTIN: Why'd you go out to the desert in the first place?

LEE: I was on my way to see the old man.

AUSTIN: You mean you just passed through there?

LEE: Yeah. That's right. Three months of passin' through.

AUSTIN: Three months?

LEE: Somethin' like that. Maybe more. Why?

AUSTIN: You lived on the Mojave for three months?

LEE: Yeah. What'sa' matter with that?

AUSTIN: By yourself?

LEE: Mostly. Had a couple a' visitors. Had that dog for a while.

AUSTIN: Didn't you miss people?

LEE: (*laughs*) People?

AUSTIN: Yeah. I mean I go crazy if I have to spend three nights in a motel by myself.

LEE: Yer not in a motel now.

AUSTIN: No, I know. But sometimes I have to stay in motels.

LEE: Well, they got people in motels don't they?

AUSTIN: Strangers.

LEE: Yer friendly aren't ya'? Aren't you the friendly type?

(*pause*)

AUSTIN: I'm going to have somebody coming by here later, Lee.

LEE: Ah! Lady friend?

AUSTIN: No, a producer.

LEE: Aha! What's he produce?

AUSTIN: Film. Movies. You know.

LEE: Oh, movies. Motion Pictures! A Big Wig huh?

AUSTIN: Yeah.

LEE: What's he comin' by here for?

AUSTIN: We have to talk about a project.

LEE: Whadya' mean, "a project"? What's "a project"?

AUSTIN: A script.

LEE: Oh. That's what yer doin' with all these papers?

AUSTIN: Yeah.

LEE: Well, what's the project about?

AUSTIN: We're uh—it's a period piece.

LEE: What's "a period piece"?

AUSTIN: Look, it doesn't matter. The main thing is we need to discuss this alone. I mean—

LEE: Oh, I get it. You want me outa' the picture.

AUSTIN: Not exactly. I just need to be alone with him for a couple of hours. So we can talk.

LEE: Yer afraid I'll embarrass ya' huh?

AUSTIN: I'm not afraid you'll embarrass me!

LEE: Well, I tell ya' what— Why don't you just gimme the keys to yer car and I'll be back here around six o'clock or so. That give ya' enough time?

AUSTIN: I'm not loaning you my car, Lee.

LEE: You want me to just git lost huh? Take a hike? Is that it? Pound the pavement for a few hours while you bullshit yer way into a million bucks.

AUSTIN: Look, it's going to be hard enough for me to face this character on my own without—

LEE: You don't know this guy?

AUSTIN: No I don't know—He's a producer. I mean I've been meeting with him for months but you never get to know a producer.

LEE: Yer tryin' to hustle him? Is that it?

AUSTIN: I'm not trying to hustle him! I'm trying to work out a deal! It's not easy.

LEE: What kinda' deal?

AUSTIN: Convince him it's a worthwhile story.

LEE: He's not convinced? How come he's comin' over here if he's not convinced? I'll convince him for ya'.

AUSTIN: You don't understand the way things work down here.

LEE: How do things work down here?

(*pause*)

AUSTIN: Look, if I loan you my car will you have it back here by six?

LEE: On the button. With a full tank a' gas.

AUSTIN: (*digging in his pocket for keys*) Forget about the gas.

LEE: Hey, these days gas is gold, old buddy.

(AUSTIN *hands the keys to* LEE)

You remember that car I used to loan you?

AUSTIN: Yeah.

LEE: Forty Ford. Flathead.

AUSTIN: Yeah.

LEE: Sucker hauled ass didn't it?

AUSTIN: Lee, it's not that I don't want to loan you my car—

LEE: You are loanin' me yer car.

(LEE *gives* AUSTIN *a pat on the shoulder, pause*)

AUSTIN: I know. I just wish—

LEE: What? You wish what?

AUSTIN: I don't know. I wish I wasn't— I wish I didn't have to be doing business down here. I'd like to just spend some time with you.

LEE: I thought it was "Art" you were doin'.

(LEE *moves across kitchen toward exit, tosses keys in his hand*)

AUSTIN: Try to get it back here by six, okay?

LEE: No sweat. Hey, ya' know, if that uh—story of yours

doesn't go over with the guy—tell him I got a couple a' "projects" he might be interested in. Real commercial. Full a' suspense. True-to-life stuff.

(LEE *exits,* AUSTIN *stares after* LEE *then turns, goes to papers at table, leafs through pages, lights fade to black*)

SCENE THREE

Afternoon. Alcove, SAUL KIMMER *and* AUSTIN *seated across from each other at table.*

SAUL: Well, to tell you the truth Austin, I have never felt so confident about a project in quite a long time.

AUSTIN: Well, that's good to hear, Saul.

SAUL: I am absolutely convinced we can get this thing off the ground. I mean we'll have to make a sale to television and that means getting a major star. Somebody bankable. But I think we can do it. I really do.

AUSTIN: Don't you think we need a first draft before we approach a star?

SAUL: No, no, not at all. I don't think it's necessary. Maybe a brief synopsis. I don't want you to touch the typewriter until we have some seed money.

AUSTIN: That's fine with me.

SAUL: I mean it's a great story. Just the story alone. You've really managed to capture something this time.

AUSTIN: I'm glad you like it, Saul.

(LEE *enters abruptly into kitchen carrying a stolen television set, short pause*)

LEE: Aw shit, I'm sorry about that. I am really sorry Austin.

AUSTIN: (*standing*) That's all right.

LEE: (*moving toward them*) I mean I thought it was way past six already. You said to have it back here by six.

AUSTIN: We were just finishing up. (*to Saul*) This is my, uh—brother, Lee.

SAUL: (*standing*) Oh, I'm very happy to meet you.

(LEE *sets T.V. on sink counter, shakes hands with* SAUL)

LEE: I can't tell ya' how happy I am to meet you sir.

SAUL: Saul Kimmer.

LEE: Mr. Kipper.

SAUL: Kimmer.

AUSTIN: Lee's been living out on the desert and he just uh—

SAUL: Oh, that's terrific! (*to* LEE) Palm Springs?

LEE: Yeah. Yeah, right. Right around in that area. Near uh— Bob Hope Drive there.

SAUL: Oh I love it out there. I just love it. The air is wonderful.

LEE: Yeah. Sure is. Healthy.

SAUL: And the golf. I don't know if you play golf, but the golf is just about the best.

LEE: I play a lota' golf.

SAUL: Is that right?

LEE: Yeah. In fact I was hoping I'd run into somebody out here who played a little golf. I've been lookin' for a partner.

SAUL: Well, I uh—

AUSTIN: Lee's just down for a visit while our mother's in Alaska.

SAUL: Oh, your mother's in Alaska?

AUSTIN: Yes. She went up there on a little vacation. This is her place.

SAUL: I see. Well isn't that something. Alaska.

LEE: What kinda' handicap do ya' have, Mr. Kimmer?

SAUL: Oh I'm just a Sunday duffer really. You know.

LEE: That's good 'cause I haven't swung a club in months.

SAUL: Well we ought to get together sometime and have a little game. Austin, do you play?

(SAUL *mimes a Johnny Carson golf swing for* AUSTIN)

AUSTIN: No. I don't uh—I've watched it on T.V.

LEE: (*to* SAUL) How 'bout tomorrow morning? Bright and early. We could get out there and put in eighteen holes before breakfast.

SAUL: Well, I've got uh—I have several appointments—

LEE: No, I mean real early. Crack a'dawn. While the dew's still thick on the fairway.

SAUL: Sounds really great.

LEE: Austin could be our caddie.

SAUL: Now that's an idea. (*laughs*)

AUSTIN: I don't know the first thing about golf.

LEE: There's nothin' to it. Isn't that right, Saul? He'd pick it up in fifteen minutes.

SAUL: Sure. Doesn't take long. 'Course you have to play for years to find your true form. (*chuckles*)

LEE: (*to* AUSTIN) We'll give ya' a quick run-down on the club faces. The irons, the woods. Show ya' a couple pointers on the basic swing. Might even let ya' hit the ball a couple times. Whadya' think, Saul?

SAUL: Why not. I think it'd be great. I haven't had any exercise in weeks.

LEE: 'At's the spirit! We'll have a little orange juice right afterwards.

(*pause*)

SAUL: Orange juice?

LEE: Yeah! Vitamin C! Nothin' like a shot a' orange juice after a round a' golf. Hot shower. Snappin' towels at each others' privates. Real sense a' fraternity.

SAUL: (*smiles at* AUSTIN) Well, you make it sound very inviting, I must say. It really does sound great.

LEE: Then it's a date.

SAUL: Well, I'll call the country club and see if I can arrange something.

LEE: Great! Boy, I sure am sorry that I busted in on ya' all in the middle of yer meeting.

SAUL: Oh that's quite all right. We were just about finished anyway.

LEE: I can wait out in the other room if you want.

SAUL: No really—

LEE: Just got Austin's color T.V. back from the shop. I can watch a little amateur boxing now.

(LEE *and* AUSTIN *exchange looks*)

SAUL: Oh— Yes.

LEE: You don't fool around in Television, do you Saul?

SAUL: Uh— I have in the past. Produced some T.V. Specials. Network stuff. But it's mainly features now.

LEE: That's where the big money is, huh?

SAUL: Yes. That's right.

AUSTIN: Why don't I call you tomorrow, Saul and we'll get together. We can have lunch or something.

SAUL: That'd be terrific.

LEE: Right after the golf.

(*pause*)

SAUL: What?

LEE: You can have lunch right after the golf.

SAUL: Oh, right.

LEE: Austin was tellin' me that yer interested in stories.

SAUL: Well, we develop certain projects that we feel have commercial potential.

LEE: What kinda' stuff do ya' go in for?

SAUL: Oh, the usual. You know. Good love interest. Lots of action. (*chuckles at* AUSTIN)

LEE: Westerns?

SAUL: Sometimes.

AUSTIN: I'll give you a ring, Saul.

(AUSTIN *tries to move* SAUL *across the kitchen but* LEE *blocks their way*)

LEE: I got a Western that'd knock yer lights out.

SAUL: Oh really?

LEE: Yeah. Contemporary Western. Based on a true story. 'Course I'm not a writer like my brother here. I'm not a man of the pen.

SAUL: Well—

LEE: I mean I can tell ya' a story off the tongue but I can't put it down on paper. That don't make any difference though does it?

SAUL: No, not really.

LEE: I mean plenty a' guys have stories don't they? True-life stories. Musta' been a lota' movies made from real life.

SAUL: Yes. I suppose so.

LEE: I haven't seen a good Western since "Lonely Are the Brave." You remember that movie?

SAUL: No, I'm afraid I—

LEE: Kirk Douglas. Helluva' movie. You remember that movie, Austin?

AUSTIN: Yes.

LEE: (*to* SAUL) The man dies for the love of a horse.

SAUL: Is that right.

LEE: Yeah. Ya' hear the horse screamin' at the end of it. Rain's comin' down. Horse is screamin'. Then there's a shot. BLAM! Just a single shot like that. Then nothin' but the sound of rain. And Kirk Douglas is ridin' in the ambulance. Ridin' away from the scene of the accident. And when he hears that shot he knows that his horse has died. He knows. And you see his eyes. And his eyes die. Right inside his face. And then his eyes close. And you know that he's died too. You know that Kirk Douglas has died from the death of his horse.

SAUL: (*eyes* AUSTIN *nervously*) Well, it sounds like a great movie. I'm sorry I missed it.

LEE: Yeah, you shouldn't a' missed that one.

SAUL: I'll have to try to catch it some time. Arrange a screening or something. Well, Austin, I'll have to hit the freeway before rush hour.

AUSTIN: (*ushers him toward exit*) It's good seeing you, Saul.

(AUSTIN *and* SAUL *shake hands*)

LEE: So ya' think there's room for a real Western these days? A true-to-life Western?

SAUL: Well, I don't see why not. Why don't you uh—tell the story to Austin and have him write a little outline.

LEE: You'd take a look at it then?

SAUL: Yes. Sure. I'll give it a read-through. Always eager for new material. (*smiles at* AUSTIN)

LEE: That's great! You'd really read it then huh?

SAUL: It would just be my opinion of course.

LEE: That's all I want. Just an opinion. I happen to think it has a lota' possibilities.

SAUL: Well, it was great meeting you and I'll—

(SAUL *and* LEE *shake*)

LEE: I'll call you tomorrow about the golf.

SAUL: Oh. Yes, right.

LEE: Austin's got your number, right?

SAUL: Yes.

LEE: So long Saul. (*gives* SAUL *a pat on the back*)

(SAUL *exits*, AUSTIN *turns to* LEE, *looks at T.V. then back to* LEE)

AUSTIN: Give me the keys.

(AUSTIN *extends his hand toward* LEE, LEE *doesn't move, just stares at* AUSTIN, *smiles, lights to black*)

SCENE FOUR

Night. Coyotes in distance, fade, sound of typewriter in dark, crickets, candlelight in alcove, dim light in kitchen, lights reveal AUSTIN *at glass table typing,* LEE *sits across from him, foot on table, drinking beer and whiskey, the T.V. is still on sink counter,* AUSTIN *types for a while, then stops.*

LEE: All right, now read it back to me.

AUSTIN: I'm not reading it back to you, Lee. You can read it when we're finished. I can't spend all night on this.

LEE: You got better things to do?

AUSTIN: Let's just go ahead. Now what happens when he leaves Texas?

LEE: Is he ready to leave Texas yet? I didn't know we were that far along. He's not ready to leave Texas.

AUSTIN: He's right at the border.

LEE: (*sitting up*) No, see this is one a' the crucial parts. Right here. (*taps paper with beer can*) We can't rush through this. He's not right at the border. He's a good fifty miles from the border. A lot can happen in fifty miles.

AUSTIN: It's only an outline. We're not writing an entire script now.

LEE: Well ya' can't leave things out even if it is an outline. It's one a' the most important parts. Ya' can't go leavin' it out.

AUSTIN: Okay, okay. Let's just—get it done.

LEE: All right. Now. He's in the truck and he's got his horse trailer and his horse.

AUSTIN: We've already established that.

LEE: And he sees this other guy comin' up behind him in another truck. And that truck is pullin' a gooseneck.

AUSTIN: What's a gooseneck?

LEE: Cattle trailer. You know the kind with a gooseneck, goes right down in the bed a' the pick-up.

AUSTIN: Oh. All right. (*types*)

LEE: It's important.

AUSTIN: Okay. I got it.

LEE: All these details are important.

(AUSTIN *types as they talk*)

AUSTIN: I've got it.

LEE: And this other guy's got his horse all saddled up in the back a' the gooseneck.

AUSTIN: Right.

LEE: So both these guys have got their horses right along with 'em, see.

AUSTIN: I understand.

LEE: Then this first guy suddenly realizes two things.

AUSTIN: The guy in front?

LEE: Right. The guy in front realizes two things almost at the same time. Simultaneous.

AUSTIN: What were the two things?

LEE: Number one, he realizes that the guy behind him is the husband of the woman he's been—

(LEE *makes gesture of screwing by pumping his arm*)

AUSTIN: (*sees* LEE'S *gesture*) Oh. Yeah.

LEE: And number two, he realizes he's in the middle of Tornado Country.

AUSTIN: What's "Tornado Country"?

LEE: Panhandle.

AUSTIN: Panhandle?

LEE: Sweetwater. Around in that area. Nothin'. Nowhere. And number three—

AUSTIN: I thought there was only two.

LEE: There's three. There's a third unforeseen realization.

AUSTIN: And what's that?

LEE: That he's runnin' outa' gas.

AUSTIN: (*stops typing*) Come on, Lee.

(AUSTIN *gets up, moves to kitchen, gets a glass of water*)

LEE: Whadya' mean, "come on"? That's what it is. Write it down! He's runnin' outa' gas.

AUSTIN: It's too—

LEE: What? It's too what? It's too real! That's what ya' mean isn't it? It's too much like real life!

AUSTIN: It's not like real life! It's not enough like real life. Things don't happen like that.

LEE: What! Men don't fuck other men's women?

AUSTIN: Yes. But they don't end up chasing each other across the Panhandle. Through "Tornado Country."

LEE: They do in this movie!

AUSTIN: And they don't have horses conveniently along with them when they run out of gas! And they don't run out of gas either!

LEE: These guys run outa' gas! This is my story and one a' these guys runs outa' gas!

AUSTIN: It's just a dumb excuse to get them into a chase scene. It's contrived.

LEE: It is a chase scene! It's already a chase scene. They been chasin' each other fer days.

AUSTIN: So now they're supposed to abandon their trucks, climb on their horses and chase each other into the mountains?

LEE: (*standing suddenly*) There aren't any mountains in the Panhandle! It's flat!

(LEE *turns violently toward windows in alcove and throws beer can at them*)

LEE: Goddamn these crickets! (*yells at crickets*) Shut up out there! (*pause, turns back toward table*) This place is like a fuckin' rest home here. How're you supposed to think!

AUSTIN: You wanna' take a break?

LEE: No, I don't wanna' take a break! I wanna' get this done! This is my last chance to get this done.

AUSTIN: (*moves back into alcove*) All right. Take it easy.

LEE: I'm gonna' be leavin' this area. I don't have time to mess around here.

AUSTIN: Where are you going?

LEE: Never mind where I'm goin'! That's got nothin' to do with you. I just gotta' get this done. I'm not like you. Hangin' around bein' a parasite offa' other fools. I gotta' do this thing and get out.

(*pause*)

AUSTIN: A parasite? Me?

LEE: Yeah, you!

AUSTIN: After you break into people's houses and take their televisions?

LEE: They don't need their televisions! I'm doin' them a service.

AUSTIN: Give me back my keys, Lee.

LEE: Not until you write this thing! You're gonna' write this outline thing for me or that car's gonna' wind up in Arizona with a different paint job.

AUSTIN: You think you can force me to write this? I was doing you a favor.

LEE: Git off yer high horse will ya'! Favor! Big favor. Handin' down favors from the mountain top.

AUSTIN: Let's just write it, okay? Let's sit down and not get upset and see if we can just get through this.

(AUSTIN *sits at typewriter*)

(*long pause*)

LEE: Yer not gonna' even show it to him, are ya'?

AUSTIN: What?

LEE: This outline. You got no intention of showin' it to him. Yer just doin' this 'cause yer afraid a' me.

AUSTIN: You can show it to him yourself.

LEE: I will, boy! I'm gonna' read it to him on the golf course.

AUSTIN: And I'm not afraid of you either.

LEE: Then how come yer doin' it?

AUSTIN: (*pause*) So I can get my keys back.

(*pause as* LEE *takes keys out of his pocket slowly and throws them on table, long pause,* AUSTIN *stares at keys*)

LEE: There. Now you got yer keys back.

(AUSTIN *looks up at* LEE *but doesn't take keys*)

LEE: Go ahead. There's yer keys.

(AUSTIN *slowly takes keys off table and puts them back in his own pocket*)

Now what're you gonna' do? Kick me out?

AUSTIN: I'm not going to kick you out, Lee.

LEE: You couldn't kick me out, boy.

AUSTIN: I know.

LEE: So you can't even consider that one. (*pause*) You could call the police. That'd be the obvious thing.

AUSTIN: You're my brother.

LEE: That don't mean a thing. You go down to the L.A. Police Department there and ask them what kinda' people kill each other the most. What do you think they'd say?

AUSTIN: Who said anything about killing?

LEE: Family people. Brothers. Brothers-in-law. Cousins. Real American-type people. They kill each other in the heat mostly. In the Smog-Alerts. In the Brush Fire Season. Right about this time a' year.

AUSTIN: This isn't the same.

LEE: Oh no? What makes it different?

AUSTIN: We're not insane. We're not driven to acts of violence like that. Not over a dumb movie script. Now sit down.

(*long pause,* LEE *considers which way to go with it*)

LEE: Maybe not. (*he sits back down at table across from* AUSTIN) Maybe you're right. Maybe we're too intelligent, huh? (*pause*) We got our heads on our shoulders. One of us has even got a Ivy League diploma. Now that means somethin' don't it? Doesn't that mean somethin'?

AUSTIN: Look, I'll write this thing for you, Lee. I don't mind writing it. I just don't want to get all worked up about it. It's not worth it. Now, come on. Let's just get through it, okay?

LEE: Nah. I think there's easier money. Lotsa' places I could pick up thousands. Maybe millions. I don't need this shit. I could go up to Sacramento Valley and steal me a diesel. Ten thousand a week dismantling one a' those suckers. Ten thousand a week!

(LEE *opens another beer, puts his foot back up on table*)

AUSTIN: No, really, look, I'll write it out for you. I think it's a great idea.

LEE: Nah, you got yer own work to do. I don't wanna' interfere with yer life.

AUSTIN: I mean it'd be really fantastic if you could sell this. Turn it into a movie. I mean it.

(*pause*)

LEE: Ya' think so huh?

AUSTIN: Absolutely. You could really turn your life around, you know. Change things.

LEE: I could get me a house maybe.

AUSTIN: Sure you could get a house. You could get a whole ranch if you wanted to.

LEE: (*laughs*) A ranch? I could get a ranch?

AUSTIN: 'Course you could. You know what a screenplay sells
for these days?

LEE: No. What's it sell for?

AUSTIN: A lot. A whole lot of money.

LEE: Thousands?

AUSTIN: Yeah. Thousands.

LEE: Millions?

AUSTIN: Well—

LEE: We could get the old man outa' hock then.

AUSTIN: Maybe.

LEE: Maybe? Whadya' mean, maybe?

AUSTIN: I mean it might take more than money.

LEE: You were just tellin' me it'd change my whole life around.
Why wouldn't it change his?

AUSTIN: He's different.

LEE: Oh, he's of a different ilk huh?

AUSTIN: He's not gonna' change. Let's leave the old man out of
it.

LEE: That's right. He's not gonna' change but I will. I'll just
turn myself right inside out. I could be just like you then,
huh? Sittin' around dreamin' stuff up. Gettin' paid to dream.
Ridin' back and forth on the freeway just dreamin' my fool
head off.

AUSTIN: It's not all that easy.

LEE: It's not, huh?

AUSTIN: No. There's a lot of work involved.

LEE: What's the toughest part? Deciding whether to jog or
play tennis?

(*long pause*)

AUSTIN: Well, look. You can stay here—do whatever you
want to. Borrow the car. Come in and out. Doesn't matter to
me. It's not my house. I'll help you write this thing or—not.
Just let me know what you want. You tell me.

LEE: Oh. So now suddenly you're at my service. Is that it?

AUSTIN: What do you want to do Lee?

(*long pause*, LEE *stares at him then turns and dreams at windows*)

LEE: I tell ya' what I'd do if I still had that dog. Ya' wanna'
know what I'd do?

AUSTIN: What?

LEE: Head out to Ventura. Cook up a little match. God that little dog could bear down. Lota' money in dog fightin'. Big money.

(*pause*)

AUSTIN: Why don't we try to see this through, Lee. Just for the hell of it. Maybe you've really got something here. What do you think?

(*pause*, LEE *considers*)

LEE: Maybe so. No harm in tryin' I guess. You think it's such a hot idea. Besides, I always wondered what'd be like to be you.

AUSTIN: You did?

LEE: Yeah, sure. I used to picture you walkin' around some campus with yer arms fulla' books. Blondes chasin' after ya'.

AUSTIN: Blondes? That's funny.

LEE: What's funny about it?

AUSTIN: Because I always used to picture you somewhere.

LEE: Where'd you picture me?

AUSTIN: Oh, I don't know. Different places. Adventures. You were always on some adventure.

LEE: Yeah.

AUSTIN: And I used to say to myself, "Lee's got the right idea. He's out there in the world and here I am. What am I doing?"

LEE: Well you were settin' yourself up for somethin'.

AUSTIN: I guess.

LEE: We better get started on this thing then.

AUSTIN: Okay.

(AUSTIN *sits up at typewriter, puts new paper in*)

LEE: Oh. Can I get the keys back before I forget?

(AUSTIN *hesitates*)

You said I could borrow the car if I wanted, right? Isn't that what you said?

AUSTIN: Yeah. Right.

(AUSTIN *takes keys out of his pocket, sets them on table,* LEE *takes keys slowly, plays with them in his hand*)

LEE: I could get a ranch, huh?

AUSTIN: Yeah. We have to write it first though.

LEE: Okay. Let's write it.

(*lights start dimming slowly to end of scene as* AUSTIN *types,* LEE *speaks*)

So they take off after each other straight into an endless black prairie. The sun is just comin' down and they can feel the night on their backs. What they don't know is that each one of 'em is afraid, see. Each one separately thinks that he's the only one that's afraid. And they keep ridin' like that straight into the night. Not knowing. And the one who's chasin' doesn't know where the other one is taking him. And the one who's being chased doesn't know where he's going.

(*lights to black, typing stops in the dark, crickets fade*)

ACT TWO

SCENE FIVE

Morning. LEE *at the table in alcove with a set of golf clubs in a fancy leather bag,* AUSTIN *at sink washing a few dishes.*

AUSTIN: He really liked it, huh?

LEE: He wouldn't a' gave me these clubs if he didn't like it.

AUSTIN: He gave you the clubs?

LEE: Yeah. I told ya' he gave me the clubs. The bag too.

AUSTIN: I thought he just loaned them to you.

LEE: He said it was part a' the advance. A little gift like. Gesture of his good faith.

AUSTIN: He's giving you an advance?

LEE: Now what's so amazing about that? I told ya' it was a good story. You even said it was a good story.

AUSTIN: Well that is really incredible Lee. You know how many guys spend their whole lives down here trying to break into this business? Just trying to get in the door?

LEE: (*pulling clubs out of bag, testing them*) I got no idea. How many?

(*pause*)

AUSTIN: How much of an advance is he giving you?

LEE: Plenty. We were talkin' big money out there. Ninth hole is where I sealed the deal.

AUSTIN: He made a firm commitment?

LEE: Absolutely.

AUSTIN: Well, I know Saul and he doesn't fool around when he says he likes something.

LEE: I thought you said you didn't know him.

AUSTIN: Well, I'm familiar with his tastes.

28

LEE: I let him get two up on me goin' into the back nine. He was sure he had me cold. You shoulda' seen his face when I pulled out the old pitching wedge and plopped it pin-high, two feet from the cup. He 'bout shit his pants. "Where'd a guy like you ever learn how to play golf like that?" he says.

(LEE *laughs*, AUSTIN *stares at him*)

AUSTIN: 'Course there's no contract yet. Nothing's final until it's on paper.

LEE: It's final, all right. There's no way he's gonna' back out of it now. We gambled for it.

AUSTIN: Saul, gambled?

LEE: Yeah, sure. I mean he liked the outline already so he wasn't risking that much. I just guaranteed it with my short game.

(*pause*)

AUSTIN: Well, we should celebrate or something. I think Mom left a bottle of champagne in the refrigerator. We should have a little toast.

(AUSTIN *gets glasses from cupboard, goes to refrigerator, pulls out bottle of champagne*)

LEE: You shouldn't oughta' take her champagne, Austin. She's gonna' miss that.

AUSTIN: Oh, she's not going to mind. She'd be glad we put it to good use. I'll get her another bottle. Besides, it's perfect for the occasion.

(*pause*)

LEE: Yer gonna' get a nice fee fer writin' the script a' course. Straight fee.

(AUSTIN *stops, stares at* LEE, *puts glasses and bottle on table, pause*)

AUSTIN: I'm writing the script?

LEE: That's what he said. Said we couldn't hire a better screen-writer in the whole town.

AUSTIN: But I'm already working on a script. I've got my own project. I don't have time to write two scripts.

LEE: No, he said he was gonna' drop that other one.

(*pause*)

AUSTIN: What? You mean mine? He's going to drop mine and do yours instead?

LEE: (*smiles*) Now look, Austin, it's jest beginner's luck ya' know. I mean I sank a fifty foot putt for this deal. No hard feelings.

(AUSTIN *goes to phone on wall, grabs it, starts dialing*)

He's not gonna' be in, Austin. Told me he wouldn't be in 'till late this afternoon.

AUSTIN: (*stays on phone, dialing, listens*) I can't believe this. I just can't believe it. Are you sure he said that? Why would he drop mine?

LEE: That's what he told me.

AUSTIN: He can't do that without telling me first. Without talking to me at least. He wouldn't just make a decision like that without talking to me!

LEE: Well I was kinda' surprised myself. But he was real enthusiastic about my story.

(AUSTIN *hangs up phone violently, paces*)

AUSTIN: What'd he say! Tell me everything he said!

LEE: I been tellin' ya'! He said he liked the story a whole lot. It was the first authentic Western to come along in a decade.

AUSTIN: He liked that story! Your story?

LEE: Yeah! What's so surprisin' about that?

AUSTIN: It's stupid! It's the dumbest story I ever heard in my life.

LEE: Hey, hold on! That's my story yer talkin' about!

AUSTIN: It's a bullshit story! It's idiotic. Two lamebrains chasing each other across Texas! Are you kidding? Who do you think's going to go see a film like that?

LEE: It's not a film! It's a movie. There's a big difference. That's somethin' Saul told me.

AUSTIN: Oh he did, huh?

LEE: Yeah, he said, "In this business we make movies, American movies. Leave the films to the French."

AUSTIN: So you got real intimate with old Saul huh? He started pouring forth his vast knowledge of Cinema.

LEE: I think he liked me a lot, to tell ya' the truth. I think he felt I was somebody he could confide in.

AUSTIN: What'd you do, beat him up or something?

LEE: (*stands fast*) Hey, I've about had it with the insults buddy!
You think yer the only one in the brain department here? Yer
the only one that can sit around and cook things up? There's
other people got ideas too, ya' know!

AUSTIN: You must've done something. Threatened him or
something. Now what'd you do Lee?

LEE: I convinced him!

(LEE *makes sudden menacing lunge toward* AUSTIN, *wielding golf
club above his head, stops himself, frozen moment, long pause,* LEE
lowers club)

AUSTIN: Oh, Jesus. You didn't hurt him did you?

(*long silence,* LEE *sits back down at table*)

Lee! Did you hurt him?

LEE: I didn't do nothin' to him! He liked my story. Pure and
simple. He said it was the best story he's come across in a
long, long time.

AUSTIN: That's what he told me about my story! That's the
same thing he said to me.

LEE: Well, he musta' been lyin'. He musta' been lyin' to one of
us anyway.

AUSTIN: You can't come into this town and start pushing people
around. They're gonna' put you away!

LEE: I never pushed anybody around! I beat him fair and
square. (*pause*) They can't touch me anyway. They can't put
a finger on me. I'm gone. I can come in through the window
and go out through the door. They never knew what hit 'em.
You, yer stuck. Yer the one that's stuck. Not me. So don't be
warnin' me what to do in this town.

(*pause,* AUSTIN *crosses to table, sits at typewriter, rests*)

AUSTIN: Lee, come on, level with me will you? It doesn't
make any sense that suddenly he'd throw my idea out the
window. I've been talking to him for months. I've got too
much at stake. Everything's riding on this project.

LEE: What's yer idea?

AUSTIN: It's just a simple love story.

LEE: What kinda' love story?

AUSTIN: (*stands, crosses into kitchen*) I'm not telling you!

LEE: Ha! 'Fraid I'll steal it huh? Competition's gettin' kinda' close to home isn't it?

AUSTIN: Where did Saul say he was going?

LEE: He was gonna' take my story to a couple studios.

AUSTIN: That's *my* outline you know! I wrote that outline! You've got no right to be peddling it around.

LEE: You weren't ready to take credit for it last night.

AUSTIN: Give me my keys!

LEE: What?

AUSTIN: The keys! I want my keys back!

LEE: Where you goin'?

AUSTIN: Just give me my keys! I gotta' take a drive. I gotta' get out of here for a while.

LEE: Where you gonna' go, Austin?

AUSTIN: (*pause*) I might just drive out to the desert for a while. I gotta' think.

LEE: You can think here just as good. This is the perfect setup for thinkin'. We got some writin' to do here, boy. Now let's just have us a little toast. Relax. We're partners now.

(LEE *pops the cork of the champagne bottle, pours two drinks as the lights fade to black*)

SCENE SIX

Afternoon. LEE *and* SAUL *in kitchen,* AUSTIN *in alcove*

LEE: Now you tell him. You tell him, Mr. Kipper.

SAUL: Kimmer.

LEE: Kimmer. You tell him what you told me. He don't believe me.

AUSTIN: I don't want to hear it.

SAUL: It's really not a big issue, Austin. I was simply amazed by your brother's story and—

AUSTIN: Amazed? You lost a bet! You gambled with my material!

SAUL: That's really beside the point, Austin. I'm ready to go all the way with your brother's story. I think it has a great deal of merit.

AUSTIN: I don't want to hear about it, okay? Go tell it to the

executives! Tell it to somebody who's going to turn it into a
package deal or something. A T.V. series. Don't tell it to
me.

SAUL: But I want to continue with your project too, Austin. It's
not as though we can't do both. We're big enough for that
aren't we?

AUSTIN: "We"? *I* can't do both! I don't know about "we."

LEE: (*to* SAUL) See, what'd I tell ya'. He's totally unsympathetic.

SAUL: Austin, there's no point in our going to another screenwriter for this. It just doesn't make sense. You're brothers.
You know each other. There's a familiarity with the material
that just wouldn't be possible otherwise.

AUSTIN: There's no familiarity with the material! None! I don't
know what "Tornado Country" is. I don't know what a
"gooseneck" is. And I don't want to know! (*pointing to* LEE)
He's a hustler! He's a bigger hustler than you are! If you
can't see that, then—

LEE: (*to* AUSTIN) Hey, now hold on. I didn't have to bring this
bone back to you, boy. I persuaded Saul here that you were
the right man for the job. You don't have to go throwin' up
favors in my face.

AUSTIN: Favors! I'm the one who wrote the fuckin' outline! You
can't even spell.

SAUL: (*to* AUSTIN) Your brother told me about the situation with
your father.

(*pause*)

AUSTIN: What? (*looks at* LEE)

SAUL: That's right. Now we have a clear-cut deal here, Austin.
We have big studio money standing behind this thing. Just
on the basis of your outline.

AUSTIN: (*to* SAUL) What'd he tell you about my father?

SAUL: Well—that he's destitute. He needs money.

LEE: That's right. He does.

(AUSTIN *shakes his head, stares at them both*)

AUSTIN: (*to* LEE) And this little assignment is supposed to go
toward the old man? A charity project? Is that what this is?
Did you cook this up on the ninth green too?

SAUL: It's a big slice, Austin.

AUSTIN: (*to* LEE) I gave him money! I already gave him money.
You know that. He drank it all up!

LEE: This is a different deal here.

SAUL: We can set up a trust for your father. A large sum of
money. It can be doled out to him in parcels so he can't
misuse it.

AUSTIN: Yeah, and who's doing the doling?

SAUL: Your brother volunteered.

(AUSTIN *laughs*)

LEE: That's right. I'll make sure he uses it for groceries.

AUSTIN: (*to* SAUL) I'm not doing this script! I'm not writing this
crap for you or anybody else. You can't blackmail me into it.
You can't threaten me into it. There's no way I'm doing it.
So just give it up. Both of you.

(*long pause*)

SAUL: Well, that's it then. I mean this is an easy three hundred grand. Just for a first draft. It's incredible, Austin. We've
got three different studios all trying to cut each other's throats
to get this material. In one morning. That's how hot it is.

AUSTIN: Yeah, well you can afford to give me a percentage on
the outline then. And you better get the genius here an agent
before he gets burned.

LEE: Saul's gonna' be my agent. Isn't that right, Saul?

SAUL: That's right. (*to* AUSTIN) Your brother has really got
something, Austin. I've been around too long not to recognize it. Raw talent.

AUSTIN: He's got a lota' balls is what he's got. He's taking you
right down the river.

SAUL: Three hundred thousand, Austin. Just for a first draft.
Now you've never been offered that kind of money before.

AUSTIN: I'm not writing it.

(*pause*)

SAUL: I see. Well—

LEE: We'll just go to another writer then. Right, Saul? Just hire
us somebody with some enthusiasm. Somebody who can
recognize the value of a good story.

SAUL: I'm sorry about this, Austin.

AUSTIN: Yeah.

SAUL: I mean I was hoping we could continue both things but
now I don't see how it's possible.

AUSTIN: So you're dropping my idea altogether. Is that it? Just trade horses in midstream? After all these months of meetings.

SAUL: I wish there was another way.

AUSTIN: I've got everything riding on this, Saul. You know that. It's my only shot. If this falls through—

SAUL: I have to go with what my instincts tell me—

AUSTIN: Your instincts!

SAUL: My gut reaction.

AUSTIN: You lost! That's your gut reaction. You lost a gamble. Now you're trying to tell me you like his story? How could you possibly fall for that story? It's as phony as Hoppalong Cassidy. What do you see in it? I'm curious.

SAUL: It has the ring of truth, Austin.

AUSTIN: (*laughs*) Truth?

LEE: It is true.

SAUL: Something about the real West.

AUSTIN: Why? Because it's got horses? Because it's got grown men acting like little boys?

SAUL: Something about the land. Your brother is speaking from experience.

AUSTIN: So am I!

SAUL: But nobody's interested in love these days, Austin. Let's face it.

LEE: That's right.

AUSTIN: (*to* SAUL) He's been camped out on the desert for three months. Talking to cactus. What's he know about what people wanna' see on the screen! I drive on the freeway every day. I swallow the smog. I watch the news in color. I shop in the Safeway. I'm the one who's in touch! Not him!

SAUL: I have to go now, Austin.

(SAUL *starts to leave*)

AUSTIN: There's no such thing as the West anymore! It's a dead issue! It's dried up, Saul, and so are you.

(SAUL *stops and turns to* AUSTIN)

SAUL: Maybe you're right. But I have to take the gamble, don't I?

AUSTIN: You're a fool to do this, Saul.

SAUL: I've always gone on my hunches. Always. And I've never been wrong. (*to* LEE) I'll talk to you tomorrow, Lee.

LEE: All right, Mr. Kimmer.
SAUL: Maybe we could have some lunch.
LEE: Fine with me. (*smiles at* AUSTIN)
SAUL: I'll give you a ring.

(SAUL *exits, lights to black as brothers look at each other from a distance*)

SCENE SEVEN

Night. Coyotes, crickets, sound of typewriter in dark, candlelight up on LEE *at typewriter struggling to type with one finger system,* AUSTIN *sits sprawled out on kitchen floor with whiskey bottle, drunk.*

AUSTIN: (*singing, from floor*)
   "Red sails in the sunset
   Way out on the blue
   Please carry my loved one
   Home safely to me

   Red sails in the sunset—"
LEE: (*slams fist on table*) Hey! Knock it off will ya'! I'm tryin' to concentrate here.
AUSTIN: (*laughs*) You're tryin' to concentrate?
LEE: Yeah. That's right.
AUSTIN: Now you're tryin' to concentrate.
LEE: Between you, the coyotes and the crickets a thought don't have much of a chance.
AUSTIN: "Between me, the coyotes and the crickets." What a great title.
LEE: I don't need a title! I need a thought.
AUSTIN: (*laughs*) A thought! Here's a thought for ya'—
LEE: I'm not askin' fer yer thoughts! I got my own. I can do this thing on my own.
AUSTIN: You're going to write an entire script on your own?
LEE: That's right.

   (*pause*)

AUSTIN: Here's a thought. Saul Kimmer—
LEE: Shut up will ya'!

AUSTIN: He thinks we're the same person.

LEE: Don't get cute.

AUSTIN: He does! He's lost his mind. Poor old Saul. (*giggles*) Thinks we're one and the same.

LEE: Why don't you ease up on that champagne.

AUSTIN: (*holding up bottle*) This isn't champagne anymore. We went through the champagne a long time ago. This is serious stuff. The days of champagne are long gone.

LEE: Well, go outside and drink it.

AUSTIN: I'm enjoying your company, Lee. For the first time since your arrival I am finally enjoying your company. And now you want me to go outside and drink alone?

LEE: That's right.

(LEE *reads through paper in typewriter, makes an erasure*)

AUSTIN: You think you'll make more progress if you're alone? You might drive yourself crazy.

LEE: I could have this thing done in a night if I had a little silence.

AUSTIN: Well you'd still have the crickets to contend with. The coyotes. The sounds of the Police Helicopters prowling above the neighborhood. Slashing their searchlights down through the streets. Hunting for the likes of you.

LEE: I'm a screenwriter now! I'm legitimate.

AUSTIN: (*laughing*) A screenwriter!

LEE: That's right. I'm on salary. That's more'n I can say for you. I got an advance coming.

AUSTIN: This is true. This is very true. An advance. (*pause*) Well, maybe I oughta' go out and try my hand at your trade. Since you're doing so good at mine.

LEE: Ha!

(LEE *attempts to type some more but gets the ribbon tangled up, starts trying to re-thread it as they continue talking*)

AUSTIN: Well why not? You don't think I've got what it takes to sneak into people's houses and steal their T.V.s?

LEE: You couldn't steal a toaster without losin' yer lunch.

(AUSTIN *stands with a struggle, supports himself by the sink*)

AUSTIN: You don't think I could sneak into somebody's house and steal a toaster?

LEE: Go take a shower or somethin' will ya!

(LEE *gets more tangled up with the typewriter ribbon, pulling it out of the machine as though it was fishing line*)

AUSTIN: You really don't think I could steal a crumby toaster? How much you wanna' bet I can't steal a toaster! How much? Go ahead! You're a gambler aren't you? Tell me how much yer willing to put on the line. Some part of your big advance? Oh, you haven't got that yet have you. I forgot.

LEE: All right. I'll bet you your car that you can't steal a toaster without gettin' busted.

AUSTIN: You already got my car!

LEE: Okay, your house then.

AUSTIN: What're you gonna' give me! I'm not talkin' about my house and my car, I'm talkin' about what are you gonna' give me. You don't have nothin' to give me.

LEE: I'll give you—shared screen credit. How 'bout that? I'll have it put in the contract that this was written by the both of us.

AUSTIN: I don't want my name on that piece of shit! I want something of value. You got anything of value? You got any tidbits from the desert? Any Rattlesnake bones? I'm not a greedy man. Any little personal treasure will suffice.

LEE: I'm gonna' just kick yer ass out in a minute.

AUSTIN: Oh, so now you're gonna' kick me out! Now I'm the intruder. I'm the one who's invading your precious privacy.

LEE: I'm trying to do some screenwriting here!!

(LEE *stands, picks up typewriter, slams it down hard on table, pause, silence except for crickets*)

AUSTIN: Well, you got everything you need. You got plenty a' coffee? Groceries. You got a car. A contract. (*pause*) Might need a new typewriter ribbon but other than that you're pretty well fixed. I'll just leave ya' alone for a while.

(AUSTIN *tries to steady himself to leave,* LEE *makes a move toward him*)

LEE: Where you goin'?

AUSTIN: Don't worry about me. I'm not the one to worry about.

(AUSTIN *weaves toward exit, stops*)

LEE: What're you gonna' do? Just go wander out into the night?

AUSTIN: I'm gonna' make a little tour.

LEE: Why don't ya' just go to bed for Christ's sake. Yer makin' me sick.

AUSTIN: I can take care a' myself. Don't worry about me.

(AUSTIN *weaves badly in another attempt to exit, he crashes to the floor*, LEE *goes to him but remains standing*)

LEE: You want me to call your wife for ya' or something?

AUSTIN: (*from floor*) My wife?

LEE: Yeah. I mean maybe she can help ya' out. Talk to ya' or somethin'.

AUSTIN: (*struggles to stand again*) She's five hundred miles away. North. North of here. Up in the North country where things are calm. I don't need any help. I'm gonna' go outside and I'm gonna' steal a toaster. I'm gonna' steal some other stuff too. I might even commit bigger crimes. Bigger than you ever dreamed of. Crimes beyond the imagination!

(AUSTIN *manages to get himself vertical, tries to head for exit again*)

LEE: Just hang on a minute, Austin.

AUSTIN: Why? What for? You don't need my help, right? You got a handle on the project. Besides, I'm lookin' forward to the smell of the night. The bushes. Orange blossoms. Dust in the driveways. Rain bird sprinklers. Lights in people's houses. You're right about the lights, Lee. Everybody else is livin' the life. Indoors. Safe. This is a Paradise down here. You know that? We're livin' in a Paradise. We've forgotten about that.

LEE: You sound just like the old man now.

AUSTIN: Yeah, well we all sound alike when we're sloshed. We just sorta' echo each other.

LEE: Maybe if we could work on this together we could bring him back out here. Get him settled down some place.

(AUSTIN *turns violently toward* LEE, *takes a swing at him, misses and crashes to the floor again*, LEE *stays standing*)

AUSTIN: I don't want him out here! I've had it with him! I went all the way out there! I went out of my way. I gave him money and all he did was play Al Jolson records and spit at me! I gave him money!

(*pause*)

LEE: Just help me a little with the characters, all right? You know how to do it, Austin.

AUSTIN: (*on floor, laughs*) The characters!

LEE: Yeah. You know. The way they talk and stuff. I can hear it in my head but I can't get it down on paper.

AUSTIN: What characters?

LEE: The guys. The guys in the story.

AUSTIN: Those aren't characters.

LEE: Whatever you call 'em then. I need to write somethin' out.

AUSTIN: Those are illusions of characters.

LEE: I don't give a damn what ya' call 'em! You know what I'm talkin' about!

AUSTIN: Those are fantasies of a long lost boyhood.

LEE: I gotta' write somethin' out on paper!!

(*pause*)

AUSTIN: What for? Saul's gonna' get you a fancy screenwriter isn't he?

LEE: I wanna' do it myself!

AUSTIN: Then do it! Yer on your own now, old buddy. You bulldogged yer way into contention. Now you gotta' carry it through.

LEE: I will but I need some advice. Just a couple a' things. Come on, Austin. Just help me get 'em talkin' right. It won't take much.

AUSTIN: Oh, now you're having a little doubt huh? What happened? The pressure's on, boy. This is it. You gotta' come up with it now. You don't come up with a winner on your first time out they just cut your head off. They don't give you a second chance ya' know.

LEE: I got a good story! I know it's a good story. I just need a little help is all.

AUSTIN: Not from me. Not from yer little old brother. I'm retired.

LEE: You could save this thing for me, Austin. I'd give ya' half the money. I would. I only need half anyway. With this kinda' money I could be a long time down the road. I'd never bother ya' again. I promise. You'd never even see me again.

AUSTIN: (*still on floor*) You'd disappear?

LEE: I would for sure.

AUSTIN: Where would you disappear to?

LEE: That don't matter. I got plenty a' places.

AUSTIN: Nobody can disappear. The old man tried that. Look where it got him. He lost his teeth.

LEE: He never had any money.

AUSTIN: I don't mean that. I mean his teeth! His real teeth. First he lost his real teeth, then he lost his false teeth. You never knew that did ya'? He never confided in you.

LEE: Nah, I never knew that.

AUSTIN: You wanna' drink?

(AUSTIN *offers bottle to* LEE, LEE *takes it, sits down on kitchen floor with* AUSTIN, *they share the bottle*)

Yeah, he lost his real teeth one at a time. Woke up every morning with another tooth lying on the mattress. Finally, he decides he's gotta' get 'em all pulled out but he doesn't have any money. Middle of Arizona with no money and no insurance and every morning another tooth is lying on the mattress. (*takes a drink*) So what does he do?

LEE: I dunno'. I never knew about that.

AUSTIN: He begs the government. G.I. Bill or some damn thing. Some pension plan he remembers in the back of his head. And they send him out the money.

LEE: They did?

(*they keep trading the bottle between them, taking drinks*)

AUSTIN: Yeah. They send him the money but it's not enough money. Costs a lot to have all yer teeth yanked. They charge by the individual tooth, ya' know. I mean one tooth isn't equal to another tooth. Some are more expensive. Like the big ones in the back—

LEE: So what happened?

AUSTIN: So he locates a Mexican dentist in Juarez who'll do the whole thing for a song. And he takes off hitchhiking to the border.

LEE: Hitchhiking?

AUSTIN: Yeah. So how long you think it takes him to get to the border? A man his age.

LEE: I dunno.

AUSTIN: Eight days it takes him. Eight days in the rain and the sun and every day he's droppin' teeth on the blacktop and nobody'll pick him up 'cause his mouth's full a' blood.

(*pause, they drink*)

So finally he stumbles into the dentist. Dentist takes all his money and all his teeth. And there he is, in Mexico, with his gums sewed up and his pockets empty.

(*long silence*, AUSTIN *drinks*)

LEE: That's it?

AUSTIN: Then I go out to see him, see. I go out there and I take him out for a nice Chinese dinner. But he doesn't eat. All he wants to do is drink Martinis outa' plastic cups. And he takes his teeth out and lays 'em on the table 'cause he can't stand the feel of 'em. And we ask the waitress for one a' those doggie bags to take the Chop Suey home in. So he drops his teeth in the doggie bag along with the Chop Suey. And then we go out to hit all the bars up and down the highway. Says he wants to introduce me to all his buddies. And in one a' those bars, in one a' those bars up and down the highway, he left that doggie bag with his teeth laying in the Chop Suey.

LEE: You never found it?

AUSTIN: We went back but we never did find it. (*pause*) Now that's a true story. True to life.

(*they drink as lights fade to black*)

SCENE EIGHT

Very early morning, between night and day. No crickets, coyotes yapping feverishly in distance before light comes up, a small fire blazes up in the dark from alcove area, sound of LEE *smashing typewriter with a golf club, lights coming up,* LEE *seen smashing typewriter methodically then dropping pages of his script into a burning bowl set on the floor of alcove, flames leap up,* AUSTIN *has a whole bunch of stolen toasters lined up on the sink counter along with* LEE'S *stolen T.V., the toasters are of a wide variety of models, mostly chrome,* AUSTIN *goes up and down the line of toasters, breathing on them and polishing them with a dish towel, both men are drunk, empty whiskey bottles and beer cans litter floor of kitchen, they share a half empty bottle on one of the chairs in the alcove,* LEE *keeps periodically taking deliberate ax-chops at the typewriter using a nine-iron as* AUSTIN *speaks, all of their mother's house plants are dead and drooping.*

AUSTIN: (*polishing toasters*) There's gonna' be a general lack of toast in the neighborhood this morning. Many, many unhappy, bewildered breakfast faces. I guess it's best not to even think of the victims. Not to even entertain it. Is that the right psychology?

LEE: (*pauses*) What?

AUSTIN: Is that the correct criminal psychology? Not to think of the victims?

LEE: What victims?

(LEE *takes another swipe at typewriter with nine-iron, adds pages to the fire*)

AUSTIN: The victims of crime. Of breaking and entering. I mean is it a prerequisite for a criminal not to have a conscience?

LEE: Ask a criminal.

(*pause,* LEE *stares at* AUSTIN)

What're you gonna' do with all those toasters? That's the dumbest thing I ever saw in my life.

AUSTIN: I've got hundreds of dollars worth of household appliances here. You may not realize that.

LEE: Yeah, and how many hundreds of dollars did you walk right past?

AUSTIN: It was toasters you challenged me to. Only toasters. I ignored every other temptation.

LEE: I never challenged you! That's no challenge. Anybody can steal a toaster.

(LEE *smashes typewriter again*)

AUSTIN: You don't have to take it out on my typewriter ya' know. It's not the machine's fault that you can't write. It's a sin to do that to a good machine.

LEE: A sin?

AUSTIN: When you consider all the writers who never even had a machine. Who would have given an eyeball for a good typewriter. Any typewriter.

(LEE *smashes typewriter again*)

AUSTIN: (*polishing toasters*) All the ones who wrote on match-book covers. Paper bags. Toilet paper. Who had their writing destroyed by their jailers. Who persisted beyond all odds. Those writers would find it hard to understand your actions.

(LEE *comes down on typewriter with one final crushing blow of the nine-iron then collapses in one of the chairs, takes a drink from bottle, pause*)

AUSTIN: (*after pause*) Not to mention demolishing a perfectly good golf club. What about all the struggling golfers? What about Lee Trevino? What do you think he would've said when he was batting balls around with broomsticks at the age of nine. Impoverished.

(*pause*)

LEE: What time is it anyway?
AUSTIN: No idea. Time stands still when you're havin' fun.
LEE: Is it too late to call a woman? You know any women?
AUSTIN: I'm a married man.
LEE: I mean a local woman.

(AUSTIN *looks out at light through window above sink*)

AUSTIN: It's either too late or too early. You're the nature enthusiast. Can't you tell the time by the light in the sky? Orient yourself around the North Star or something?
LEE: I can't tell anything.
AUSTIN: Maybe you need a little breakfast. Some toast! How 'bout some toast?

(AUSTIN *goes to cupboard, pulls out loaf of bread and starts dropping slices into every toaster,* LEE *stays sitting, drinks, watches* AUSTIN)

LEE: I don't need toast. I need a woman.
AUSTIN: A woman isn't the answer. Never was.
LEE: I'm not talkin' about permanent. I'm talkin' about temporary.
AUSTIN: (*putting toast in toasters*) We'll just test the merits of these little demons. See which brands have a tendency to burn. See which one can produce a perfectly golden piece of fluffy toast.

LEE: How much gas you got in yer car?

AUSTIN: I haven't driven my car for days now. So I haven't had an opportunity to look at the gas gauge.

LEE: Take a guess. You think there's enough to get me to Bakersfield?

AUSTIN: Bakersfield? What's in Bakersfield?

LEE: Just never mind what's in Bakersfield! You think there's enough goddamn gas in the car!

AUSTIN: Sure.

LEE: Sure. You could care less, right. Let me run outa' gas on the Grapevine. You could give a shit.

AUSTIN: I'd say there was enough gas to get you just about anywhere, Lee. With your determination and guts.

LEE: What the hell time is it anyway?

(LEE *pulls out his wallet, starts going through dozens of small pieces of paper with phone numbers written on them, drops some on the floor, drops others in the fire*)

AUSTIN: Very early. This is the time of morning when the coyotes kill people's cocker spaniels. Did you hear them? That's what they were doing out there. Luring innocent pets away from their homes.

LEE: (*searching through his papers*) What's the area code for Bakersfield? You know?

AUSTIN: You could always call the operator.

LEE: I can't stand that voice they give ya'.

AUSTIN: What voice?

LEE: That voice that warns you that if you'd only tried harder to find the number in the phone book you wouldn't have to be calling the operator to begin with.

(LEE *gets up, holding a slip of paper from his wallet, stumbles toward phone on wall, yanks receiver, starts dialing*)

AUSTIN: Well I don't understand why you'd want to talk to anybody else anyway. I mean you can talk to me. I'm your brother.

LEE: (*dialing*) I wanna' talk to a woman. I haven't heard a woman's voice in a long time.

AUSTIN: Not since the Botanist?

LEE: What?

AUSTIN: Nothing. (*starts singing as he tends toast*)

"Red sails in the sunset
Way out on the blue
Please carry my loved one
Home safely to me."

LEE: Hey, knock it off will ya'! This is long distance here.

AUSTIN: Bakersfield?

LEE: Yeah, Bakersfield. It's Kern County.

AUSTIN: Well, what County are *we* in?

LEE: You better get yourself a 7-Up, boy.

AUSTIN: One County's as good as another.

(AUSTIN *hums "Red Sails" softly as* LEE *talks on phone*)

LEE: (*to phone*) Yeah, operator look—first off I wanna' know the area code for Bakersfield. Right. Bakersfield! Okay. Good. Now I wanna' know if you can help me track somebody down. (*pause*) No, no I mean a phone number. Just a phone number. Okay. (*holds a piece of paper up and reads it*) Okay, the name is Melly Ferguson. Melly. (*pause*) I dunno'. Melly. Maybe. Yeah. Maybe Melanie. Yeah. Melanie Ferguson. Okay. (*pause*) What? I can't hear ya' so good. Sounds like yer under the ocean. (*pause*) You got ten Melanie Fergusons? How could that be? Ten Melanie Fergusons in Bakersfield? Well gimme all of 'em then. (*pause*) What d'ya' mean? Gimmie all ten Melanie Fergusons! That's right. Just a second. (*to* AUSTIN) Gimme a pen.

AUSTIN: I don't have a pen.

LEE: Gimme a pencil then!

AUSTIN: I don't have a pencil.

LEE: (*to phone*) Just a second, operator. (*to* AUSTIN) Yer a writer and ya' don't have a pen or a pencil!

AUSTIN: I'm not a writer. You're a writer.

LEE: I'm on the phone here! Get me a pen or a pencil.

AUSTIN: I gotta' watch the toast.

LEE: (*to phone*) Hang on a second, operator.

(LEE *lets the phone drop then starts pulling all the drawers in the kitchen out on the floor and dumping the contents, searching for a pencil,* AUSTIN *watches him casually*)

LEE: (*crashing through drawers, throwing contents around kitchen*) This is the last time I try to live with people, boy! I can't believe it. Here I am! Here I am again in a desperate situation! This would never happen out on the desert. I would never be in this kinda' situation out on the desert. Isn't there a pen or a pencil in this house! Who lives in this house anyway!

AUSTIN: Our mother.

LEE: How come she don't have a pen or a pencil! She's a social person isn't she? Doesn't she have to make shopping lists? She's gotta' have a pencil. (*finds a pencil*) Aaha! (*he rushes back to phone, picks up receiver*) All right operator. Operator? Hey! Operator! Goddamnit!

(LEE *rips the phone off the wall and throws it down, goes back to chair and falls into it, drinks, long pause*)

AUSTIN: She hung up?

LEE: Yeah, she hung up. I knew she was gonna' hang up. I could hear it in her voice.

(LEE *starts going through his slips of paper again*)

AUSTIN: Well, you're probably better off staying here with me anyway. I'll take care of you.

LEE: I don't need takin' care of! Not by you anyway.

AUSTIN: Toast is almost ready.

(AUSTIN *starts buttering all the toast as it pops up*)

LEE: I don't want any toast!

(*long pause*)

AUSTIN: You gotta' eat something. Can't just drink. How long have we been drinking, anyway?

LEE: (*looking through slips of paper*) Maybe it was Fresno. What's the area code for Fresno? How could I have lost that number! She was beautiful.

(*pause*)

AUSTIN: Why don't you just forget about that, Lee. Forget about the woman.

LEE: She had green eyes. You know what green eyes do to me?

AUSTIN: I know but you're not gonna' get it on with her now anyway. It's dawn already. She's in Bakersfield for Christ's sake.

(*long pause,* LEE *considers the situation*)

LEE: Yeah. (*looks at windows*) It's dawn?

AUSTIN: Let's just have some toast and—

LEE: What is this bullshit with the toast anyway! You make it sound like salvation or something. I don't want any goddamn toast! How many times I gotta' tell ya'! (LEE *gets up, crosses upstage to windows in alcove, looks out,* AUSTIN *butters toast*)

AUSTIN: Well it is like salvation sort of. I mean the smell. I love the smell of toast. And the sun's coming up. It makes me feel like anything's possible. Ya' know?

LEE: (*back to* AUSTIN, *facing windows upstage*) So go to church why don't ya'.

AUSTIN: Like a beginning. I love beginnings.

LEE: Oh yeah. I've always been kinda' partial to endings myself.

AUSTIN: What if I come with you, Lee?

LEE: (*pause as* LEE *turns toward* AUSTIN) What?

AUSTIN: What if I come with you out to the desert?

LEE: Are you kiddin'?

AUSTIN: No. I'd just like to see what it's like.

LEE: You wouldn't last a day out there pal.

AUSTIN: That's what you said about the toasters. You said I couldn't steal a toaster either.

LEE: A toaster's got nothin' to do with the desert.

AUSTIN: I could make it, Lee. I'm not that helpless. I can cook.

LEE: Cook?

AUSTIN: I can.

LEE: So what! You can cook. Toast.

AUSTIN: I can make fires. I know how to get fresh water from condensation.

(AUSTIN *stacks buttered toast up in a tall stack on plate*)

(LEE *slams table*)

LEE: It's not somethin' you learn out of a Boy Scout handbook!

AUSTIN: Well how do you learn it then! How're you supposed to learn it!

(*pause*)

LEE: Ya' just learn it, that's all. Ya' learn it 'cause ya' have to learn it. You don't *have* to learn it.

AUSTIN: You could teach me.

LEE: (*stands*) What're you, crazy or somethin'? You went to college. Here, you are down here, rollin' in bucks. Floatin' up and down in elevators. And you wanna' learn how to live on the desert!

AUSTIN: I do, Lee. I really do. There's nothin' down here for me. There never was. When we were kids here it was different. There was a life here then. But now—I keep comin' down here thinkin' it's the fifties or somethin'. I keep finding myself getting off the freeway at familiar landmarks that turn out to be unfamiliar. On the way to appointments. Wandering down streets I thought I recognized that turn out to be replicas of streets I remember. Streets I misremember. Streets I can't tell if I lived on or saw in a postcard. Fields that don't even exist anymore.

LEE: There's no point cryin' about that now.

AUSTIN: There's nothin' real down here, Lee! Least of all me!

LEE: Well I can't save you from that!

AUSTIN: You can let me come with you.

LEE: No dice, pal.

AUSTIN: You could let me come with you, Lee!

LEE: Hey, do you actually think I chose to live out in the middle a' nowhere? Do ya'? Ya' think it's some kinda' philosophical decision I took or somethin'? I'm livin' out there 'cause I can't make it here! And yer bitchin' to me about all yer success!

AUSTIN: I'd cash it all in in a second. That's the truth.

LEE: (*pause, shakes his head*) I can't believe this.

AUSTIN: Let me go with you.

LEE: Stop sayin' that will ya'! Yer worse than a dog.

(AUSTIN *offers out the plate of neatly stacked toast to* LEE)

AUSTIN: You want some toast?

(LEE *suddenly explodes and knocks the plate out of* AUSTIN'S *hand, toast goes flying, long frozen moment where it appears* LEE *might go all the way this time when* AUSTIN *breaks it by slowly lowering himself to his knees and begins gathering the scattered toast from the floor and stacking it back on the plate,* LEE *begins to circle* AUSTIN *in a slow, predatory way, crushing pieces of toast in his wake, no words for a while,* AUSTIN *keeps gathering toast, even the crushed pieces*)

LEE: Tell ya' what I'll do, little brother. I might just consider makin' you a deal. Little trade. (AUSTIN *continues gathering toast as* LEE *circles him through this*) You write me up this screenplay thing just like I tell ya'. I mean you can use all yer usual tricks and stuff. Yer fancy language. Yer artistic hocus pocus. But ya' gotta' write everything like I say. Every move. Every time they run outa' gas, they run outa' gas. Every time they wanna' jump on a horse, they do just that. If they wanna' stay in Texas, by God they'll stay in Texas! (*Keeps circling*) And you finish the whole thing up for me. Top to bottom. And you put my name on it. And I own all the rights. And every dime goes in my pocket. You do that and I'll sure enough take ya' with me to the desert. (LEE *stops, pause, looks down at* AUSTIN) How's that sound?

(*pause as* AUSTIN *stands slowly holding plate of demolished toast, their faces are very close, pause*)

AUSTIN: It's a deal.

(LEE *stares straight into* AUSTIN'S *eyes, then he slowly takes a piece of toast off the plate, raises it to his mouth and takes a huge crushing bite never taking his eyes off* AUSTIN'S, *as* LEE *crunches into the toast the lights black out*)

SCENE NINE

Mid-day. No sound, blazing heat, the stage is ravaged; bottles, toasters, smashed typewriter, ripped out telephone, etc. All the debris from previous scene is now starkly visible in intense yellow light, the effect should be like a desert junkyard at high noon, the coolness of the preceding scenes is totally obliterated. AUSTIN *is seated at table in alcove, shirt open, pouring with sweat, hunched over a writing notebook, scribbling notes desperately with a ballpoint pen.* LEE *with no shirt, beer in hand, sweat pouring down his chest, is walking a slow circle around the table, picking his way through the objects, sometimes kicking them aside.*

LEE: (*as he walks*) All right, read it back to me. Read it back to me!

AUSTIN: (*scribbling at top speed*) Just a second.

LEE: Come on, come on! Just read what ya' got.

AUSTIN: I can't keep up! It's not the same as if I had a typewriter.

LEE: Just read what we got so far. Forget about the rest.

AUSTIN: All right. Let's see—okay—(*wipes sweat from his face, reads as* LEE *circles*) Luke says uh—

LEE: Luke?

AUSTIN: Yeah.

LEE: His name's Luke? All right, all right—we can change the names later. What's he say? Come on, come on.

AUSTIN: He says uh—(*reading*) "I told ya' you were a fool to follow me in here. I know this prairie like the back a' my hand."

LEE: No, no, no! That's not what I said. I never said that.

AUSTIN: That's what I wrote.

LEE: It's not what I said. I never said "like the back a' my hand." That's stupid. That's one a' those—whadya' call it? Whadya' call that?

AUSTIN: What?

LEE: Whadya' call it when somethin's been said a thousand times before. Whadya' call that?

AUSTIN: Um—a cliché?

LEE: Yeah. That's right. Cliché. That's what that is. A cliché. "The back a' my hand." That's stupid.

AUSTIN: That's what you said.

LEE: I never said that! And even if I did, that's where yer supposed to come in. That's where yer supposed to change it to somethin' better.

AUSTIN: Well how am I supposed to do that and write down what you say at the same time?

LEE: Ya' just do, that's all! You hear a stupid line you change it. That's yer job.

AUSTIN: All right. (*makes more notes*)

LEE: What're you changin' it to?

AUSTIN: I'm not changing it. I'm just trying to catch up.

LEE: Well change it! We gotta' change that, we can't leave that in there like that. ". . . the back a' my hand." That's dumb.

AUSTIN: (*stops writing, sits back*) All right.

LEE: (*pacing*) So what'll we change it to?

AUSTIN: Um—How 'bout—"I'm on intimate terms with this prairie."

LEE: (*to himself considering line as he walks*) "I'm on intimate terms with this prairie." Intimate terms, intimate terms. Intimate—that means like uh—sexual right?

AUSTIN: Well—yeah—or—

LEE: He's on sexual terms with the prairie? How dya' figure that?

AUSTIN: Well it doesn't necessarily have to mean sexual.

LEE: What's it mean then?

AUSTIN: It means uh—close—personal—

LEE: All right. How's it sound? Put it into the uh—the line there. Read it back. Let's see how it sounds. (*to himself*) "Intimate terms."

AUSTIN: (*scribbles in notebook*) Okay. It'd go something like this: (*reads*) "I told ya' you were a fool to follow me in here. I'm on intimate terms with this prairie."

LEE: That's good. I like that. That's real good.

AUSTIN: You do?

LEE: Yeah. Don't you?

AUSTIN: Sure.

LEE: Sounds original now. "Intimate terms." That's good. Okay. Now we're cookin! That has a real ring to it.

(AUSTIN *makes more notes,* LEE *walks around, pours beer on his arms and rubs it over his chest feeling good about the new progress, as he does this* MOM *enters unobtrusively down left with her luggage, she stops and stares at the scene still holding luggage as the two men continue, unaware of her presence,* AUSTIN *absorbed in his writing,* LEE *cooling himself off with beer*)

LEE: (*continues*) "He's on intimate terms with this prairie." Sounds real mysterious and kinda' threatening at the same time.

AUSTIN: (*writing rapidly*) Good.

LEE: Now—(LEE *turns and suddenly sees* MOM, *he stares at her for a while, she stares back,* AUSTIN *keeps writing feverishly, not noticing,* LEE *walks slowly over to* MOM *and takes a closer look, long pause*)

LEE: Mom?

(AUSTIN *looks up suddenly from his writing, sees* MOM, *stands quickly, long pause,* MOM *surveys the damage*)

AUSTIN: Mom. What're you doing back?

MOM: I'm back.

LEE: Here, lemme take those for ya.

(LEE *sets beer on counter than takes both her bags but doesn't know where to set them down in the sea of junk so he just keeps holding them*)

AUSTIN: I wasn't expecting you back so soon. I thought uh— How was Alaska?

MOM: Fine.

LEE: See any igloos?

MOM: No. Just glaciers.

AUSTIN: Cold huh?

MOM: What?

AUSTIN: It must've been cold up there?

MOM: Not really.

LEE: Musta' been colder than this here. I mean we're havin' a real scorcher here.

MOM: Oh? (*she looks at damage*)

LEE: Yeah. Must be in the hundreds.

AUSTIN: You wanna' take your coat off, Mom?

MOM: No. (*pause, she surveys space*) What happened in here?

AUSTIN: Oh um— Me and Lee were just sort of celebrating and uh—

MOM: Celebrating?

AUSTIN: Yeah. Uh— Lee sold a screenplay. A story, I mean.

MOM: Lee did?

AUSTIN: Yeah.

MOM: Not you?

AUSTIN: No. Him.

MOM: (*to* LEE) You sold a screenplay?

LEE: Yeah. That's right. We're just sorta' finishing it up right now. That's what we're doing here.

AUSTIN: Me and Lee are going out to the desert to live.

MOM: You and Lee?

AUSTIN: Yeah. I'm taking off with Lee.

MOM: (*she looks back and forth at each of them, pause*) You gonna go live with your father?

AUSTIN: No. We're going to a different desert Mom.

MOM: I see. Well, you'll probably wind up on the same desert sooner or later. What're all these toasters doing here?

AUSTIN: Well—we had kind of a contest.

MOM: Contest?

LEE: Yeah.

AUSTIN: Lee won.

MOM: Did you win a lot of money, Lee?

LEE: Well not yet. It's comin' in any day now.

MOM: (*to* LEE) What happened to your shirt?

LEE: Oh. I was sweatin' like a pig and I took it off.

(AUSTIN *grabs* LEE'S *shirt off the table and tosses it to him*, LEE *sets down suitcases and puts his shirt on*)

MOM: Well it's one hell of a mess in here isn't it?

AUSTIN: Yeah, I'll clean it up for you, Mom. I just didn't know you were coming back so soon.

MOM: I didn't either.

AUSTIN: What happened?

MOM: Nothing. I just started missing all my plants.

(*she notices dead plants*)

AUSTIN: Oh.

MOM: Oh, they're all dead aren't they. (*she crosses toward them, examines them closely*) You didn't get a chance to water I guess.

AUSTIN: I was doing it and then Lee came and—

LEE: Yeah I just distracted him a whole lot here, Mom. It's not his fault.

(*pause, as* MOM *stares at plants*)

MOM: Oh well, one less thing to take care of I guess. (*turns toward brothers*) Oh, that reminds me— You boys will probably never guess who's in town. Try and guess.

(*long pause, brothers stare at her*)

AUSTIN: Whadya' mean, Mom?

MOM: Take a guess. Somebody very important has come to town. I read it, coming down on the Greyhound.

LEE: Somebody very important?

MOM: See if you can guess. You'll never guess.

AUSTIN: Mom—we're trying to uh—(*points to writing pad*)

MOM: Picasso. (*pause*) Picasso's in town. Isn't that incredible? Right now.

(*pause*)

AUSTIN: Picasso's dead, Mom.

MOM: No, he's not dead. He's visiting the museum. I read it on the bus. We have to go down there and see him.

AUSTIN: Mom—

MOM: This is the chance of a lifetime. Can you imagine? We could all go down and meet him. All three of us.

LEE: Uh— I don't think I'm really up fer meetin' anybody right now. I'm uh— What's his name?

MOM: Picasso! Picasso! You've never heard of Picasso? Austin, you've heard of Picasso.

AUSTIN: Mom, we're not going to have time.

MOM: It won't take long. We'll just hop in the car and go down there. An opportunity like this doesn't come along every day.

AUSTIN: We're gonna' be leavin' here, Mom!

(*pause*)

MOM: Oh.

LEE: Yeah.

(*pause*)

MOM: You're both leaving?

LEE: (*looks at* AUSTIN) Well we were thinkin' about that before but now I—

AUSTIN: No, we are! We're both leaving. We've got it all planned.

MOM: (*to* AUSTIN) Well you can't leave. You have a family.

AUSTIN: I'm leaving. I'm getting out of here.

LEE: (*to* MOM) I don't really think Austin's cut out for the desert do you?

MOM: No. He's not.

AUSTIN: I'm going with you, Lee!

MOM: He's too thin.

LEE: Yeah, he'd just burn up out there.

AUSTIN: (*to* LEE) We just gotta' finish this screenplay and then we're gonna' take off. That's the plan. That's what you said. Come on, let's get back to work, Lee.

LEE: I can't work under these conditions here. It's too hot.

AUSTIN: Then we'll do it on the desert.

LEE: Don't be tellin' me what we're gonna do!

MOM: Don't shout in the house.

LEE: We're just gonna' have to postpone the whole deal.

AUSTIN: I can't postpone it! It's gone past postponing! I'm doing everything you said. I'm writing down exactly what you tell me.

LEE: Yeah, but you were right all along see. It is a dumb story.
"Two lamebrains chasin' each other across Texas." That's
what you said, right?

AUSTIN: I never said that.

(LEE *sneers in* AUSTIN'S *face then turns to* MOM)

LEE: I'm gonna' just borrow some a' your antiques, Mom.
You don't mind do ya'? Just a few plates and things. Silverware.

(LEE *starts going through all the cupboards in kitchen pulling out
plates and stacking them on counter as* MOM *and* AUSTIN *watch*)

MOM: You don't have any utensils on the desert?

LEE: Nah, I'm fresh out.

AUSTIN: (*to* LEE) What're you doing?

MOM: Well some of those are very old. Bone China.

LEE: I'm tired of eatin' outa' my bare hands, ya' know. It's not
civilized.

AUSTIN: (*to* LEE) What're you doing? We made a deal!

MOM: Couldn't you borrow the plastic ones instead? I have
plenty of plastic ones.

LEE: (*as he stacks plates*) It's not the same. Plastic's not the same
at all. What I need is somethin' authentic. Somethin' to keep
me in touch. It's easy to get outa' touch out there. Don't
worry I'll get em' back to ya'.

(AUSTIN *rushes up to* LEE, *grabs him by shoulders*)

AUSTIN: You can't just drop the whole thing, Lee!

(LEE *turns, pushes* AUSTIN *in the chest knocking him backwards into
the alcove,* MOM *watches numbly,* LEE *returns to collecting the plates,
silverware, etc.*)

MOM: You boys shouldn't fight in the house. Go outside and
fight.

LEE: I'm not fightin'. I'm leavin'.

MOM: There's been enough damage done already.

LEE: (*his back to* AUSTIN *and* MOM, *stacking dishes on counter*) I'm
clearin' outa' here once and for all. All this town does is drive
a man insane. Look what it's done to Austin there. I'm not
lettin' that happen to me. Sell myself down the river. No sir.
I'd rather be a hundred miles from nowhere than let that
happen to me.

(*during this* AUSTIN *has picked up the ripped-out phone from the floor and wrapped the cord tightly around both his hands, he lunges at* LEE *whose back is still to him, wraps the cord around* LEE'S *neck, plants a foot in* LEE'S *back and pulls back on the cord, tightening it,* LEE *chokes desperately, can't speak and can't reach* AUSTIN *with his arms,* AUSTIN *keeps applying pressure on* LEE'S *back with his foot, bending him into the sink,* MOM *watches*)

AUSTIN: (*tightening cord*) You're not goin' anywhere! You're not takin' anything with you. You're not takin' my car! You're not takin' the dishes! You're not takin' anything! You're stayin' right here!

MOM: You'll have to stop fighting in the house. There's plenty of room outside to fight. You've got the whole outdoors to fight in.

(LEE *tries to tear himself away, he crashes across the stage like an enraged bull dragging* AUSTIN *with him, he snorts and bellows but* AUSTIN *hangs on and manages to keep clear of* LEE'S *attempts to grab him, they crash into the table, to the floor,* LEE *is face down thrashing wildly and choking,* AUSTIN *pulls cord tighter, stands with one foot planted on* LEE'S *back and the cord stretched taut*)

AUSTIN: (*holding cord*) Gimme back my keys, Lee! Take the keys out! Take 'em out!

(LEE *desperately tries to dig in his pockets, searching for the car keys,* MOM *moves closer*)

MOM: (*calmly to* AUSTIN) You're not killing him are you?

AUSTIN: I don't know. I don't know if I'm killing him. I'm stopping him. That's all. I'm just stopping him.

(LEE *thrashes but* AUSTIN *is relentless*)

MOM: You oughta' let him breathe a little bit.

AUSTIN: Throw the keys out, Lee!

(LEE *finally gets keys out and throws them on floor but out of* AUSTIN'S *reach,* AUSTIN *keeps pressure on cord, pulling* LEE'S *neck back,* LEE *gets one hand to the cord but can't relieve the pressure*)

Reach me those keys would ya', Mom.

MOM: (*not moving*) Why are you doing this to him?

AUSTIN: Reach me the keys!

MOM: Not until you stop choking him.

AUSTIN: I can't stop choking him! He'll kill me if I stop choking him!

MOM: He won't kill you. He's your brother.

AUSTIN: Just get me the keys would ya'!

(*pause.* MOM *picks keys up off floor, hands them to* AUSTIN)

AUSTIN: (*to* MOM) Thanks.

MOM: Will you let him go now?

AUSTIN: I don't know. He's not gonna' let me get outa' here.

MOM: Well you can't kill him.

AUSTIN: I can kill him! I can easily kill him. Right now. Right here. All I gotta' do is just tighten up. See? (*he tightens cord,* LEE *thrashes wildly,* AUSTIN *releases pressure a little, maintaining control*) Ya' see that?

MOM: That's a savage thing to do.

AUSTIN: Yeah well don't tell me I can't kill him because I can. I can just twist. I can just keep twisting. (AUSTIN *twists the cord tighter,* LEE *weakens, his breathing changes to a short rasp*)

MOM: Austin!

(AUSTIN *relieves pressure,* LEE *breathes easier but* AUSTIN *keeps him under control*)

AUSTIN: (*eyes on* LEE, *holding cord*) I'm goin' to the desert. There's nothing stopping me. I'm going by myself to the desert.

(MOM *moving toward her luggage*)

MOM: Well, I'm going to go check into a motel. I can't stand this anymore.

AUSTIN: Don't go yet!

(MOM *pauses*)

MOM: I can't stay here. This is worse than being homeless.

AUSTIN: I'll get everything fixed up for you, Mom. I promise. Just stay for a while.

MOM: (*picking up luggage*) You're going to the desert.

AUSTIN: Just wait!

(LEE *thrashes,* AUSTIN *subdues him,* MOM *watches holding luggage, pause*)

MOM: It was the worst feeling being up there. In Alaska. Staring out a window. I never felt so desperate before. That's why when I saw that article on Picasso I thought—

AUSTIN: Stay here, Mom. This is where you live.

(*she looks around the stage*)

MOM: I don't recognize it at all.

(*she exits with luggage,* AUSTIN *makes a move toward her but* LEE *starts to struggle and* AUSTIN *subdues him again with cord, pause*)

AUSTIN: (*holding cord*) Lee? I'll make ya' a deal. You let me get outa' here. Just let me get to my car. All right, Lee? Gimme a little headstart and I'll turn you loose. Just gimme a little headstart. All right?

(LEE *makes no response,* AUSTIN *slowly releases tension cord, still nothing from* LEE)

AUSTIN: Lee?

(LEE *is motionless,* AUSTIN *very slowly begins to stand, still keeping a tenuous hold on the cord and his eyes riveted to* LEE *for any sign of movement,* AUSTIN *slowly drops the cord and stands, he stares down at* LEE *who appears to be dead*)

AUSTIN: (*whispers*) Lee?

(*pause,* AUSTIN *considers, looks toward exit, back to* LEE, *then makes a small movement as if to leave. Instantly* LEE *is on his feet and moves toward exit, blocking* AUSTIN'S *escape. They square off to each other, keeping a distance between them. Pause, a single coyote heard in distance, lights fade softly into moonlight, the figures of the brothers now appear to be caught in a vast desert-like landscape, they are very still but watchful for the next move, lights go slowly to black as the after-image of the brothers pulses in the dark, coyote fades*)

BURIED CHILD

Pulitzer Prize 1979

While the rain of your fingertips falls,
while the rain of your bones falls,
and your laughter and marrow fall down,
you come flying.

PABLO NERUDA

DODGE: *in his seventies*
HALIE: *his wife Mid-sixties*
TILDEN: *their oldest son*
BRADLEY: *their next oldest son, an amputee*
VINCE: *Tilden's son*
SHELLY: *Vince's girl friend*
FATHER DEWIS: *a Protestant minister*

Buried Child was first produced at the Magic Theatre, San Francisco, on June 27, 1978. It was directed by Robert Woodruff with the following cast:

DODGE	Joseph Gistirak
HALIE	Catherine Willis
TILDEN	Dennis Ludlow
BRADLEY	William M. Carr
SHELLY	Betsy Scott
VINCE	Barry Lane
FATHER DEWIS	Rj Frank

The New York premiere was directed by Robert Woodruff with the following cast:

DODGE	Richard Hamilton
HALIE	Jacqueline Brookes
TILDEN	Tom Noonan
BRADLEY	Jay O. Sanders
SHELLY	Mary McDonnell
VINCE	Christopher McCann
FATHER DEWIS	Bill Wiley

ACT ONE

SCENE: *Day. Old wooden staircase down left with pale, frayed carpet laid down on the steps. The stairs lead off stage left up into the wings with no landing. Up right is an old, dark green sofa with the stuffing coming out in spots. Stage right of the sofa is an upright lamp with a faded yellow shade and a small night table with several small bottles of pills on it. Down right of the sofa, with the screen facing the sofa, is a large, old-fashioned brown T.V. A flickering blue light comes from the screen, but no image, no sound. In the dark, the light of the lamp and the T.V. slowly brighten in the black space. The space behind the sofa, upstage, is a large, screened-in porch with a board floor. A solid interior door to stage right of the sofa, leading into the room on stage; and another screen door up left, leading from the porch to the outside. Beyond that are the shapes of dark elm trees.*

    Gradually the form of DODGE *is made out, sitting on the couch, facing the T.V., the blue light flickering on his face. He wears a well-worn T-shirt, suspenders, khaki work pants and brown slippers. He's covered himself in an old brown blanket. He's very thin and sickly looking, in his late seventies. He just stares at the T.V. More light fills the stage softly. The sound of light rain.* DODGE *slowly tilts his head back and stares at the ceiling for a while, listening to the rain. He lowers his head again and stares at the T.V. He turns his head slowly to the left and stares at the cushion of the sofa next to the one he's sitting on. He pulls his left arm out from under the blanket, slides his hand under the cushion, and pulls out a bottle of whiskey. He looks down left toward the staircase, listens, then uncaps the bottle, takes a*

63

*long swig and caps it again. He puts the bottle back under the cushion
and stares at the T.V. He starts to cough slowly and softly. The
coughing gradually builds. He holds one hand to his mouth and tries to
stifle it. The coughing gets louder, then suddenly stops when he hears the
sound of his wife's voice coming from the top of the staircase.*

HALIE'S VOICE: Dodge?

(DODGE *just stares at the T.V. Long pause. He stifles two short
coughs.*)

HALIE'S VOICE: Dodge! You want a pill, Dodge?

(*He doesn't answer. Takes the bottle out again and takes another
long swig. Puts the bottle back, stares at T.V., pulls blanket up
around his neck.*)

HALIE'S VOICE: You know what it is, don't you? It's the rain!
Weather. That's it. Every time. Every time you get like
this, it's the rain. No sooner does the rain start then you
start. (*pause*) Dodge?

(*He makes no reply. Pulls a pack of cigarettes out from his sweater
and lights one. Stares at T.V. pause.*)

HALIE'S VOICE: You should see it coming down up here. Just
coming down in sheets. Blue sheets. The bridge is pretty
near flooded. What's it like down there? Dodge?

(DODGE *turns his head back over his left shoulder and takes a look
out through the porch. He turns back to the T.V.*)

DODGE: (*to himself*) Catastrophic.
HALIE'S VOICE: What? What'd you say, Dodge?
DODGE: (*louder*) It looks like rain to me! Plain old rain!
HALIE'S VOICE: Rain? Of course it's rain! Are you having a
seizure or something! Dodge? (*pause*) I'm coming down there
in about five minutes if you don't answer me!
DODGE: Don't come down.
HALIE'S VOICE: What!
DODGE: (*louder*) Don't come down!

(*He has another coughing attack. Stops.*)

HALIE'S VOICE: You should take a pill for that! I don't see why

you just don't take a pill. Be done with it once and for all.
Put a stop to it.

(*He takes bottle out again. Another swig. Returns bottle.*)

HALIE'S VOICE: It's not Christian, but it works. It's not necessarily Christian, that is. We don't know. There's some things
the ministers can't even answer. I, personally, can't see
anything wrong with it. Pain is pain. Pure and simple. Suffer-
ing is a different matter. That's entirely different. A pill
seems as good an answer as any. Dodge? (*pause*) Dodge, are
you watching baseball?

DODGE: No.

HALIE'S VOICE: What?

DODGE: (*louder*) No!

HALIE'S VOICE: What're you watching? You shouldn't be watching anything that'll get you excited! No horse racing!

DODGE: They don't race on Sundays.

HALIE'S VOICE: What?

DODGE: (*louder*) They don't race on Sundays!

HALIE'S VOICE: Well they shouldn't race on Sundays.

DODGE: Well they don't!

HALIE'S VOICE: Good. I'm amazed they still have that kind of
legislation. That's amazing.

DODGE: Yeah, it's amazing.

HALIE'S VOICE: What?

DODGE: (*louder*) It is amazing!

HALIE'S VOICE: It is. It truly is. I would've thought these days
they'd be racing on Christmas even. A big flashing Christmas
tree right down at the finish line.

DODGE: (*shakes his head*) No.

HALIE'S VOICE: They used to race on New Year's! I remember
that.

DODGE: They never raced on New Year's!

HALIE'S VOICE: Sometimes they did.

DODGE: They never did!

HALIE'S VOICE: Before we were married they did!

(DODGE *waves his hand in disgust at the staircase. Leans back in
sofa. Stares at T.V.*)

HALIE'S VOICE: I went once. With a man.

DODGE: (*mimicking her*) Oh, a "man."

HALIE'S VOICE: What?

DODGE: Nothing!

HALIE'S VOICE: A wonderful man. A breeder.

DODGE: A what?

HALIE'S VOICE: A breeder! A horse breeder! Thoroughbreds.

DODGE: Oh, Thoroughbreds. Wonderful.

HALIE'S VOICE: That's right. He knew everything there was to know.

DODGE: I bet he taught you a thing or two huh? Gave you a good turn around the old stable!

HALIE'S VOICE: Knew everything there was to know about horses. We won bookoos of money that day.

DODGE: What?

HALIE'S VOICE: Money! We won every race I think.

DODGE: Bookoos?

HALIE'S VOICE: Every single race.

DODGE: Bookoos of money?

HALIE'S VOICE: It was one of those kind of days.

DODGE: New Year's!

HALIE'S VOICE: Yes! It might've been Florida. Or California! One of those two.

DODGE: Can I take my pick?

HALIE'S VOICE: It was Florida!

DODGE: Aha!

HALIE'S VOICE: Wonderful! Absolutely wonderful! The sun was just gleaming. Flamingos. Bougainvilleas. Palm trees.

DODGE: (*to himself, mimicking her*) Bougainvilleas. Palm trees.

HALIE'S VOICE: Everything was dancing with life! There were all kinds of people from everywhere. Everyone was dressed to the nines. Not like today. Not like they dress today.

DODGE: When was this anyway?

HALIE'S VOICE: This was long before I knew you.

DODGE: Must've been.

HALIE'S VOICE: Long before. I was escorted.

DODGE: To Florida?

HALIE'S VOICE: Yes. Or it might've been California. I'm not sure which.

DODGE: All that way you were escorted?

HALIE'S VOICE: Yes.

DODGE: And he never laid a finger on you I suppose? (*long silence*) Halie?

(*No answer. Long pause.*)

HALIE'S VOICE: Are you going out today?

DODGE: (*gesturing toward rain*) In this?

HALIE'S VOICE: I'm just asking a simple question.

DODGE: I rarely go out in the bright sunshine, why would I go out in this?

HALIE'S VOICE: I'm just asking because I'm not doing any shopping today. And if you need anything you should ask Tilden.

DODGE: Tilden's not here!

HALIE'S VOICE: He's in the kitchen.

(DODGE *looks toward stage left, then back toward T.V.*)

DODGE: All right.

HALIE'S VOICE: What?

DODGE: (*louder*) All right!

HALIE'S VOICE: Don't scream. It'll only get your coughing started.

DODGE: All right.

HALIE'S VOICE: Just tell Tilden what you want and he'll get it. (*pause*) Bradley should be over later.

DODGE: Bradley?

HALIE'S VOICE: Yes. To cut your hair.

DODGE: My hair? I don't need my hair cut!

HALIE'S VOICE: It won't hurt!

DODGE: I don't need it!

HALIE'S VOICE: It's been more than two weeks Dodge.

DODGE: I don't need it!

HALIE'S VOICE: I have to meet Father Dewis for lunch.

DODGE: You tell Bradley that if he shows up here with those clippers, I'll kill him!

HALIE'S VOICE: I won't be very late. No later than four at the very latest.

DODGE: You tell him! Last time he left me almost bald! And I wasn't even awake! I was sleeping! I woke up and he'd already left!

HALIE'S VOICE: That's not my fault!

DODGE: You put him up to it!

HALIE'S VOICE: I never did!

DODGE: You did too! You had some fancy, stupid meeting planned! Time to dress up the corpse for company! Lower the ears a little! Put up a little front! Surprised you didn't

tape a pipe to my mouth while you were at it! That woulda'
looked nice! Huh? A pipe? Maybe a bowler hat! Maybe a
copy of The Wall Street Journal casually placed on my lap!

HALIE'S VOICE: You always imagine the worst things of people!

DODGE: That's not the worst! That's the least of the worst!

HALIE'S VOICE: I don't need to hear it! All day long I hear things
like that and I don't need to hear more.

DODGE: You better tell him!

HALIE'S VOICE: You tell him yourself! He's your own son. You
should be able to talk to your own son.

DODGE: Not while I'm sleeping! He cut my hair while I was
sleeping!

HALIE'S VOICE: Well he won't do it again.

DODGE: There's no guarantee.

HALIE'S VOICE: I promise he won't do it without your consent.

DODGE: (after pause) There's no reason for him to even come
over here.

HALIE'S VOICE: He feels responsible.

DODGE: For my hair?

HALIE'S VOICE: For your appearance.

DODGE: My appearance is out of his domain! It's even out of
mine! In fact, it's disappeared! I'm an invisible man!

HALIE'S VOICE: Don't be ridiculous.

DODGE: He better not try it. That's all I've got to say.

HALIE'S VOICE: Tilden will watch out for you.

DODGE: Tilden won't protect me from Bradley!

HALIE'S VOICE: Tilden's the oldest. He'll protect you.

DODGE: Tilden can't even protect himself!

HALIE'S VOICE: Not so loud! He'll hear you. He's right in the
kitchen.

DODGE: (yelling off left) Tilden!

HALIE'S VOICE: Dodge, what are you trying to do?

DODGE: (yelling off left) Tilden, get in here!

HALIE'S VOICE: Why do you enjoy stirring things up?

DODGE: I don't enjoy anything!

HALIE'S VOICE: That's a terrible thing to say.

DODGE: Tilden!

HALIE'S VOICE: That's the kind of statement that leads people
right to the end of their rope.

DODGE: Tilden!

HALIE'S VOICE: It's no wonder people turn to Christ!

DODGE: TILDEN!!

HALIE'S VOICE: It's no wonder the messengers of God's word are shouted down in public places!

DODGE: TILDEN!!!!

(DODGE *goes into a violent, spasmodic coughing attack as* TILDEN *enters from stage left, his arms loaded with fresh ears of corn.* TILDEN *is* DODGE'S *oldest son, late forties, wears heavy construction boots, covered with mud, dark green work pants, a plaid shirt and a faded brown windbreaker. He has a butch haircut, wet from the rain. Something about him is profoundly burned out and displaced. He stops center stage with the ears of corn in his arms and just stares at* DODGE *until he slowly finishes his coughing attack.* DODGE *looks up at him slowly. He stares at the corn. Long pause as they watch each other.*)

HALIE'S VOICE: Dodge, if you don't take that pill nobody's going to force you.

(*The two men ignore the voice.*)

DODGE: (*to* TILDEN) Where'd you get that?

TILDEN: Picked it.

DODGE: You picked all that?

(TILDEN *nods.*)

DODGE: You expecting company?

TILDEN: No.

DODGE: Where'd you pick it from?

TILDEN: Right out back.

DODGE: Out back where?

TILDEN: Right out in back.

DODGE: There's nothing out there!

TILDEN: There's corn.

DODGE: There hasn't been corn out there since about nineteen thirty-five! That's the last time I planted corn out there!

TILDEN: It's out there now.

DODGE: (*yelling at stairs*) Halie!

HALIE'S VOICE: Yes dear!

DODGE: Tilden's brought a whole bunch of corn in here! There's no corn out in back is there?

TILDEN: (*to himself*) There's tons of corn.

HALIE'S VOICE: Not that I know of!

DODGE: That's what I thought.

HALIE'S VOICE: Not since about nineteen thirty-five!

DODGE: (*to* TILDEN) That's right. Nineteen thirty-five.

TILDEN: It's out there now.

DODGE: You go and take that corn back to wherever you got it from!

TILDEN: (*After pause, staring at* DODGE) It's picked. I picked it all in the rain. Once it's picked you can't put it back.

DODGE: I haven't had trouble with neighbors here for fifty-seven years. I don't even know who the neighbors are! And I don't wanna know! Now go put that corn back where it came from!

(TILDEN *stares at* DODGE *then walks slowly over to him and dumps all the corn on* DODGE'S *lap and steps back.* DODGE *stares at the corn then back to* TILDEN. *Long pause.*)

DODGE: Are you having trouble here, Tilden! Are you in some kind of trouble?

TILDEN: I'm not in any trouble.

DODGE: You can tell me if you are. I'm still your father.

TILDEN: I know you're still my father.

DODGE: I know you had a little trouble back in New Mexico. That's why you came out here.

TILDEN: I never had any trouble.

DODGE: Tilden, your mother told me all about it.

TILDEN: What'd she tell you?

(TILDEN *pulls some chewing tobacco out of his jacket and bites off a plug.*)

DODGE: I don't have to repeat what she told me! She told me all about it!

TILDEN: Can I bring my chair in from the kitchen?

DODGE: What?

TILDEN: Can I bring in my chair from the kitchen?

DODGE: Sure. Bring your chair in.

(TILDEN *exits left.* DODGE *pushes all the corn off his lap onto the floor. He pulls the blanket off angrily and tosses it at one end of the sofa, pulls out the bottle and takes another swig.* TILDEN *enters again from left with a milking stool and a pail.* DODGE *hides the bottle quickly under the cushion before* TILDEN *sees it.* TILDEN *sets the stool down by the sofa, sits on it, puts the pail in front of him on the floor.* TILDEN *starts picking up the ears of corn one at a time and husking them. He throws the husks and silk in the center of the stage and drops the ears into the pail each time he cleans one. He repeats this process as they talk.*)

DODGE: (*after pause*) Sure is nice-looking corn.

TILDEN: It's the best.

DODGE: Hybrid?

TILDEN: What?

DODGE: Some kinda fancy hybrid?

TILDEN: You planted it. I don't know what it is.

DODGE: (*pause*) Tilden, look, you can't stay here forever. You know that, don't you?

TILDEN: (*spits in spittoon*) I'm not.

DODGE: I know you're not. I'm not worried about that. That's not the reason I brought it up.

TILDEN: What's the reason?

DODGE: The reason is I'm wondering what you're gonna do.

TILDEN: You're not worried about me, are you?

DODGE: I'm not worried about you.

TILDEN: You weren't worried about me when I wasn't here. When I was in New Mexico.

DODGE: No, I wasn't worried about you then either.

TILDEN: You shoulda worried about me then.

DODGE: Why's that? You didn't do anything down there, did you?

TILDEN: I didn't do anything.

DODGE: Then why should I have worried about you?

TILDEN: Because I was lonely.

DODGE: Because you were lonely?

TILDEN: Yeah. I was more lonely than I've ever been before.

DODGE: Why was that?

TILDEN: (*pause*) Could I have some of that whiskey you've got?

DODGE: What whiskey? I haven't got any whiskey.

TILDEN: You've got some under the sofa.

DODGE: I haven't got anything under the sofa! Now mind your own damn business! Jesus God, you come into the house outa the middle of nowhere, haven't heard or seen you in twenty years and suddenly you're making accusations.

TILDEN: I'm not making accusations.

DODGE: You're accusing me of hoarding whiskey under the sofa!

TILDEN: I'm not accusing you.

DODGE: You just got through telling me I had whiskey under the sofa!

HALIE'S VOICE: Dodge?

DODGE: (*to* TILDEN) Now she knows about it!

TILDEN: She doesn't know about it.

HALIE'S VOICE: Dodge, are you talking to yourself down there?

DODGE: I'm talking to Tilden!

HALIE'S VOICE: Tilden's down there?

DODGE: He's right here!

HALIE'S VOICE: What?

DODGE: (*louder*) He's right here!

HALIE'S VOICE: What's he doing?

DODGE: (*to* TILDEN) Don't answer her.

TILDEN: (*to* DODGE) I'm not doing anything wrong.

DODGE: I know you're not.

HALIE'S VOICE: What's he doing down there!

DODGE: (*to* TILDEN) Don't answer.

TILDEN: I'm not.

HALIE'S VOICE: Dodge!

(*The men sit in silence.* DODGE *lights a cigarette.* TILDEN *keeps husking corn, spits tobacco now and then in spittoon.*)

HALIE'S VOICE: Dodge! He's not drinking anything, is he? You see to it that he doesn't drink anything! You've gotta watch out for him. It's our responsibility. He can't look after himself anymore, so we have to do it. Nobody else will do it. We can't just send him away somewhere. If we had lots of money we could send him away. But we don't. We never will. That's why we have to stay healthy. You and me. Nobody's going to look after us. Bradley can't look after us. Bradley can hardly look after himself. I was always hoping that Tilden would look out for Bradley when they got older. After Bradley lost his leg. Tilden's the oldest. I always thought he'd be the one to take responsibility. I had no idea in the world that Tilden would be so much trouble. Who would've dreamed. Tilden was an All-American, don't forget. Don't forget that. Fullback. Or quarterback. I forget which.

TILDEN: (*to himself*) Fullback. (*still husking*)

HALIE'S VOICE: Then when Tilden turned out to be so much trouble, I put all my hopes on Ansel. Of course Ansel wasn't

as handsome, but he was smart. He was the smartest probably.
I think he probably was. Smarter than Bradley, that's for
sure. Didn't go and chop his leg off with a chain saw. Smart
enough not to go and do that. I think he was smarter than
Tilden too. Especially after Tilden got in all that trouble.
Doesn't take brains to go to jail. Anybody knows that. Course
then when Ansel died that left us all alone. Same as being
alone. No different. Same as if they'd all died. He was the
smartest. He could've earned lots of money. Lots and lots of
money.

(HALIE *enters slowly from the top of the staircase as she continues
talking. Just her feet are seen at first as she makes her way down the
stairs, a step at a time. She appears dressed completely in black, as
though in mourning. Black handbag, hat with a veil, and pulling on
elbow length black gloves. She is about sixty-five with pure white
hair. She remains absorbed in what she's saying as she descends the
stairs and doesn't really notice the two men who continue sitting
there as they were before she came down, smoking and husking.*)

HALIE: He would've took care of us, too. He would've seen to it
that we were repaid. He was like that. He was a hero. Don't
forget that. A genuine hero. Brave. Strong. And very
intelligent. Ansel could've been a great man. One of the
greatest. I only regret that he didn't die in action. It's not
fitting for a man like that to die in a motel room. A soldier.
He could've won a medal. He could've been decorated for
valor. I've talked to Father Dewis about putting up a plaque
for Ansel. He thinks it's a good idea. He agrees. He knew
Ansel when he used to play basketball. Went to every game.
Ansel was his favorite player. He even recommended to the
City Council that they put up a statue of Ansel. A big, tall
statue with a basketball in one hand and a rifle in the other.
That's how much he thinks of Ansel.

(HALIE *reaches the stage and begins to wander around, still absorbed
in pulling on her gloves, brushing lint off her dress and continuously
talking to herself as the men just sit.*)

HALIE: Of course, he'd still be alive today if he hadn't married
into the Catholics. The Mob. How in the world he never
opened his eyes to that is beyond me. Just beyond me.
Everyone around him could see the truth. Even Tilden.

Tilden told him time and again. Catholic women are the
Devil incarnate. He wouldn't listen. He was blind with love.
Blind. I knew. Everyone knew. The wedding was more like
a funeral. You remember? All those Italians. All that horrible
black, greasy hair. The smell of cheap cologne. I think even
the priest was wearing a pistol. When he gave her the ring I
knew he was a dead man. I knew it. As soon as he gave her
the ring. But then it was the honeymoon that killed him.
The honeymoon. I knew he'd never come back from the
honeymoon. I kissed him and he felt like a corpse. All white.
Cold. Icy blue lips. He never used to kiss like that. Never
before. I knew then that she'd cursed him. Taken his soul. I
saw it in her eyes. She smiled at me with that Catholic sneer
of hers. She told me with her eyes that she'd murder him in
his bed. Murder my son. She told me. And there was nothing
I could do. Absolutely nothing. He was going with her,
thinking he was free. Thinking it was love. What could I do?
I couldn't tell him she was a witch. I couldn't tell him that.
He'd have turned on me. Hated me. I couldn't stand him
hating me and then dying before he ever saw me again.
Hating me in his death bed. Hating me and loving her! How
could I do that? I had to let him go. I had to. I watched him
leave. I watched him throw gardenias as he helped her into
the limousine. I watched his face disappear behind the glass.

(*She stops abruptly and stares at the corn husks. She looks around
the space as though just waking up. She turns and looks hard at*
TILDEN *and* DODGE *who continue sitting calmly. She looks again at
the corn husks.*)

HALIE: (*pointing to the husks*) What's this in my house! (*kicks husks*)
What's all this!

(TILDEN *stops husking and stares at her.*)

HALIE: (*to* DODGE) And you encourage him!

(DODGE *pulls blanket over him again.*)

DODGE: You're going out in the rain?
HALIE: It's not raining.

(TILDEN *starts husking again.*)

DODGE: Not in Florida it's not.

HALIE: We're not in Florida!

DODGE: It's not raining at the race track.

HALIE: Have you been taking those pills? Those pills always make you talk crazy. Tilden, has he been taking those pills?

TILDEN: He hasn't took anything.

HALIE: (*to* DODGE) What've you been taking?

DODGE: It's not raining in California or Florida or the race track. Only in Illinois. This is the only place it's raining. All over the rest of the world it's bright golden sunshine.

(HALIE *goes to the night table next to the sofa and checks the bottle of pills.*)

HALIE: Which ones did you take? Tilden, you must've seen him take something.

TILDEN: He never took a thing.

HALIE: Then why's he talking crazy?

TILDEN: I've been here the whole time.

HALIE: Then you've both been taking something!

TILDEN: I've just been husking the corn.

HALIE: Where'd you get that corn anyway? Why is the house suddenly full of corn?

DODGE: Bumper crop!

HALIE: (*moving center*) We haven't had corn here for over thirty years.

TILDEN: The whole back lot's full of corn. Far as the eye can see.

DODGE: (*to* HALIE) Things keep happening while you're upstairs, ya know. The world doesn't stop just because you're upstairs. Corn keeps growing. Rain keeps raining.

HALIE: I'm not unaware of the world around me! Thank you very much. It so happens that I have an over-all view from the upstairs. The back yard's in plain view of my window. And there's no corn to speak of. Absolutely none!

DODGE: Tilden wouldn't lie. If he says there's corn, there's corn.

HALIE: What's the meaning of this corn Tilden!

TILDEN: It's a mystery to me. I was out in back there. And the rain was coming down. And I didn't feel like coming back inside. I didn't feel the cold so much. I didn't mind the wet. So I was just walking. I was muddy but I didn't mind the mud so much. And I looked up. And I saw this stand of corn. In fact I was standing in it. So, I was standing in it.

HALIE: There isn't any corn outside, Tilden! There's no corn! Now, you must've either stolen this corn or you bought it.

DODGE: He doesn't have any money.

HALIE: (*to* TILDEN) So you stole it!

TILDEN: I didn't steal it. I don't want to get kicked out of Illinois. I was kicked out of New Mexico and I don't want to get kicked out of Illinois.

HALIE: You're going to get kicked out of this house, Tilden, if you don't tell me where you got that corn!

(TILDEN *starts crying softly to himself but keeps husking corn. Pause.*)

DODGE: (*to* HALIE) Why'd you have to tell him that? Who cares where he got the corn? Why'd you have to go and tell him that?

HALIE: (*to* DODGE) It's your fault you know! You're the one that's behind all this! I suppose you thought it'd be funny! Some joke! Cover the house with corn husks. You better get this cleaned up before Bradley sees it.

DODGE: Bradley's not getting in the front door!

HALIE: (*kicking husks, striding back and forth*) Bradley's going to be very upset when he sees this. He doesn't like to see the house in disarray. He can't stand it when one thing is out of place. The slightest thing. You know how he gets.

DODGE: Bradley doesn't even live here!

HALIE: It's his home as much as ours. He was born in this house!

DODGE: He was born in a hog wallow.

HALIE: Don't you say that! Don't you ever say that!

DODGE: He was born in a goddamn hog wallow! That's where he was born and that's where he belongs! He doesn't belong in this house!

HALIE: (*she stops*) I don't know what's come over you, Dodge. I don't know what in the world's come over you. You've become an evil man. You used to be a good man.

DODGE: Six of one, a half dozen of another.

HALIE: You sit here day and night, festering away! Decomposing! Smelling up the house with your putrid body! Hacking your head off till all hours of the morning! Thinking up mean, evil, stupid things to say about your own flesh and blood!

DODGE: He's not my flesh and blood! My flesh and blood's buried in the back yard!

(*They freeze. Long pause. The men stare at her.*)

HALIE: (*quietly*) That's enough, Dodge. That's quite enough. I'm going out now. I'm going to have lunch with Father Dewis. I'm going to ask him about a monument. A statue. At least a plaque.

(*She crosses to the door up right. She stops.*)

HALIE: If you need anything, ask Tilden. He's the oldest. I've left some money on the kitchen table.
DODGE: I don't need anything.
HALIE: No, I suppose not. (*she opens the door and looks out through porch*) Still raining. I love the smell just after it stops. The ground. I won't be too late.

(*She goes out door and closes it. She's still visible on the porch as she crosses toward stage left screen door. She stops in the middle of the porch, speaks to* DODGE *but doesn't turn to him.*)

HALIE: Dodge, tell Tilden not to go out in the back lot anymore. I don't want him back there in the rain.
DODGE: You tell him. He's sitting right here.
HALIE: He never listens to me Dodge. He's never listened to me in the past.
DODGE: I'll tell him.
HALIE: We have to watch him just like we used to now. Just like we always have. He's still a child.
DODGE: I'll watch him.
HALIE: Good.

(*She crosses to screen door, left, takes an umbrella off a hook and goes out the door. The door slams behind her. Long pause.* TILDEN *husks corn, stares at pail.* DODGE *lights a cigarette, stares at T.V.*)

TILDEN: (*still husking*) You shouldn't a told her that.
DODGE: (*staring at T.V.*) What?
TILDEN: What you told her. You know.
DODGE: What do you know about it?
TILDEN: I know. I know all about it. We all know.
DODGE: So what difference does it make? Everybody knows, everybody's forgot.

TILDEN: She hasn't forgot.

DODGE: She should've forgot.

TILDEN: It's different for a woman. She couldn't forget that. How could she forget that?

DODGE: I don't want to talk about it!

TILDEN: What do you want to talk about?

DODGE: I don't want to talk about anything! I don't want to talk about troubles or what happened fifty years ago or thirty years ago or the race track or Florida or the last time I seeded the corn! I don't want to talk!

TILDEN: You don't wanna die do you?

DODGE: No, I don't wanna die either.

TILDEN: Well, you gotta talk or you'll die.

DODGE: Who told you that?

TILDEN: That's what I know. I found that out in New Mexico. I thought I was dying but I just lost my voice.

DODGE: Were you with somebody?

TILDEN: I was alone. I thought I was dead.

DODGE: Might as well have been. What'd you come back here for?

TILDEN: I didn't know where to go.

DODGE: You're a grown man. You shouldn't be needing your parents at your age. It's unnatural. There's nothing we can do for you now anyway. Couldn't you make a living down there? Couldn't you find some way to make a living? Support yourself? What'd'ya come back here for? You expect us to feed you forever?

TILDEN: I didn't know where else to go.

DODGE: I never went back to my parents. Never. Never even had the urge. I was independent. Always independent. Always found a way.

TILDEN: I didn't know what to do. I couldn't figure anything out.

DODGE: There's nothing to figure out. You just forge ahead. What's there to figure out?

(TILDEN *stands*.)

TILDEN: I don't know.

DODGE: Where are you going?

TILDEN: Out back.

DODGE: You're not supposed to go out there. You heard what she said. Don't play deaf with me!

TILDEN: I like it out there.

DODGE: In the rain?

TILDEN: Especially in the rain. I like the feeling of it. Feels like it always did.

DODGE: You're supposed to watch out for me. Get me things when I need them.

TILDEN: What do you need?

DODGE: I don't need anything! But I might. I might need something any second. Any second now. I can't be left alone for a minute!

(DODGE *starts to cough.*)

TILDEN: I'll be right outside. You can just yell.

DODGE: (*between coughs*) No! It's too far! You can't go out there! It's too far! You might not ever hear me!

TILDEN: (*moving to pills*) Why don't you take a pill? You want a pill?

(DODGE *coughs more violently, throws himself back against sofa, clutches his throat.* TILDEN *stands by helplessly.*)

DODGE: Water! Get me some water!

(TILDEN *rushes off left.* DODGE *reaches out for the pills, knocking some bottles to the floor, coughing in spasms. He grabs a small bottle, takes out pills and swallows them.* TILDEN *rushes back on with a glass of water.* DODGE *takes it and drinks, his coughing subsides.*)

TILDEN: You all right now?

(DODGE *nods. Drinks more water.* TILDEN *moves in closer to him.* DODGE *sets glass of water on the night table. His coughing is almost gone.*)

TILDEN: Why don't you lay down for a while? Just rest a little.

(TILDEN *helps* DODGE *lay down on the sofa. Covers him with blanket.*)

DODGE: You're not going outside are you?

TILDEN: No.

DODGE: I don't want to wake up and find you not here.

TILDEN: I'll be here.

(TILDEN *tucks blanket around* DODGE)

DODGE: You'll stay right here?

TILDEN: I'll stay in my chair.

DODGE: That's not a chair. That's my old milking stool.

TILDEN: I know.

DODGE: Don't call it a chair.

TILDEN: I won't.

(TILDEN *tries to take* DODGE'S *baseball cap off.*)

DODGE: What're you doing! Leave that on me! Don't take that offa me! That's my cap!

(TILDEN *leaves the cap on* DODGE)

TILDEN: I know.

DODGE: Bradley'll shave my head if I don't have that on. That's my cap.

TILDEN: I know it is.

DODGE: Don't take my cap off.

TILDEN: I won't.

DODGE: You stay right here now.

TILDEN: (*sits on stool*) I will.

DODGE: Don't go outside. There's nothing out there.

TILDEN: I won't.

DODGE: Everything's in here. Everything you need. Money's on the table. T.V. Is the T.V. on?

TILDEN: Yeah.

DODGE: Turn it off! Turn the damn thing off! What's it doing on?

TILDEN: (*shuts off T.V., light goes out*) You left it on.

DODGE: Well turn it off.

TILDEN: (*sits on stool again*) It's off.

DODGE: Leave it off.

TILDEN: I will.

DODGE: When I fall asleep you can turn it on.

TILDEN: Okay.

DODGE: You can watch the ball game. Red Sox. You like the Red Sox don't you?

TILDEN: Yeah.

DODGE: You can watch the Red Sox. Pee Wee Reese. Pee Wee Reese. You remember Pee Wee Reese?

TILDEN: No.

DODGE: Was he with the Red Sox?

TILDEN: I don't know.

DODGE: Pee Wee Reese. (*falling asleep*) You can watch the Cardinals. You remember Stan Musial.

TILDEN: No.

DODGE: Stan Musial. (*falling into sleep*) Bases loaded. Top a' the sixth. Bases loaded. Runner on first and third. Big fat knuckle ball. Floater. Big as a blimp. Cracko! Ball just took off like a rocket. Just pulverized. I marked it. Marked it with my eyes. Straight between the clock and the Burma Shave ad. I was the first kid out there. First kid. I had to fight hard for that ball. I wouldn't give it up. They almost tore the ears right off me. But I wouldn't give it up.

(DODGE *falls into deep sleep.* TILDEN *just sits staring at him for a while. Slowly he leans toward the sofa, checking to see if* DODGE *is well asleep. He reaches slowly under the cushion and pulls out the bottle of booze.* DODGE *sleeps soundly.* TILDEN *stands quietly, staring at* DODGE *as he uncaps the bottle and takes a long drink. He caps the bottle and sticks it in his hip pocket. He looks around at the husks on the floor and then back to* DODGE. *He moves center stage and gathers an armload of corn husks then crosses back to the sofa. He stands holding the husks over* DODGE *and looking down at him he gently spreads the corn husks over the whole length of* DODGE'S *body. He stands back and looks at* DODGE. *Pulls out bottle, takes another drink, returns bottle to his hip pocket. He gathers more husks and repeats the procedure until the floor is clean of corn husks and* DODGE *is completely covered in them except for his head.* TILDEN *takes another long drink, stares at* DODGE *sleeping then quietly exits stage left. Long pause as the sound of rain continues.* DODGE *sleeps on. The figure of* BRADLEY *appears up left, outside the screen porch door. He holds a wet newspaper over his head as a protection from the rain. He seems to be struggling with the door then slips and almost falls to the ground.* DODGE *sleeps on, undisturbed.*)

BRADLEY: Sonuvabitch! Sonuvagoddamnbitch!

(BRADLEY *recovers his footing and makes it through the screen door onto the porch. He throws the newspaper down, shakes the water out of his hair, and brushes the rain off of his shoulders. He is a big man dressed in a gray sweat shirt, black suspenders, baggy dark blue pants and black janitor's shoes. His left leg is wooden, having been amputated above the knee. He moves with an exaggerated, almost*

*mechanical limp. The squeaking sounds of leather and metal accom-
pany his walk coming from the harness and hinges of the false leg.
His arms and shoulders are extremely powerful and muscular due to
a lifetime dependency on the upper torso doing all the work for the
legs. He is about five years younger than* TILDEN. *He moves labori-
ously to the stage right door and enters, closing the door behind him.
He doesn't notice* DODGE *at first. He moves toward the staircase.*)

BRADLEY: (*calling to upstairs*) Mom!

(*He stops and listens. Turns upstage and sees* DODGE *sleeping.
Notices corn husks. He moves slowly toward sofa. Stops next to pail
and looks into it. Looks at husks.* DODGE *stays asleep. Talks to
himself.*)

BRADLEY: What in the hell is this?

(*He looks at* DODGE'S *sleeping face and shakes his head in disgust.
He pulls out a pair of black electric hair clippers from his pocket.
Unwinds the cord and crosses to the lamp. He jabs his wooden leg
behind the knee, causing it to bend at the joint and awkwardly kneels
to plug the cord into a floor outlet. He pulls himself to his feet again
by using the sofa as leverage. He moves to* DODGE'S *head and again
jabs his false leg. Goes down on one knee. He violently knocks away
some of the corn husks then jerks off* DODGE'S *baseball cap and
throws it down center stage.* DODGE *stays asleep.* BRADLEY *switches
on the clippers. Lights start dimming.* BRADLEY *cuts* DODGE'S *hair
while he sleeps. Lights dim slowly to black with the sound of clippers
and rain.*)

ACT TWO

SCENE: *Same set as act 1. Night. Sounds of rain.* DODGE *still asleep on sofa. His hair is cut extremely short and in places the scalp is cut and bleeding. His cap is still center stage. All the corn and husks, pail and milking stool have been cleared away. The lights come up to the sound of a young girl laughing off stage left.* DODGE *remains asleep.* SHELLY *and* VINCE *appear up left outside the screen porch door sharing the shelter of* VINCE's *overcoat above their heads.* SHELLY *is about nineteen, black hair, very beautiful. She wears tight jeans, high heels, purple T-shirt and a short rabbit fur coat. Her makeup is exaggerated and her hair has been curled.* VINCE *is* TILDEN's *son, about twenty-two, wears a plaid shirt, jeans, dark glasses, cowboy boots and carries a black saxophone case. They shake the rain off themselves as they enter the porch through the screen door.*

SHELLY: (*laughing, gesturing to house*) This is it? I don't believe this is it!

VINCE: This is it.

SHELLY: This is the house?

VINCE: This is the house.

SHELLY: I don't believe it!

VINCE: How come?

SHELLY: It's like a Norman Rockwell cover or something.

VINCE: What's a' matter with that? It's American.

SHELLY: Where's the milkman and the little dog? What's the little dog's name? Spot. Spot and Jane. Dick and Jane and Spot.

VINCE: Knock it off.

SHELLY: Dick and Jane and Spot and Mom and Dad and Junior and Sissy!

83

(*She laughs. Slaps her knee.*)

VINCE: Come on! It's my heritage. What dya' expect?

(*She laughs more hysterically, out of control.*)

SHELLY: "And Tuffy and Toto and Dooda and Bonzo all went down one day to the corner grocery store to buy a big bag of licorice for Mr. Marshall's pussy cat!"

(*She laughs so hard she falls to her knees holding her stomach.* VINCE *stands there looking at her.*

VINCE: Shelly will you get up!

(*She keeps laughing. Staggers to her feet. Turning in circles holding her stomach.*)

SHELLY: (*continuing her story in kid's voice*) "Mr. Marshall was on vacation. He had no idea that the four little boys had taken such a liking to his little kitty cat."

VINCE: Have some respect would ya'!

SHELLY: (*trying to control herself*) I'm sorry.

VINCE: Pull yourself together.

SHELLY: (*salutes him*) Yes sir.

(*She giggles.*)

VINCE: Jesus Christ, Shelly.

SHELLY: (*pause, smiling*) And Mr. Marshall—

VINCE: Cut it out.

(*She stops. Stands there staring at him. Stifles a giggle.*)

VINCE: (*after pause*) Are you finished?

SHELLY: Oh brother!

VINCE: I don't wanna go in there with you acting like an idiot.

SHELLY: Thanks.

VINCE: Well, I don't.

SHELLY: I won't embarrass you. Don't worry.

VINCE: I'm not worried.

SHELLY: You are too.

VINCE: Shelly look, I just don't wanna go in there with you giggling your head off. They might think something's wrong with you.

SHELLY: There is.

VINCE: There is not!

SHELLY: Something's definitely wrong with me.

VINCE: There is not!

SHELLY: There's something wrong with you too.

VINCE: There's nothing wrong with me either!

SHELLY: You wanna know what's wrong with you?

VINCE: What?

(SHELLY *laughs*.)

VINCE: (*crosses back left toward screen door*) I'm leaving!

SHELLY: (*stops laughing*) Wait! Stop! Stop! (VINCE *stops*) What's wrong with you is that you take the situation too seriously.

VINCE: I just don't want to have them think that I've suddenly arrived out of the middle of nowhere completely deranged.

SHELLY: What do you want them to think then?

VINCE: (*pause*) Nothing. Let's go in.

(*He crosses porch toward stage right interior door.* SHELLY *follows him. The stage right door opens slowly.* VINCE *sticks his head in, doesn't notice* DODGE *sleeping. Calls out toward staircase.*)

VINCE: Grandma!

(SHELLY *breaks into laughter, unseen behind* VINCE. VINCE *pulls his head back outside and pulls door shut. We hear their voices again without seeing them.*)

SHELLY'S VOICE: (*stops laughing*) I'm sorry. I'm sorry Vince. I really am. I really am sorry. I won't do it again. I couldn't help it.

VINCE'S VOICE: It's not all that funny.

SHELLY'S VOICE: I know it's not. I'm sorry.

VINCE'S VOICE: I mean this is a tense situation for me! I haven't seen them for over six years. I don't know what to expect.

SHELLY'S VOICE: I know. I won't do it again.

VINCE'S VOICE: Can't you bite your tongue or something?

SHELLY'S VOICE: Just don't say "Grandma," okay? (*she giggles, stops*) I mean if you say "Grandma" I don't know if I can stop myself.

VINCE'S VOICE: Well try!

SHELLY'S VOICE: Okay. Sorry.

(*Door opens again.* VINCE *sticks his head in then enters.* SHELLY *follows behind him.* VINCE *crosses to staircase, sets down saxophone*

case and overcoat, looks up staircase. SHELLY *notices* DODGE'S
baseball cap. Crosses to it. Picks it up and puts it on her head.
VINCE *goes up the stairs and disappears at the top.* SHELLY *watches
him then turns and sees* DODGE *on the sofa. She takes off the baseball
cap.*)

VINCE'S VOICE: (*from above stairs*) Grandma!

(SHELLY *crosses over to* DODGE *slowly and stands next to him. She
stands at his head, reaches out slowly and touches one of the cuts. The
second she touches his head,* DODGE *jerks up to a sitting position on
the sofa, eyes open.* SHELLY *gasps.* DODGE *looks at her, sees his cap
in her hands, quickly puts his hand to his bare head. He glares at*
SHELLY *then whips the cap out of her hands and puts it on.* SHELLY
backs away from him. DODGE *stares at her.*)

SHELLY: I'm uh—with Vince.

(DODGE *just glares at her.*)

SHELLY: He's upstairs.

(DODGE *looks at the staircase then back to* SHELLY.)

SHELLY: (*calling upstairs*) Vince!
VINCE'S VOICE: Just a second!
SHELLY: You better get down here!
VINCE'S VOICE: Just a minute! I'm looking at the pictures.

(DODGE *keeps staring at her.*)

SHELLY: (*to* DODGE) We just got here. Pouring rain on the
freeway so we thought we'd stop by. I mean Vince was
planning on stopping anyway. He wanted to see you. He said
he hadn't seen you in a long time.

(*Pause.* DODGE *just keeps staring at her.*)

SHELLY: We were going all the way through to New Mexico.
To see his father. I guess his father lives out there. We
thought we'd stop by and see you on the way. Kill two birds
with one stone, you know? (*she laughs,* DODGE *stares, she stops
laughing*) I mean Vince has this thing about his family now. I
guess it's a new thing with him. I kind of find it hard to relate
to. But he feels it's important. You know. I mean he feels he
wants to get to know you all again. After all this time.

(*Pause.* DODGE *just stares at her. She moves nervously to staircase and yells up to* VINCE.)

SHELLY: Vince will you come down here please!

(VINCE *comes half way down the stairs.*)

VINCE: I guess they went out for a while.

(SHELLY *points to sofa and* DODGE. VINCE *turns and sees* DODGE. *He comes all the way down staircase and crosses to* DODGE. SHELLY *stays behind near staircase, keeping her distance.*)

VINCE: Grandpa?

(DODGE *looks up at him, not recognizing him.*)

DODGE: Did you bring the whiskey?

(VINCE *looks back at* SHELLY *then back to* DODGE.)

VINCE: Grandpa, it's Vince. I'm Vince. Tilden's son. You remember?

(DODGE *stares at him.*)

DODGE: You didn't do what you told me. You didn't stay here with me.
VINCE: Grandpa, I haven't been here until just now. I just got here.
DODGE: You left. You went outside like we told you not to do. You went out there in back. In the rain.

(VINCE *looks back at* SHELLY. *She moves slowly toward sofa.*)

SHELLY: Is he okay?
VINCE: I don't know. (*takes off his shades*) Look, Grandpa, don't you remember me? Vince. Your Grandson.

(DODGE *stares at him then takes off his baseball cap.*)

DODGE: (*points to his head*) See what happens when you leave me alone? See that? That's what happens.

(VINCE *looks at his head.* VINCE *reaches out to touch his head.* DODGE *slaps his hand away with the cap and puts it back on his head.*)

VINCE: What's going on Grandpa? Where's Halie?
DODGE: Don't worry about her. She won't be back for days. She

says she'll be back but she won't be. (*he starts laughing*)
There's life in the old girl yet! (*stops laughing*)

VINCE: How did you do that to your head?

DODGE: I didn't do it! Don't be ridiculous!

VINCE: Well who did then?

(*Pause.* DODGE *stares at* VINCE.)

DODGE: Who do you think did it? Who do you think?

(SHELLY *moves toward* VINCE.)

SHELLY: Vince, maybe we oughta' go. I don't like this. I
mean this isn't my idea of a good time.

VINCE: (*to* SHELLY) Just a second. (*to* DODGE) Grandpa, look, I
just got here. I just now got here. I haven't been here for six
years. I don't know anything that's happened.

(*Pause,* DODGE *stares at him.*)

DODGE: You don't know anything?

VINCE: No.

DODGE: Well that's good. That's good. It's much better not to
know anything. Much, much better.

VINCE: Isn't there anybody here with you?

(DODGE *turns slowly and looks off to stage left.*)

DODGE: Tilden's here.

VINCE: No, Grandpa, Tilden's in New Mexico. That's where I
was going. I'm going out there to see him.

(DODGE *turns slowly back to* VINCE.)

DODGE: Tilden's here.

(VINCE *backs away and joins* SHELLY. DODGE *stares at them.*)

SHELLY: Vince, why don't we spend the night in a motel and
come back in the morning? We could have breakfast. Maybe
everything would be different.

VINCE: Don't be scared. There's nothing to be scared of. He's
just old.

SHELLY: I'm not scared!

DODGE: You two are not my idea of the perfect couple!

SHELLY: (*after pause*) Oh really? Why's that?

VINCE: Shh! Don't aggravate him.

DODGE: There's something wrong between the two of you. Something not compatible.

VINCE: Grandpa, where did Halie go? Maybe we should call her.

DODGE: What are you talking about? Do you know what you're talking about? Are you just talking for the sake of talking? Lubricating the gums?

VINCE: I'm trying to figure out what's going on here!

DODGE: Is that it?

VINCE: Yes. I mean I expected everything to be different.

DODGE: Who are you to expect anything? Who are you supposed to be?

VINCE: I'm Vince! Your Grandson!

DODGE: Vince. My Grandson.

VINCE: Tilden's son.

DODGE: Tilden's son, Vince.

VINCE: You haven't seen me for a long time.

DODGE: When was the last time?

VINCE: I don't remember.

DODGE: You don't remember?

VINCE: No.

DODGE: You don't remember. How am I supposed to remember if you don't remember?

SHELLY: Vince, come on. This isn't going to work out.

VINCE: (*to* SHELLY) Just take it easy.

SHELLY: I'm taking it easy! He doesn't even know who you are!

VINCE: (*crossing toward* DODGE) Grandpa, look—

DODGE: Stay where you are! Keep your distance!

(VINCE *stops. Looks back at* SHELLY *then to* DODGE.)

SHELLY: Vince, this is really making me nervous. I mean he doesn't even want us here. He doesn't even like us.

DODGE: She's a beautiful girl.

VINCE: Thanks.

DODGE: Very Beautiful Girl.

SHELLY: Oh my God.

DODGE: (*to* SHELLY) What's your name?

SHELLY: Shelly.

DODGE: Shelly. That's a man's name isn't it?

SHELLY: Not in this case.

DODGE: (*to* VINCE) She's a smart-ass too.

SHELLY: Vince! Can we go?

DODGE: She wants to go. She just got here and she wants to go.

VINCE: This is kind of strange for her.

DODGE: She'll get used to it. (*to* SHELLY) What part of the country do you come from?

SHELLY: Originally?

DODGE: That's right. Originally. At the very start.

SHELLY: L.A.

DODGE: L.A. Stupid country.

SHELLY: I can't stand this Vince! This is really unbelievable!

DODGE: It's stupid! L.A. is stupid! So is Florida! All those Sunshine States. They're all stupid. Do you know why they're stupid?

SHELLY: Illuminate me.

DODGE: I'll tell you why. Because they're full of smart-asses! That's why.

(SHELLY *turns her back to* DODGE, *crosses to staircase and sits on bottom step.*)

DODGE: (*to* VINCE) Now she's insulted.

VINCE: Well you weren't very polite.

DODGE: She's insulted! Look at her! In my house she's insulted! She's over there sulking because I insulted her!

SHELLY: (*to* VINCE) This is really terrific. This is wonderful. And you were worried about me making the right first impression!

DODGE: (*to* VINCE) She's a fireball isn't she? Regular fireball. I had some a' them in my day. Temporary stuff. Never lasted more than a week.

VINCE: Grandpa—

DODGE: Stop calling me Grandpa will ya'! It's sickening. "Grandpa." I'm nobody's Grandpa!

(DODGE *starts feeling around under the cushion for the bottle of whiskey.* SHELLY *gets up from the staircase.*)

SHELLY: (*to* VINCE) Maybe you've got the wrong house. Did you ever think of that? Maybe this is the wrong address!

VINCE: It's not the wrong address! I recognize the yard.

SHELLY: Yeah but do you recognize the people? He says he's not your Grandfather.

DODGE: (*digging for bottle*) Where's that bottle!

VINCE: He's just sick or something. I don't know what's happened to him.

DODGE: Where's my goddamn bottle!

(DODGE *gets up from sofa and starts tearing the cushions off it and throwing them downstage, looking for the whiskey.*)

SHELLY: Can't we just drive on to New Mexico? This is terrible, Vince! I don't want to stay here. In this house. I thought it was going to be turkey dinners and apple pie and all that kinda stuff.

VINCE: Well I hate to disappoint you!

SHELLY: I'm not disappointed! I'm fuckin' terrified! I wanna' go!

(DODGE *yells toward stage left.*)

DODGE: Tilden! Tilden!

(DODGE *keeps ripping away at the sofa looking for his bottle, he knocks over the night stand with the bottles.* VINCE *and* SHELLY *watch as he starts ripping the stuffing out of the sofa.*)

VINCE: (*to* SHELLY) He's lost his mind or something. I've got to try to help him.

SHELLY: You help him! I'm leaving!

(SHELLY *starts to leave.* VINCE *grabs her. They struggle as* DODGE *keeps ripping away at the sofa and yelling.*)

DODGE: Tilden! Tilden get your ass in here! Tilden!

SHELLY: Let go of me!

VINCE: You're not going anywhere! You're going to stay right here!

SHELLY: Let go of me you sonuvabitch! I'm not your property!

(*Suddenly* TILDEN *walks on from stage left just as he did before. This time his arms are full of carrots.* DODGE, VINCE *and* SHELLY *stop suddenly when they see him. They all stare at* TILDEN *as he crosses slowly center stage with the carrots and stops.* DODGE *sits on sofa, exhausted.*)

DODGE: (*panting, to* TILDEN) Where in the hell have you been?

TILDEN: Out back.

DODGE: Where's my bottle?

TILDEN: Gone.

(TILDEN *and* VINCE *stare at each other.* SHELLY *backs away.*)

DODGE: (*to* TILDEN) You stole my bottle!
VINCE: (*to* TILDEN) Dad?

(TILDEN *just stares at* VINCE.)

DODGE: You had no right to steal my bottle! No right at all!
VINCE: (*to* TILDEN) It's Vince. I'm Vince.

(TILDEN *stares at* VINCE *then looks at* DODGE *then turns to* SHELLY.)

TILDEN: (*after pause*) I picked these carrots. If anybody wants
any carrots, I picked 'em.
SHELLY: (*to* VINCE) This is your father?
VINCE: (*to* TILDEN) Dad, what're you doing here?

(TILDEN *just stares at* VINCE, *holding carrots,* DODGE *pulls the
blanket back over himself.*)

DODGE: (*to* TILDEN) You're going to have to get me another
bottle! You gotta get me a bottle before Halie comes back!
There's money on the table. (*points to stage left kitchen*)
TILDEN: (*shaking his head*) I'm not going down there. Into town.

(SHELLY *crosses to* TILDEN. TILDEN *stares at her.*)

SHELLY: (*to* TILDEN) Are you Vince's father?
TILDEN: (*to* SHELLY) Vince?
SHELLY: (*pointing to* VINCE) This is supposed to be your son! Is
he your son! Do you recognize him! I'm just along for the
ride here. I thought everybody knew each other!

(TILDEN *stares at* VINCE. DODGE *wraps himself up in the blanket
and sits on sofa staring at the floor.*)

TILDEN: I had a son once but we buried him.

(DODGE *quickly looks at* TILDEN. SHELLY *looks to* VINCE.)

DODGE: You shut up about that! You don't know anything
about that!
VINCE: Dad, I thought you were in New Mexico. We were
going to drive down there and see you.
TILDEN: Long way to drive.
DODGE: (*to* TILDEN) You don't know anything about that! That
happened before you were born! Long before!
VINCE: What's happened, Dad? What's going on here? I thought
everything was all right. What's happened to Halie?

TILDEN: She left.

SHELLY: (*to* TILDEN) Do you want me to take those carrots for you?

(TILDEN *stares at her. She moves in close to him. Holds out her arms.* TILDEN *stares at her arms then slowly dumps the carrots into her arms.* SHELLY *stands there holding the carrots.*)

TILDEN: (*to* SHELLY) You like carrots?

SHELLY: Sure. I like all kinds of vegetables.

DODGE: (*to* TILDEN) You gotta get me a bottle before Halie comes back!

(DODGE *hits sofa with his fist.* VINCE *crosses up to* DODGE *and tries to console him.* SHELLY *and* TILDEN *stay facing each other.*)

TILDEN: (*to* SHELLY) Back yard's full of carrots. Corn. Potatoes.

SHELLY: You're Vince's father, right?

TILDEN: All kinds of vegetables. You like vegetables?

SHELLY: (*laughs*) Yeah. I love vegetables.

TILDEN: We could cook these carrots ya' know. You could cut 'em up and we could cook 'em.

SHELLY: All right.

TILDEN: I'll get you a pail and a knife.

SHELLY: Okay.

TILDEN: I'll be right back. Don't go.

(TILDEN *exits off stage left.* SHELLY *stands center, arms full of carrots.* VINCE *stands next to* DODGE. SHELLY *looks toward* VINCE *then down at the carrots.*)

DODGE: (*to* VINCE) You could get me a bottle. (*pointing off left*) There's money on the table.

VINCE: Grandpa why don't you lay down for a while?

DODGE: I don't wanna lay down for a while! Every time I lay down something happens! (*whips off his cap, points at his head*) Look what happens! That's what happens! (*pulls his cap back on*) You go lie down and see what happens to you! See how you like it! They'll steal your bottle! They'll cut your hair! They'll murder your children! That's what'll happen.

VINCE: Just relax for a while.

DODGE: (*pause*) You could get me a bottle ya' know. There's nothing stopping you from getting me a bottle.

SHELLY: Why don't you get him a bottle, Vince? Maybe it would help everybody identify each other.

DODGE: (*pointing to* SHELLY) There, see? She thinks you should get me a bottle.

(VINCE *crosses to* SHELLY.)

VINCE: What're you doing with those carrots.

SHELLY: I'm waiting for your father.

DODGE: She thinks you should get me a bottle!

VINCE: Shelly put the carrots down will ya'! We gotta deal with the situation here! I'm gonna need your help.

SHELLY: I'm helping.

VINCE: You're only adding to the problem! You're making things worse! Put the carrots down!

(VINCE *tries to knock the carrots out of her arms. She turns away from him, protecting the carrots.*)

SHELLY: Get away from me! Stop it!

(VINCE *stands back from her. She turns to him still holding the carrots.*)

VINCE: (*to* SHELLY) Why are you doing this! Are you trying to make fun of me? This is my family you know!

SHELLY: You coulda' fooled me! I'd just as soon not be here myself. I'd just as soon be a thousand miles from here. I'd rather be anywhere but here. You're the one who wants to stay. So I'll stay. I'll stay and I'll cut the carrots. And I'll cook the carrots. And I'll do whatever I have to do to survive. Just to make it through this.

VINCE: Put the carrots down Shelly.

(TILDEN *enters from left with pail, milking stool and a knife. He sets the stool and pail center stage for* SHELLY. SHELLY *looks at* VINCE *then sits down on stool, sets the carrots on the floor and takes the knife from* TILDEN. *She looks at* VINCE *again then picks up a carrot, cuts the ends off, scrapes it and drops it in pail. She repeats this,* VINCE *glares at her. She smiles.*)

DODGE: She could get me a bottle. She's the type a' girl that could get me a bottle. Easy. She'd go down there. Slink up to the counter. They'd probably give her two bottles for the price of one. She could do that.

(SHELLY *laughs. Keeps cutting carrots.* VINCE *crosses up to* DODGE, *looks at him.* TILDEN *watches* SHELLY'S *hands. Long pause.*)

VINCE: (*to* DODGE) I haven't changed that much. I mean physically. Physically I'm just about the same. Same size. Same weight. Everything's the same.

(DODGE *keeps staring at* SHELLY *while* VINCE *talks to him.*)

DODGE: She's a beautiful girl. Exceptional.

(VINCE *moves in front of* DODGE *to block his view of* SHELLY. DODGE *keeps craning his head around to see her as* VINCE *demonstrates tricks from his past.*)

VINCE: Look. Look at this. Do you remember this? I used to bend my thumb behind my knuckles. You remember? I used to do it at the dinner table.

(VINCE *bends a thumb behind his knuckles for* DODGE *and holds it out to him.* DODGE *takes a short glance then looks back at* SHELLY. VINCE *shifts position and shows him something else.*)

VINCE: What about this?

(VINCE *curls his lips back and starts drumming on his teeth with his fingernails making little tapping sounds.* DODGE *watches a while.* TILDEN *turns toward the sound.* VINCE *keeps it up. He sees* TILDEN *taking notice and crosses to* TILDEN *as he drums on his teeth.* DODGE *turns T.V. on. Watches it.*)

VINCE: You remember this Dad?

(VINCE *keeps on drumming for* TILDEN. TILDEN *watches a while, fascinated, then turns back to* SHELLY. VINCE *keeps up the drumming on his teeth, crosses back to* DODGE *doing it.* SHELLY *keeps working on carrots, talking to* TILDEN.)

SHELLY: (*to* TILDEN) He drives me crazy with that sometimes.
VINCE: (*to* DODGE) I know! Here's one you'll remember. You used to kick me out of the house for this one.

(VINCE *pulls his shirt out of his belt and holds it tucked under his chin with his stomach exposed. He grabs the flesh on either side of his belly button and pushes it in and out to make it look like a mouth talking. He watches his belly button and makes a deep sounding cartoon voice to synchronize with the movement. He demonstrates it to* DODGE *then crosses down to* TILDEN *doing it. Both* DODGE *and* TILDEN *take short, uninterested glances then ignore him.*)

VINCE: (*deep cartoon voice*) "Hello. How are you? I'm fine. Thank you very much. It's so good to see you looking well this fine Sunday morning. I was going down to the hardware store to fetch a pail of water."

SHELLY: Vince, don't be pathetic will ya'!

(VINCE *stops. Tucks his shirt back in.*)

SHELLY: Jesus Christ. They're not gonna play. Can't you see that?

(SHELLY *keeps cutting carrots.* VINCE *slowly moves toward* TILDEN. TILDEN *keeps watching* SHELLY. DODGE *watches T.V.*)

VINCE: (*to* SHELLY) I don't get it. I really don't get it. Maybe it's me. Maybe I forgot something.

DODGE: (*from sofa*) You forgot to get me a bottle! That's what you forgot. Anybody in this house could get me a bottle. Anybody! But nobody will. Nobody understands the urgency! Peelin' carrots is more important. Playin' piano on your teeth! Well I hope you all remember this when you get up in years. When you find yourself immobilized. Dependent on the whims of others.

(VINCE *moves up toward* DODGE. *Pause as he looks at him.*)

VINCE: I'll get you a bottle.

DODGE: You will?

VINCE: Sure.

(SHELLY *stands holding knife and carrot.*)

SHELLY: You're not going to leave me here are you?

VINCE: (*moving to her*) You suggested it! You said, "why don't I go get him a bottle." So I'll go get him a bottle!

SHELLY: But I can't stay here.

VINCE: What is going on! A minute ago you were ready to cut carrots all night!

SHELLY: That was only if you stayed. Something to keep me busy, so I wouldn't be so nervous. I don't want to stay here alone.

DODGE: Don't let her talk you out of it! She's a bad influence. I could see it the minute she stepped in here.

SHELLY: (*to* DODGE) You were asleep!

TILDEN: (*to* SHELLY) Don't you want to cut carrots anymore?

SHELLY: Sure. Sure I do.

(SHELLY *sits back down on stool and continues cutting carrots. Pause.* VINCE *moves around, stroking his hair, staring at* DODGE *and* TILDEN. VINCE *and* SHELLY *exchange glances.* DODGE *watches T.V.*)

VINCE: Boy! This is amazing. This is truly amazing. (*keeps moving around*) What is this anyway? Am I in a time warp or something? Have I committed an unpardonable offence? It's true, I'm not married. (SHELLY *looks at him, then back to carrots*) But I'm also not divorced. I have been known to plunge into sinful infatuation with the Alto Saxophone. Sucking on number 5 reeds deep into the wee, wee hours.

SHELLY: Vince, what are you doing that for? They don't care about any of that. They just don't recognize you, that's all.

VINCE: How could they not recognize me! How in the hell could they not recognize me! I'm their son!

DODGE: (*watching T.V.*) You're no son of mine. I've had sons in my time and you're not one of 'em.

(*Long pause.* VINCE *stares at* DODGE *then looks at* TILDEN. *He turns to* SHELLY.)

VINCE: Shelly, I gotta go out for a while. I just gotta go out. I'll get a bottle and I'll come right back. You'll be o.k. here. Really.

SHELLY: I don't know if I can handle this, Vince.

VINCE: I just gotta think or something. I don't know. I gotta put this all together.

SHELLY: Can't we just go?

VINCE: No! I gotta find out what's going on.

SHELLY: Look, you think you're bad off, what about me? Not only don't they recognize me but I've never seen them before in my life. I don't know who these guys are. They could be anybody!

VINCE: They're not anybody!

SHELLY: That's what you say.

VINCE: They're my family for Christ's sake! I should know who my own family is! Now give me a break. It won't take that long. I'll just go out and I'll come right back. Nothing'll happen. I promise.

(SHELLY *stares at him. Pause*)

SHELLY: All right.

VINCE: Thanks. (*he crosses up to* DODGE) I'm gonna go out now, Grandpa, and I'll pick you up a bottle. Okay?

DODGE: Change of heart huh? (*pointing off left*) Money's on the table. In the kitchen.

(VINCE *moves toward* SHELLY.)

VINCE: (*to* SHELLY) You be all right?

SHELLY: (*cutting carrots*) Sure. I'm fine. I'll just keep real busy while you're gone.

(VINCE *looks at* TILDEN *who keeps staring down at* SHELLY'S *hands.*)

DODGE: Persistence see? That's what it takes. Persistence. Persistence, fortitude and determination. Those are the three virtues. You stick with those three and you can't go wrong.

VINCE: (*to* TILDEN) You want anything, Dad?

TILDEN: (*looks up at* VINCE) Me?

VINCE: From the store? I'm gonna get Grandpa a bottle.

TILDEN: He's not supposed to drink. Halie wouldn't like it.

VINCE: He wants a bottle.

TILDEN: He's not supposed to drink.

DODGE: (*to* VINCE) Don't negotiate with him! Don't make any transactions until you've spoken to me first! He'll steal you blind!

VINCE: (*to* DODGE) Tilden says you're not supposed to drink.

DODGE: Tilden's lost his marbles! Look at him! He's around the bend. Take a look at him.

(VINCE *stares at* TILDEN. TILDEN *watches* SHELLY'S *hands as she keeps cutting carrots.*)

DODGE: Now look at me. Look here at me!

(VINCE *looks back to* DODGE.)

DODGE: Now, between the two of us, who do you think is more trustworthy? Him or me? Can you trust a man who keeps bringing in vegetables from out of nowhere? Take a look at him.

(VINCE *looks back at* TILDEN.)

SHELLY: Go get the bottle, Vince.

VINCE: (*to* SHELLY) You sure you'll be all right?

SHELLY: I'll be fine. I feel right at home now.

VINCE: You do?

SHELLY: I'm fine. Now that I've got the carrots everything is all right.

VINCE: I'll be right back.

(VINCE *crosses stage left.*)

DODGE: Where are you going?

VINCE: I'm going to get the money.

DODGE: Then where are you going?

VINCE: Liquor store.

DODGE: Don't go anyplace else. Don't go off some place and drink. Come right back here.

VINCE: I will.

(VINCE *exits stage left.*)

DODGE: (*calling after* VINCE) You've got responsibility now! And don't go out the back way either! Come out through this way! I wanna' see you when you leave! Don't go out the back!

VINCE'S VOICE: (*off left*) I won't!

(DODGE *turns and looks at* TILDEN *and* SHELLY.)

DODGE: Untrustworthy. Probably drown himself if he went out the back. Fall right in a hole. I'd never get my bottle.

SHELLY: I wouldn't worry about Vince. He can take care of himself.

DODGE: Oh he can, huh? Independent.

(VINCE *comes on again from stage left with two dollars in his hand. He crosses stage right past* DODGE.)

DODGE: (*to* VINCE) You got the money?

VINCE: Yeah. Two bucks.

DODGE: Two bucks. Two bucks is two bucks. Don't sneer.

VINCE: What kind do you want?

DODGE: Whiskey! Gold Star Sour Mash. Use your own discretion.

VINCE: Okay.

(VINCE *crosses to stage right door. Opens it. Stops when he hears* TILDEN.)

TILDEN: (*to* VINCE) You drove all the way from New Mexico?

(VINCE *turns and looks at* TILDEN. *They stare at each other.* VINCE *shakes his head, goes out the door, crosses porch and exits out screen door.* TILDEN *watches him go. Pause.*)

SHELLY: You really don't recognize him? Either one of you?

(TILDEN *turns again and stares at* SHELLY'S *hands as she cuts carrots.*)

DODGE: (*watching T.V.*) Recognize who?
SHELLY: Vince.
DODGE: What's to recognize?

(DODGE *lights a cigarette, coughs slightly and stares at T.V.*)

SHELLY: It'd be cruel if you recognized him and didn't tell him. Wouldn't be fair.

(DODGE *just stares at T.V., smoking.*)

TILDEN: I thought I recognized him. I thought I recognized something about him.
SHELLY: You did?
TILDEN: I thought I saw a face inside his face.
SHELLY: Well it was probably that you saw what he used to look like. You haven't seen him for six years.
TILDEN: I haven't?
SHELLY: That's what he says.

(TILDEN *moves around in front of her as she continues with carrots.*)

TILDEN: Where was it I saw him last?
SHELLY: I don't know. I've only known him for a few months. He doesn't tell me everything.
TILDEN: He doesn't?
SHELLY: Not stuff like that.
TILDEN: What does he tell you?
SHELLY: You mean in general?
TILDEN: Yeah.

(TILDEN *moves around behind her.*)

SHELLY: Well he tells me all kinds of things.
TILDEN: Like what?
SHELLY: I don't know! I mean I can't just come right out and tell you how he feels.

TILDEN: How come?

(TILDEN *keeps moving around her slowly in a circle.*)

SHELLY: Because it's stuff he told me privately!

TILDEN: And you can't tell me?

SHELLY: I don't even know you!

DODGE: Tilden, go out in the kitchen and make me some coffee! Leave the girl alone.

SHELLY: (*to* DODGE) He's all right.

(TILDEN *ignores* DODGE, *keeps moving around* SHELLY. *He stares at her hair and coat.* DODGE *stares at T.V.*)

TILDEN: You mean you can't tell me anything?

SHELLY: I can tell you some things. I mean we can have a conversation.

TILDEN: We can?

SHELLY: Sure. We're having a conversation right now.

TILDEN: We are?

SHELLY: Yes. That's what we're doing.

TILDEN: But there's certain things you can't tell me, right?

SHELLY: Right.

TILDEN: There's certain things I can't tell you either.

SHELLY: How come?

TILDEN: I don't know. Nobody's supposed to hear it.

SHELLY: Well, you can tell me anything you want to.

TILDEN: I can?

SHELLY: Sure.

TILDEN: It might not be very nice.

SHELLY: That's all right. I've been around.

TILDEN: It might be awful.

SHELLY: Well, can't you tell me anything nice?

(TILDEN *stops in front of her and stares at her coat.* SHELLY *looks back at him. Long pause.*)

TILDEN: (*after pause*) Can I touch your coat?

SHELLY: My coat? (*she looks at her coat then back to* TILDEN) Sure.

TILDEN: You don't mind?

SHELLY: No. Go ahead.

(SHELLY *holds her arm out for* TILDEN *to touch.* DODGE *stays fixed on T.V.* TILDEN *moves in slowly toward* SHELLY, *staring at her arm. He reaches out very slowly and touches her arm, feels the fur gently then draws his hand back.* SHELLY *keeps her arm out.*)

SHELLY: It's rabbit.
TILDEN: Rabbit.

(*He reaches out again very slowly and touches the fur on her arm then pulls back his hand again.* SHELLY *drops her arm.*)

SHELLY: My arm was getting tired.
TILDEN: Can I hold it?
SHELLY: (*pause*) The coat? Sure.

(SHELLY *takes off her coat and hands it to* TILDEN. TILDEN *takes it slowly, feels the fur then puts it on.* SHELLY *watches as* TILDEN *strokes the fur slowly. He smiles at her. She goes back to cutting carrots.*)

SHELLY: You can have it if you want.
TILDEN: I can?
SHELLY: Yeah. I've got a raincoat in the car. That's all I need.
TILDEN: You've got a car?
SHELLY: Vince does.

(TILDEN *walks around stroking the fur and smiling at the coat.* SHELLY *watches him when he's not looking.* DODGE *sticks with T.V., stretches out on sofa wrapped in blanket.*)

TILDEN: (*as he walks around*) I had a car once! I had a white car! I drove. I went everywhere. I went to the mountains. I drove in the snow.
SHELLY: That must've been fun.
TILDEN: (*still moving, feeling coat*) I drove all day long sometimes. Across the desert. Way out across the desert. I drove past towns. Anywhere. Past palm trees. Lightning. Anything. I would drive through it. I would drive through it and I would stop and I would look around and I would drive on. I would get back in and drive! I loved to drive. There was nothing I loved more. Nothing I dreamed of was better than driving.
DODGE: (*eyes on T.V.*) Pipe down would ya'!

(TILDEN *stops. Stares at* SHELLY.)

SHELLY: Do you do much driving now?
TILDEN: Now? Now? I don't drive now.

SHELLY: How come?

TILDEN: I'm grown up now.

SHELLY: Grown up?

TILDEN: I'm not a kid.

SHELLY: You don't have to be a kid to drive.

TILDEN: It wasn't driving then.

SHELLY: What was it?

TILDEN: Adventure. I went everywhere.

SHELLY: Well you can still do that.

TILDEN: Not now.

SHELLY: Why not?

TILDEN: I just told you. You don't understand anything. If I told you something you wouldn't understand it.

SHELLY: Told me what?

TILDEN: Told you something that's true.

SHELLY: Like what?

TILDEN: Like a baby. Like a little tiny baby.

SHELLY: Like when you were little?

TILDEN: If I told you you'd make me give your coat back.

SHELLY: I won't. I promise. Tell me.

TILDEN: I can't. Dodge won't let me.

SHELLY: He won't hear you. It's okay.

(*Pause.* TILDEN *stares at her. Moves slightly toward her.*)

TILDEN: We had a baby. (*motioning to* DODGE) He did. Dodge did. Could pick it up with one hand. Put it in the other. Little baby. Dodge killed it.

(SHELLY *stands.*)

TILDEN: Don't stand up. Don't stand up!

(SHELLY *sits again.* DODGE *sits up on sofa and looks at them*)

TILDEN: Dodge drowned it.

SHELLY: Don't tell me anymore! Okay?

(TILDEN *moves closer to her.* DODGE *takes more interest.*)

DODGE: Tilden? You leave that girl alone!

TILDEN: (*pays no attention*) Never told Halie. Never told anybody. Just drowned it.

DODGE: (*shuts off T.V.*) Tilden!

TILDEN: Nobody could find it. Just disappeared. Cops looked for it. Neighbors. Nobody could find it.

(DODGE *struggles to get up from sofa.*)

DODGE: Tilden, what're you telling her! Tilden!

(DODGE *keeps struggling until he's standing.*)

TILDEN: Finally everybody just gave up. Just stopped looking. Everybody had a different answer. Kidnap. Murder. Accident. Some kind of accident.

(DODGE *struggles to walk toward* TILDEN *and falls.* TILDEN *ignores him.*)

DODGE: Tilden you shut up! You shut up about it!

(DODGE *starts coughing on the floor.* SHELLY *watches him from the stool.*)

TILDEN: Little tiny baby just disappeared. It's not hard. It's so small. Almost invisible.

(SHELLY *makes a move to help* DODGE. TILDEN *firmly pushes her back down on the stool.* DODGE *keeps coughing.*)

TILDEN: He said he had his reasons. Said it went a long way back. But he wouldn't tell anybody.

DODGE: Tilden! Don't tell her anything! Don't tell her!

TILDEN: He's the only one who knows where it's buried. The only one. Like a secret buried treasure. Won't tell any of us. Won't tell me or mother or even Bradley. Especially Bradley. Bradley tried to force it out of him but he wouldn't tell. Wouldn't even tell why he did it. One night he just did it.

(DODGE'S *coughing subsides.* SHELLY *stays on stool staring at* DODGE. TILDEN *slowly takes* SHELLY'S *coat off and holds it out to her. Long pause.* SHELLY *sits there trembling.*)

TILDEN: You probably want your coat back now.

(SHELLY *stares at coat but doesn't move to take it. The sound of* BRADLEY'S *leg squeaking is heard off left. The others on stage remain still.* BRADLEY *appears up left outside the screen door wearing a yellow rain slicker. He enters through screen door, crosses porch to stage right door and enters stage. Closes door. Takes off rain slicker and shakes it out. He sees all the others and stops.* TILDEN *turns to him.* BRADLEY *stares at* SHELLY. DODGE *remains on floor.*)

BRADLEY: What's going on here? (*motioning to* SHELLY) Who's that?

(SHELLY *stands, moves back away from* BRADLEY *as he crosses toward her. He stops next to* TILDEN. *He sees coat in* TILDEN'S *hand and grabs it away from him.*)

BRADLEY: Who's she supposed to be?
TILDEN: She's driving to New Mexico.

(BRADLEY *stares at her.* SHELLY *is frozen.* BRADLEY *limps over to her with the coat in his fist. He stops in front of her.*)

BRADLEY: (*to* SHELLY, *after pause*) Vacation?

(SHELLY *shakes her head "no," trembling.*)

BRADLEY: (*to* SHELLY, *motioning to* TILDEN) You taking him with you?

(SHELLY *shakes her head "no."* BRADLEY *crosses back to* TILDEN.)

BRADLEY: You oughta'. No use leaving him here. Doesn't do a lick a' work. Doesn't raise a finger. (*stopping, to* TILDEN) Do ya'? (*to* SHELLY) 'Course he used to be an All American. Quarterback or Fullback or somethin'. He tell you that?

(SHELLY *shakes her head "no."*)

BRADLEY: Yeah, he used to be a big deal. Wore lettermen's sweaters. Had medals hanging all around his neck. Real purty. Big deal. (*he laughs to himself, notices* DODGE *on floor, crosses to him, stops*) This one too. (*to* SHELLY) You'd never think it to look at him would ya'? All bony and wasted away.

(SHELLY *shakes her head again.* BRADLEY *stares at her, crosses back to her, clenching the coat in his fist. He stops in front of* SHELLY.)

BRADLEY: Women like that kinda' thing don't they?
SHELLY: What?
BRADLEY: Importance. Importance in a man?
SHELLY: I don't know.
BRADLEY: Yeah. You know, you know. Don't give me that. (*moves closer to* SHELLY) You're with Tilden?
SHELLY: No.

BRADLEY: (*turning to* TILDEN) Tilden! She with you?

(TILDEN *doesn't answer. Stares at floor.*)

BRADLEY: Tilden!

(TILDEN *suddenly bolts and runs off up stage left.* BRADLEY *laughs. Talks to* SHELLY. DODGE *starts moving his lips silently as though talking to someone invisible on the floor.*)

BRADLEY: (*laughing*) Scared to death! He was always scared!

(BRADLEY *stops laughing. Stares at* SHELLY.)

BRADLEY: You're scared too, right? (*laughs again*) You're scared and you don't even know me. (*stops laughing*) You don't gotta be scared.

(SHELLY *looks at* DODGE *on the floor.*)

SHELLY: Can't we do something for him?
BRADLEY: (*looking at* DODGE) We could shoot him. (*laughs*) We could drown him! What about drowning him?
SHELLY: Shut up!

(BRADLEY *stops laughing. Moves in closer to* SHELLY. *She freezes.* BRADLEY *speaks slowly and deliberately.*)

BRADLEY: Hey! Missus. Don't talk to me like that. Don't talk to me in that tone a' voice. There was a time when I had to take that tone a' voice from pretty near everyone. (*motioning to* DODGE) Him, for one! Him and that half brain that just ran outa' here. They don't talk to me like that now. Not any more. Everything's turned around now. Full circle. Isn't that funny?
SHELLY: I'm sorry.
BRADLEY: Open your mouth.
SHELLY: What?
BRADLEY: (*motioning for her to open her mouth*) Open up.

(*She opens her mouth slightly.*)

BRADLEY: Wider.

(*She opens her mouth wider.*)

BRADLEY: Keep it like that.

(*She does. Stares at* BRADLEY. *With his free hand he puts his fingers into her mouth. She tries to pull away.*)

BRADLEY: Just stay put!

(*She freezes. He keeps his fingers in her mouth. Stares at her. Pause. He pulls his hand out. She closes her mouth, keeps her eyes on him.* BRADLEY *smiles. He looks at* DODGE *on the floor and crosses over to him.* SHELLY *watches him closely.* BRADLEY *stands over* DODGE *and smiles at* SHELLY. *He holds her coat up in both hands over* DODGE, *keeps smiling at* SHELLY. *He looks down at* DODGE *then drops the coat so that it lands on* DODGE *and covers his head.* BRADLEY *keeps his hands up in the position of holding the coat, looks over at* SHELLY *and smiles. The lights black out.*)

ACT THREE

SCENE: *Same set. Morning. Bright sun. No sound of rain. Everything has been cleared up again. No sign of carrots. No pail. No stool.* VINCE'S *saxophone case and overcoat are still at the foot of the staircase.* BRADLEY *is asleep on the sofa under* DODGE'S *blanket. His head toward stage left.* BRADLEY'S *wooden leg is leaning against the sofa right by his head. The shoe is left on it. The harness hangs down.* DODGE *is sitting on the floor, propped up against the T.V. set facing stage left wearing his baseball cap.* SHELLY'S *rabbit fur coat covers his chest and shoulders. He stares off toward stage left. He seems weaker and more disoriented. The lights rise slowly to the sound of birds and remain for a while in silence on the two men.* BRADLEY *sleeps very soundly.* DODGE *hardly moves.* SHELLY *appears from stage left with a big smile, slowly crossing toward* DODGE *balancing a steaming cup of broth in a saucer.* DODGE *just stares at her as she gets closer to him.*

SHELLY: (*as she crosses*) This is going to make all the difference in the world, Grandpa. You don't mind me calling you Grandpa do you? I mean I know you minded when Vince called you that but you don't even know him.

DODGE: He skipped town with my money ya' know. I'm gonna hold you as collateral.

SHELLY: He'll be back. Don't you worry.

(*She kneels down next to* DODGE *and puts the cup and saucer in his lap.*)

DODGE: It's morning already! Not only didn't I get my bottle but he's got my two bucks!

SHELLY: Try to drink this, okay? Don't spill it.

DODGE: What is it?

108

SHELLY: Beef bouillon. It'll warm you up.

DODGE: Bouillon! I don't want any goddamn bouillon! Get that stuff away from me!

SHELLY: I just got through making it.

DODGE: I don't care if you just spent all week making it! I ain't drinking it!

SHELLY: Well, what am I supposed to do with it then? I'm trying to help you out. Besides, it's good for you.

DODGE: Get it away from me!

(SHELLY *stands up with cup and saucer.*)

DODGE: What do you know what's good for me anyway?

(*She looks at* DODGE *then turns away from him, crossing to staircase, sits on bottom step and drinks the bouillon.* DODGE *stares at her.*)

DODGE: You know what'd be good for me?

SHELLY: What?

DODGE: A little massage. A little contact.

SHELLY: Oh no. I've had enough contact for a while. Thanks anyway.

(*She keeps sipping bouillon, stays sitting. Pause as* DODGE *stares at her.*)

DODGE: Why not? You got nothing better to do. That fella's not gonna be back here. You're not expecting him to show up again are you?

SHELLY: Sure. He'll show up. He left his horn here.

DODGE: His horn? (*laughs*) You're his horn!

SHELLY: Very funny.

DODGE: He's run off with my money? He's not coming back. There.

SHELLY: He'll be back.

DODGE: You're a funny chicken, you know that?

SHELLY: Thanks.

DODGE: Full of faith. Hope. Faith and hope. You're all alike you hopers. If it's not God then it's a man. If it's not a man then it's a woman. If it's not a woman then it's the land or the future of some kind. Some kind of future.

(*Pause.*)

SHELLY: (*looking toward porch*) I'm glad it stopped raining.

DODGE: (*looks toward porch then back to her*) That's what I mean. See, you're glad it stopped raining. Now you think everything's gonna be different. Just 'cause the sun comes out.

SHELLY: It's already different. Last night I was scared.

DODGE: Scared a' what?

SHELLY: Just scared.

DODGE: Bradley? (*looks at* BRADLEY) He's a push-over. 'Specially now. All ya' gotta' do is take his leg and throw it out the back door. Helpless. Totally helpless.

(SHELLY *turns and stares at* BRADLEY'S *wooden leg then looks at* DODGE. *She sips bouillon.*)

SHELLY: You'd do that?

DODGE: Me? I've hardly got the strength to breathe.

SHELLY: But you'd actually do it if you could?

DODGE: Don't be so easily shocked, girlie. There's nothing a man can't do. You dream it up and he can do it. Anything.

SHELLY: You've tried I guess.

DODGE: Don't sit there sippin' your bouillon and judging me! This is my house!

SHELLY: I forgot.

DODGE: You forgot? Whose house did you think it was?

SHELLY: Mine.

(DODGE *just stares at her. Long pause. She sips from cup.*)

SHELLY: I know it's not mine but I had that feeling.

DODGE: What feeling?

SHELLY: The feeling that nobody lives here but me. I mean everybody's gone. You're here, but it doesn't seem like you're supposed to be. (*pointing to* BRADLEY) Doesn't seem like he's supposed to be here either. I don't know what it is. It's the house or something. Something familiar. Like I know my way around here. Did you ever get that feeling?

(DODGE *stares at her in silence. Pause.*)

DODGE: No. No, I never did.

(SHELLY *gets up. Moves around space holding cup.*)

SHELLY: Last night I went to sleep up there in that room.

DODGE: What room?

SHELLY: That room up there with all the pictures. All the crosses on the wall.

DODGE: Halie's room?

SHELLY: Yeah. Whoever "Halie" is.

DODGE: She's my wife.

SHELLY: So you remember her?

DODGE: Whad'ya mean! 'Course I remember her! She's only been gone for a day—half a day. However long it's been.

SHELLY: Do you remember her when her hair was bright red? Standing in front of an apple tree?

DODGE: What is this, the third degree or something! Who're you to be askin' me personal questions about my wife!

SHELLY: You never look at those pictures up there?

DODGE: What pictures!

SHELLY: Your whole life's up there hanging on the wall. Somebody who looks just like you. Somebody who looks just like you used to look.

DODGE: That isn't me! That never was me! This is me. Right here. This is it. The whole shootin' match, sittin' right in front of you.

SHELLY: So the past never happened as far as you're concerned?

DODGE: The past? Jesus Christ. The past. What do you know about the past?

SHELLY: Not much. I know there was a farm.

(*Pause*)

DODGE: A farm?

SHELLY: There's a picture of a farm. A big farm. A bull. Wheat. Corn.

DODGE: Corn?

SHELLY: All the kids are standing out in the corn. They're all waving these big straw hats. One of them doesn't have a hat.

DODGE: Which one was that?

SHELLY: There's a baby. A baby in a woman's arms. The same woman with the red hair. She looks lost standing out there. Like she doesn't know how she got there.

DODGE: She knows! I told her a hundred times it wasn't gonna' be the city! I gave her plenty a' warning.

SHELLY: She's looking down at the baby like it was somebody else's. Like it didn't even belong to her.

DODGE: That's about enough outa' you! You got some funny ideas. Some damn funny ideas. You think just because peo-

ple propagate they have to love their offspring? You never
seen a bitch eat her puppies? Where are you from anyway?

SHELLY: L.A. We already went through that.

DODGE: That's right, L.A. I remember.

SHELLY: Stupid country.

DODGE: That's right! No wonder.

(*Pause.*)

SHELLY: What's happened to this family anyway?

DODGE: You're in no position to ask! What do you care? You
some kinda' Social Worker?

SHELLY: I'm Vince's friend.

DODGE: Vince's friend! That's rich. That's really rich. "Vince"!
"Mr. Vince"! "Mr. Thief" is more like it! His name doesn't
mean a hoot in hell to me. Not a tinkle in the well. You
know how many kids I've spawned? Not to mention Grand
kids and Great Grand kids and Great Great Grand kids after
them?

SHELLY: And you don't remember any of them?

DODGE: What's to remember? Halie's the one with the family
album. She's the one you should talk to. She'll set you
straight on the heritage if that's what you're interested in.
She's traced it all the way back to the grave.

SHELLY: What do you mean?

DODGE: What do you think I mean? How far back can you go? A
long line of corpses! There's not a living soul behind me.
Not a one. Who's holding me in their memory? Who gives a
damn about bones in the ground?

SHELLY: Was Tilden telling the truth?

(DODGE *stops short. Stares at* SHELLY. *Shakes his head. He looks
off stage left.*)

SHELLY: Was he?

(DODGE'S *tone changes drastically.*)

DODGE: Tilden? (*turns to* SHELLY, *calmly*) Where is Tilden?

SHELLY: Last night. Was he telling the truth about the baby?

(*Pause*)

DODGE: (*turns toward stage left*) What's happened to Tilden?
Why isn't Tilden here?

SHELLY: Bradley chased him out.

DODGE: (*looking at* BRADLEY *asleep*) Bradley? Why is he on my sofa? (*turns back to* SHELLY) Have I been here all night? On the floor?

SHELLY: He wouldn't leave. I hid outside until he fell asleep.

DODGE: Outside? Is Tilden outside? He shouldn't be out there in the rain. He'll get himself into trouble. He doesn't know his way around here anymore. Not like he used to. He went out West and got himself into trouble. Got himself into bad trouble. We don't want any of that around here.

SHELLY: What did he do?

(*Pause.*)

DODGE: (*quietly stares at* SHELLY) Tilden? He got mixed up. That's what he did. We can't afford to leave him alone. Not now.

(*Sound of* HALIE *laughing comes from off left.* SHELLY *stands, looking in direction of voice, holding cup and saucer, doesn't know whether to stay or run.*)

DODGE: (*motioning to* SHELLY) Sit down! Sit back down!

(SHELLY *sits. Sound of* HALIE'S *laughter again.*)

DODGE: (*to* SHELLY *in a heavy whisper, pulling coat up around him*) Don't leave me alone now! Promise me? Don't go off and leave me alone. I need somebody here with me. Tilden's gone now and I need someone. Don't leave me! Promise!

SHELLY: (*sitting*) I won't.

(HALIE *appears outside the screen porch door, up left with* FATHER DEWIS. *She is wearing a bright yellow dress, no hat, white gloves and her arms are full of yellow roses.* FATHER DEWIS *is dressed in traditional black suit, white clerical collar and shirt. He is a very distinguished grey haired man in his sixties. They are both slightly drunk and feeling giddy. As they enter the porch through the screen door,* DODGE *pulls the rabbit fur coat over his head and hides.* SHELLY *stands again.* DODGE *drops the coat and whispers intensely to* SHELLY. *Neither* HALIE *nor* FATHER DEWIS *are aware of the people inside the house.*)

DODGE: (*to* SHELLY *in a strong whisper*) You promised!

(SHELLY *sits on stairs again.* DODGE *pulls coat back over his head.* HALIE *and* FATHER DEWIS *talk on the porch as they cross toward stage right interior door.*)

HALIE: Oh Father! That's terrible! That's absolutely terrible. Aren't you afraid of being punished?

(*She giggles*)

DEWIS: Not by the Italians. They're too busy punishing each other.

(*They both break out in giggles.*)

HALIE: What about God?

DEWIS: Well, prayerfully, God only hears what he wants to. That's just between you and me of course. In our heart of hearts we know we're every bit as wicked as the Catholics.

(*They giggle again and reach the stage right door.*)

HALIE: Father, I never heard you talk like this in Sunday sermon.

DEWIS: Well, I save all my best jokes for private company. Pearls before swine you know.

(*They enter the room laughing and stop when they see* SHELLY. SHELLY *stands.* HALIE *closes the door behind* FATHER DEWIS. DODGE'S *voice is heard under the coat, talking to* SHELLY.)

DODGE: (*under coat, to* SHELLY) Sit down, sit down! Don't let 'em buffalo you!

(SHELLY *sits on stair again.* HALIE *looks at* DODGE *on the floor then looks at* BRADLEY *asleep on sofa and sees his wooden leg. She lets out a shriek of embarrassment for* FATHER DEWIS.)

HALIE: Oh my gracious! What in the name of Judas Priest is going on in this house!

(*She hands over the roses to* FATHER DEWIS.)

HALIE: Excuse me Father.

(HALIE *crosses to* DODGE, *whips the coat off him and covers the wooden leg with it.* BRADLEY *stays asleep.*)

HALIE: You can't leave this house for a second without the Devil blowing in through the front door!

DODGE: Gimme back that coat! Gimmie back that goddamn coat before I freeze to death!

HALIE: You're not going to freeze! The sun's out in case you hadn't noticed!

DODGE: Gimme back that coat! That coat's for live flesh not dead wood!

(HALIE *whips the blanket off* BRADLEY *and throws it on* DODGE. DODGE *covers his head again with blanket.* BRADLEY'S *amputated leg can be faked by having half of it under a cushion of the sofa. He's fully clothed.* BRADLEY *sits up with a jerk when the blanket comes off him.*)

HALIE: (*as she tosses blanket*) Here! Use this! It's yours anyway! Can't you take care of yourself for once!

BRADLEY: (*yelling at* HALIE) Gimme that blanket! Gimme back that blanket! That's my blanket!

(HALIE *crosses back toward* FATHER DEWIS *who just stands there with the roses.* BRADLEY *thrashes helplessly on the sofa trying to reach blanket.* DODGE *hides himself deeper in blanket.* SHELLY *looks on from staircase, still holding cup and saucer.*)

HALIE: Believe me, Father, this is not what I had in mind when I invited you in.

DEWIS: Oh, no apologies please. I wouldn't be in the ministry if I couldn't face real life.

(*He laughs self-consciously.* HALIE *notices* SHELLY *again and crosses over to her.* SHELLY *stays sitting.* HALIE *stops and stares at her.*)

BRADLEY: I want my blanket back! Gimme my blanket!

(HALIE *turns toward* BRADLEY *and silences him.*)

HALIE: Shut up, Bradley! Right this minute! I've had enough!

(BRADLEY *slowly recoils, lies back down on sofa, turns his back toward* HALIE *and whimpers softly.* HALIE *directs her attention to* SHELLY *again. Pause.*)

HALIE: (*to* SHELLY) What're you doing with my cup and saucer?

SHELLY: (*looking at cup, back to* HALIE) I made some bouillon for Dodge.

HALIE: For Dodge?

SHELLY: Yeah.

HALIE: Well, did he drink it?
SHELLY: No.
HALIE: Did you drink it?
SHELLY: Yes.

(HALIE *stares at her. Long pause. She turns abruptly away from* SHELLY *and crosses back to* FATHER DEWIS.)

HALIE: Father, there's a stranger in my house. What would you advise? What would be the Christian thing?
DEWIS: (*squirming*) Oh, well. . . . I. . . . I really—
HALIE: We still have some whiskey, don't we?

(DODGE *slowly pulls the blanket down off his head and looks toward* FATHER DEWIS. SHELLY *stands.*)

SHELLY: Listen, I don't drink or anything. I just—

(HALIE *turns toward* SHELLY *viciously.*)

HALIE: You sit back down!

(SHELLY *sits again on stair.* HALIE *turns again to* DEWIS.)

HALIE: I think we have plenty of whiskey left! Don't we Father?
DEWIS: Well, yes. I think so. You'll have to get it. My hands are full.

(HALIE *giggles. Reaches into* DEWIS'S *pockets, searching for bottle. She smells the roses as she searches.* DEWIS *stands stiffly.* DODGE *watches* HALIE *closely as she looks for bottle.*)

HALIE: The most incredible things, roses! Aren't they incredible, Father?
DEWIS: Yes. Yes they are.
HALIE: They almost cover the stench of sin in this house. Just magnificent! The smell. We'll have to put some at the foot of Ansel's statue. On the day of the unveiling.

(HALIE *finds a silver flask of whiskey in* DEWIS'S *vest pocket. She pulls it out.* DODGE *looks on eagerly.* HALIE *crosses to* DODGE, *opens the flask and takes a sip.*)

HALIE: (*to* DODGE) Ansel's getting a statue, Dodge. Did you know that? Not a plaque but a real live statue. A full bronze. Tip to toe. A basketball in one hand and a rifle in the other.
BRADLEY: (*his back to* HALIE) He never played basketball!

HALIE: You shut up, Bradley! You shut up about Ansel! Ansel played basketball better than anyone! And you know it! He was an All American! There's no reason to take the glory away from others.

(HALIE *turns away from* BRADLEY, *crosses back toward* DEWIS *sipping on the flask and smiling.*)

HALIE: (*to Dewis*) Ansel was a great basketball player. One of the greatest.

DEWIS: I remember Ansel.

HALIE: Of course! You remember. You remember how he could play. (*she turns toward* SHELLY) Of course, nowadays they play a different brand of basketball. More vicious. Isn't that right, dear?

SHELLY: I don't know.

(HALIE *crosses to* SHELLY, *sipping on flask. She stops in front of* SHELLY.)

HALIE: Much, much more vicious. They smash into each other. They knock each other's teeth out. There's blood all over the court. Savages.

(HALIE *takes the cup from* SHELLY *and pours whiskey into it.*)

HALIE: They don't train like they used to. Not at all. They allow themselves to run amuck. Drugs and women. Women mostly.

(HALIE *hands the cup of whiskey back to* SHELLY *slowly.* SHELLY *takes it.*)

HALIE: Mostly women. Girls. Sad, pathetic little girls. (*she crosses back to* FATHER DEWIS) It's just a reflection of the times, don't you think Father? An indication of where we stand?

DEWIS: I suppose so, yes.

HALIE: Yes. A sort of a bad omen. Our youth becoming monsters.

DEWIS: Well, I uh—

HALIE: Oh you can disagree with me if you want to, Father. I'm open to debate. I think argument only enriches both sides of the question don't you? (*she moves toward* DODGE) I suppose, in the long run, it doesn't matter. When you see the way things deteriorate before your very eyes. Everything running down hill. It's kind of silly to even think about youth.

DEWIS: No, I don't think so. I think it's important to believe in certain things.

HALIE: Yes. Yes, I know what you mean. I think that's right. I think that's true. (*she looks at* DODGE) Certain basic things. We can't shake certain basic things. We might end up crazy. Like my husband. You can see it in his eyes. You can see how mad he is.

(DODGE *covers his head with the blanket again.* HALIE *takes a single rose from* DEWIS *and moves slowly over to* DODGE.)

HALIE: We can't not believe in something. We can't stop believing. We just end up dying if we stop. Just end up dead.

(HALIE *throws the rose gently onto* DODGE'S *blanket. It lands between his knees and stays there. Long pause as* HALIE *stares at the rose.* SHELLY *stands suddenly.* HALIE *doesn't turn to her but keeps staring at rose.*)

SHELLY: (*to* HALIE) Don't you wanna' know who I am! Don't you wanna know what I'm doing here! I'm not dead!

(SHELLY *crosses toward* HALIE. HALIE *turns slowly toward her.*)

HALIE: Did you drink your whiskey?

SHELLY: No! And I'm not going to either!

HALIE: Well that's a firm stand. It's good to have a firm stand.

SHELLY: I don't have any stand at all. I'm just trying to put all this together.

(HALIE *laughs and crosses back to* DEWIS.)

HALIE: (*to* DEWIS) Surprises, surprises! Did you have any idea we'd be returning to this?

SHELLY: I came here with your Grandson for a little visit! A little innocent friendly visit.

HALIE: My Grandson?

SHELLY: Yes! That's right. The one no one remembers.

HALIE: (*to* DEWIS) This is getting a little far fetched.

SHELLY: I told him it was stupid to come back here. To try to pick up from where he left off.

HALIE: Where was that?

SHELLY: Wherever he was when he left here! Six years ago! Ten years ago! Whenever it was. I told him nobody cares.

HALIE: Didn't he listen?

SHELLY: No! No he didn't. We had to stop off at every tiny little meatball town that he remembered from his boyhood! Every stupid little donut shop he ever kissed a girl in. Every Drive-In. Every Drag Strip. Every football field he ever broke a bone on.

HALIE: (*suddenly alarmed, to* DODGE) Where's Tilden?

SHELLY: Don't ignore me!

HALIE: Dodge! Where's Tilden gone?

(SHELLY *moves violently toward* HALIE.)

SHELLY: (*to* HALIE) I'm talking to you!

(BRADLEY *sits up fast on the sofa,* SHELLY *backs away.*)

BRADLEY: (*to* SHELLY) Don't you yell at my mother!

HALIE: Dodge! (*she kicks* DODGE) I told you not to let Tilden out of your sight! Where's he gone to?

DODGE: Gimme a drink and I'll yell ya'.

DEWIS: Halie, maybe this isn't the right time for a visit.

(HALIE *crosses back to* DEWIS.)

HALIE: (*to* DEWIS) I never should've left. I never, never should've left! Tilden could be anywhere by now! Anywhere! He's not in control of his faculties. Dodge knew that. I told him when I left here. I told him specifically to watch out for Tilden.

(BRADLEY *reaches down, grabs* DODGE'S *blanket and yanks it off him. He lays down on sofa and pulls the blanket over his head.*)

DODGE: He's got my blanket again! He's got my blanket!

HALIE: (*turning to* BRADLEY) Bradley! Bradley, put that blanket back!

(HALIE *moves toward* BRADLEY. SHELLY *suddenly throws the cup and saucer against the stage right door.* DEWIS *ducks. The cup and saucer smash into pieces.* HALIE *stops, turns toward* SHELLY. *Everyone freezes.* BRADLEY *slowly pulls his head out from under blanket, looks toward stage right door, then to* SHELLY. SHELLY *stares at* HALIE. DEWIS *cowers with roses.* SHELLY *moves slowly toward* HALIE. *Long pause.* SHELLY *speaks softly.*)

SHELLY: (*to* HALIE) I don't like being ignored. I don't like being

treated like I'm not here. I didn't like it when I was a
kid and I still don't like it.

BRADLEY: (*sitting up on sofa*) We don't have to tell you anything,
girl. Not a thing. You're not the police are you? You're not
the government. You're just some prostitute that Tilden
brought in here.

HALIE: Language! I won't have that language in my house!

SHELLY: (*to* BRADLEY) You stuck your hand in my mouth and you
call me a prostitute!

HALIE: Bradley! Did you put your hand in her mouth? I'm
ashamed of you. I can't leave you alone for a minute.

BRADLEY: I never did. She's lying!

DEWIS: Halie, I think I'll be running along now. I'll just put the
roses in the kitchen.

(DEWIS *moves toward stage left.* HALIE *stops him.*)

HALIE: Don't go now, Father! Not now.

BRADLEY: I never did anything, mom! I never touched her! She
propositioned me! And I turned her down. I turned her down
flat!

(SHELLY *suddenly grabs her coat off the wooden leg and takes both
the leg and coat down stage, away from* BRADLEY.)

BRADLEY: Mom! Mom! She's got my leg! She's taken my leg!
I never did anything to her! She's stolen my leg!

(BRADLEY *reaches pathetically in the air for his leg.* SHELLY *sets it
down for a second, puts on her coat fast and picks the leg up again.*
DODGE *starts coughing softly.*)

HALIE: (*to* SHELLY) I think we've had about enough of you
young lady. Just about enough. I don't know where you
came from or what you're doing here but you're no longer
welcome in this house.

SHELLY: (*laughs, holds leg*) No longer welcome!

BRADLEY: Mom! That's my leg! Get my leg back! I can't do
anything without my leg.

(BRADLEY *keeps making whimpering sounds and reaching for his
leg.*)

HALIE: Give my son back his leg. Right this very minute!

(DODGE *starts laughing softly to himself in between coughs.*)

HALIE: (*to* DEWIS) Father, do something about this would you! I'm not about to be terrorized in my own house!

BRADLEY: Gimme back my leg!

HALIE: Oh, shut up Bradley! Just shut up! You don't need your leg now! Just lay down and shut up!

(BRADLEY *whimpers. Lays down and pulls blanket around him. He keeps one arm outside blanket, reaching out toward his wooden leg.* DEWIS *cautiously approaches* SHELLY *with the roses in his arms.* SHELLY *clutches the wooden leg to her chest as though she's kidnapped it.*)

DEWIS: (*to* SHELLY) Now, honestly dear, wouldn't it be better to try to talk things out? To try to use some reason?

SHELLY: There isn't any reason here! I can't find a reason for anything.

DEWIS: There's nothing to be afraid of. These are all good people. All righteous people.

SHELLY: I'm not afraid!

DEWIS: But this isn't your house. You have to have some respect.

SHELLY: You're the strangers here, not me.

HALIE: This has gone far enough!

DEWIS: Halie, please. Let me handle this.

SHELLY: Don't come near me! Don't anyone come near me. I don't need any words from you. I'm not threatening anybody. I don't even know what I'm doing here. You all say you don't remember Vince, okay, maybe you don't. Maybe it's Vince that's crazy. Maybe he's made this whole family thing up. I don't even care anymore. I was just coming along for the ride. I thought it'd be a nice gesture. Besides, I was curious. He made all of you sound familiar to me. Every one of you. For every name, I had an image. Every time he'd tell me a name, I'd see the person. In fact, each of you was so clear in my mind that I actually believed it was you. I really believed when I walked through that door that the people who lived here would turn out to be the same people in my imagination. But I don't recognize any of you. Not one. Not even the slightest resemblance.

DEWIS: Well you can hardly blame others for not fulfilling your hallucination.

SHELLY: It was no hallucination! It was more like a prophecy. You believe in prophecy, don't you?

HALIE: Father, there's no point in talking to her any further. We're just going to have to call the police.

BRADLEY: No! Don't get the police in here. We don't want the police in here. This is our home.

SHELLY: That's right. Bradley's right. Don't you usually settle your affairs in private? Don't you usually take them out in the dark? Out in the back?

BRADLEY: You stay out of our lives! You have no business interfering!

SHELLY: I don't have any business period. I got nothing to lose.

(*She moves around, staring at each of them.*)

BRADLEY: You don't know what we've been through. You don't know anything!

SHELLY: I know you've got a secret. You've all got a secret. It's so secret in fact, you're all convinced it never happened.

(HALIE *moves to* DEWIS)

HALIE: Oh, my God, Father!

DODGE: (*laughing to himself*) She thinks she's going to get it out of us. She thinks she's going to uncover the truth of the matter. Like a detective or something.

BRADLEY: I'm not telling her anything! Nothing's wrong here! Nothing's ever been wrong! Everything's the way it's supposed to be! Nothing ever happened that's bad! Everything is all right here! We're all good people!

DODGE: She thinks she's gonna suddenly bring everything out into the open after all these years.

DEWIS: (*to* SHELLY) Can't you see that these people want to be left in peace? Don't you have any mercy? They haven't done anything to you.

DODGE: She wants to get to the bottom of it. (*to* SHELLY) That's it, isn't it? You'd like to get right down to bedrock? You want me to tell ya'? You want me to tell ya' what happened? I'll tell ya'. I might as well.

BRADLEY: No! Don't listen to him. He doesn't remember anything!

DODGE: I remember the whole thing from start to finish. I remember the day he was born.

(*pause*)

HALIE: Dodge, if you tell this thing—if you tell this, you'll be dead to me. You'll be just as good as dead.

DODGE: That won't be such a big change, Halie. See this girl, this girl here, she wants to know. She wants to know something more. And I got this feeling that it doesn't make a bit a' difference. I'd sooner tell it to a stranger than anybody else.

BRADLEY: (*to* DODGE) We made a pact! We made a pact between us! You can't break that now!

DODGE: I don't remember any pact.

BRADLEY: (*to* SHELLY) See, he doesn't remember anything. I'm the only one in the family who remembers. The only one. And I'll never tell you!

SHELLY: I'm not so sure I want to find out now.

DODGE: (*laughing to himself*) Listen to her! Now she's runnin' scared!

SHELLY: I'm not scared!

(DODGE *stops laughing, long pause.* DODGE *stares at her.*)

DODGE: You're not huh? Well, that's good. Because I'm not either. See, we were a well established family once. Well established. All the boys were grown. The farm was producing enough milk to fill Lake Michigan twice over. Me and Halie here were pointed toward what looked like the middle part of our life. Everything was settled with us. All we had to do was ride it out. Then Halie got pregnant again. Outa' the middle a' nowhere, she got pregnant. We weren't planning on havin' any more boys. We had enough boys already. In fact, we hadn't been sleepin' in the same bed for about six years.

HALIE: (*moving toward stairs*) I'm not listening to this! I don't have to listen to this!

DODGE: (*stops* HALIE) Where are you going! Upstairs! You'll just be listenin' to it upstairs! You go outside, you'll be listenin' to it outside. Might as well stay here and listen to it.

(HALIE *stays by stairs*)

BRADLEY: If I had my leg you wouldn't be saying this. You'd never get away with it if I had my leg.

DODGE: (*pointing to* SHELLY) She's got your leg. (*laughs*) She's gonna keep your leg too. (*to* SHELLY) She wants to hear this. Don't you?

SHELLY: I don't know.

DODGE: Well even if ya' don't I'm gonna' tell ya'. (*pause*) Halie had this kid. This baby boy. She had it. I let her have it on her own. All the other boys I had had the best doctors, best nurses, everything. This one I let her have by herself. This one hurt real bad. Almost killed her, but she had it anyway. It lived, see. It lived. It wanted to grow up in this family. It wanted to be just like us. It wanted to be a part of us. It wanted to pretend that I was its father. She wanted me to believe in it. Even when everyone around us knew. Everyone. All our boys knew. Tilden knew.

HALIE: You shut up! Bradley, make him shut up!

BRADLEY: I can't.

DODGE: Tilden was the one who knew. Better than any of us. He'd walk for miles with that kid in his arms. Halie let him take it. All night sometimes. He'd walk all night out there in the pasture with it. Talkin' to it. Singin' to it. Used to hear him singing to it. He'd make up stories. He'd tell that kid all kinds a' stories. Even when he knew it couldn't understand him. Couldn't understand a word he was sayin'. Never would understand him. We couldn't let a thing like that continue. We couldn't allow that to grow up right in the middle of our lives. It made everything we'd accomplished look like it was nothin'. Everything was cancelled out by this one mistake. This one weakness.

SHELLY: So you killed him?

DODGE: I killed it. I drowned it. Just like the runt of a litter. Just drowned it.

(HALIE *moves toward* BRADLEY)

HALIE: (*to* BRADLEY) Ansel would've stopped him! Ansel would've stopped him from telling these lies! He was a hero! A man! A whole man! What's happened to the men in this family! Where are the men!

(*Suddenly* VINCE *comes crashing through the screen porch door up left, tearing it off its hinges. Everyone but* DODGE *and* BRADLEY *back away from the porch and stare at* VINCE *who has landed on his stomach on the porch in a drunken stupor. He is singing loudly to himself and hauls himself slowly to his feet. He has a paper shopping bag full of empty booze bottles. He takes them out one at a time as he sings and smashes them at the opposite end of the porch, behind the solid interior door, stage right.* SHELLY *moves slowly toward stage right, holding wooden leg and watching* VINCE.)

VINCE: (*singing loudly as he hurls bottles*) "From the Halls of Montezuma to the Shores of Tripoli. We will fight our country's battles on the land and on the sea."

(*He punctuates the words "Montezuma," "Tripoli," "battles" and "sea" with a smashed bottle each. He stops throwing for a second, stares toward stage right of the porch, shades his eyes with his hand as though looking across to a battlefield, then cups his hands around his mouth and yells across the space of the porch to an imaginary army. The others watch in terror and expectation.*)

VINCE: (*to imagined Army*) Have you had enough over there! 'Cause there's a lot more here where that came from! (*pointing to paper bag full of bottles*) A helluva lot more! We got enough over here to blow ya' from here to Kingdomcome!

(*He takes another bottle, makes high whistling sound of a bomb and throws it toward stage right porch. Sound of bottle smashing against wall. This should be the actual smashing of bottles and not tape sound. He keeps yelling and heaving bottles one after another.*
VINCE *stops for a while, breathing heavily from exhaustion. Long silence as the others watch him.* SHELLY *approaches tentatively in* VINCE'S *direction, still holding* BRADLEY'S *wooden leg.*)

SHELLY: (*after silence*) Vince?

(VINCE *turns toward her. Peers through screen.*)

VINCE: Who? What? Vince who? Who's that in there?

(VINCE *pushes his face against the screen from the porch and stares in at everyone.*)

DODGE: Where's my goddamn bottle!
VINCE: (*looking in at* DODGE) What? Who is that?
DODGE: It's me! Your Grandfather! Don't play stupid with me! Where's my two bucks!
VINCE: Your two bucks?

(HALIE *moves away from* DEWIS, *upstage, peers out at* VINCE, *trying to recognize him.*)

HALIE: Vincent? Is that you, Vincent?

(SHELLY *stares at* HALIE *then looks out at* VINCE.)

VINCE: (*from porch*) Vincent who? What is this! Who are you people?

SHELLY: (*to* HALIE) Hey, wait a minute. Wait a minute! What's going on?

HALIE: (*moving closer to porch screen*) We thought you were a murderer or something. Barging in through the door like that.

VINCE: I am a murderer! Don't underestimate me for a minute! I'm the Midnight Strangler! I devour whole families in a single gulp!

(VINCE *grabs another bottle and smashes it on the porch.* HALIE *backs away.*)

SHELLY: (*approaching Halie*) You mean you know who he is?

HALIE: Of course I know who he is! That's more than I can say for you.

BRADLEY: (*sitting up on sofa*) You get off our front porch you creep! What're you doing out there breaking bottles? Who are these foreigners anyway! Where did they come from?

VINCE: Maybe I should come in there and break them!

HALIE: (*moving toward porch*) Don't you dare! Vincent, what's got into you! Why are you acting like this?

VINCE: Maybe I should come in there and usurp your territory!

(HALIE *turns back toward* DEWIS *and crosses to him.*)

HALIE: (*to* DEWIS) Father, why are you just standing around here when everything's falling apart? Can't you rectify this situation?

(DODGE *laughs, coughs.*)

DEWIS: I'm just a guest here, Halie. I don't know what my position is exactly. This is outside my parish anyway.

(VINCE *starts throwing more bottles as things continue.*)

BRADLEY: If I had my leg I'd rectify it! I'd rectify him all over the goddamn highway! I'd pull his ears out if I could reach him!

(BRADLEY *sticks his fist through the screening of the porch and reaches out for* VINCE, *grabbing at him and missing.* VINCE *jumps away from* BRADLEY'S *hand.*)

VINCE: Aaaah! Our lines have been penetrated! Tentacled animals! Beasts from the deep!

(VINCE *strikes out at* BRADLEY'S *hand with a bottle.* BRADLEY *pulls his hand back inside.*)

SHELLY: Vince! Knock it off will ya'! I want to get out of here!

(VINCE *pushes his face against screen, looks in at* SHELLY.)

VINCE: (*to* SHELLY) Have they got you prisoner in there, dear? Such a sweet young thing too. All her life in front of her. Nipped in the bud.

SHELLY: I'm coming out there, Vince! I'm coming out there and I want us to get in the car and drive away from here. Anywhere. Just away from here.

(SHELLY *moves toward* VINCE'S *saxophone case and overcoat. She sets down the wooden leg, downstage left and picks up the saxophone case and overcoat.* VINCE *watches her through the screen.*)

VINCE: (*to* SHELLY) We'll have to negotiate. Make some kind of a deal. Prisoner exchange or something. A few of theirs for one of ours. Small price to pay if you ask me.

(SHELLY *crosses toward stage right door with overcoat and case.*)

SHELLY: Just go and get the car! I'm coming out there now. We're going to leave.

VINCE: Don't come out here! Don't you dare come out here!

(SHELLY *stops short of the door, stage right.*)

SHELLY: How come?

VINCE: Off limits! Verboten! This is taboo territory. No man or woman has ever crossed the line and lived to tell the tale!

SHELLY: I'll take my chances.

(SHELLY *moves to stage right door and opens it.* VINCE *pulls out a big folding hunting knife and pulls open the blade. He jabs the blade into the screen and starts cutting a hole big enough to climb through.* BRADLEY *cowers in a corner of the sofa as* VINCE *rips at the screen.*)

VINCE: (*as he cuts screen*) Don't come out here! I'm warning you! You'll disintegrate!

(DEWIS *takes* HALIE *by the arm and pulls her toward staircase.*)

DEWIS: Halie, maybe we should go upstairs until this blows over.

HALIE: I don't understand it. I just don't understand it. He was the sweetest little boy!

(DEWIS *drops the roses beside the wooden leg at the foot of the staircase then escorts* HALIE *quickly up the stairs.* HALIE *keeps looking back at* VINCE *as they climb the stairs.*)

HALIE: There wasn't a mean bone in his body. Everyone loved Vincent. Everyone. He was the perfect baby.

DEWIS: He'll be all right after a while. He's just had a few too many that's all.

HALIE: He used to sing in his sleep. He'd sing. In the middle of the night. The sweetest voice. Like an angel. (*she stops for a moment*) I used to lie awake listening to it. I used to lie awake thinking it was all right if I died. Because Vincent was an angel. A guardian angel. He'd watch over us. He'd watch over all of us.

(DEWIS *takes her all the way up the stairs. They disappear above.* VINCE *is now climbing through the porch screen onto the sofa.* BRADLEY *crashes off the sofa, holding tight to his blanket, keeping it wrapped around him.* SHELLY *is outside on the porch.* VINCE *holds the knife in his teeth once he gets the hole wide enough to climb through.* BRADLEY *starts crawling slowly toward his wooden leg, reaching out for it.*)

DODGE: (*to* VINCE) Go ahead! Take over the house! Take over the whole goddamn house! You can have it! It's yours. It's been a pain in the neck ever since the very first mortgage. I'm gonna die any second now. Any second. You won't even notice. So I'll settle my affairs once and for all.

(As DODGE *proclaims his last will and testament,* VINCE *climbs into the room, knife in mouth, and strides slowly around the space, inspecting his inheritance. He casually notices* BRADLEY *as he crawls toward his leg.* VINCE *moves to the leg and keeps pushing it with his foot so that it's out of* BRADLEY'S *reach then goes on with his inspection. He picks up the roses and carries them around smelling them.* SHELLY *can be seen outside on the porch, moving slowly center and staring in at* VINCE. VINCE *ignores her.*)

DODGE: The house goes to my Grandson, Vincent. All the furnishings, accoutrements and paraphernalia therein. Everything tacked to the walls or otherwise resting under this roof. My tools—namely my band saw, my skill saw, my drill press, my chain saw, my lathe, my electric sander, all go to my eldest son, Tilden. That is, if he ever shows up again. My shed and gasoline powered equipment, namely my tractor, my dozer, my hand tiller plus all the attachments and riggings for the above mentioned machinery, namely my spring tooth harrow, my deep plows, my disk plows, my automatic fertilizing equipment, my reaper, my swathe, my seeder, my John Deere Harvester, my post hole digger, my jackhammer, my lathe—(*to himself*) Did I mention my lathe? I already mentioned my lathe—my Bennie Goodman records, my harnesses, my bits, my halters, my brace, my rough rasp, my forge, my welding equipment, my shoeing nails, my levels and bevels, my milking stool—no, not my milking stool—my hammers and chisels, my hinges, my cattle gates, my barbed wire, self-tapping augers, my horse hair ropes and all related materials are to be pushed into a gigantic heap and set ablaze in the very center of my fields. When the blaze is at its highest, preferably on a cold, windless night, my body is to be pitched into the middle of it and burned til nothing remains but ash.

(*Pause.* VINCE *takes the knife out of his mouth and smells the roses. He's facing toward audience and doesn't turn around to* SHELLY. *He folds up knife and pockets it.*)

SHELLY: (*from porch*) I'm leaving, Vince. Whether you come or not, I'm leaving.

VINCE: (*smelling roses*) Just put my horn on the couch there before you take off.

SHELLY: (*moving toward hole in screen*) You're not coming?

(VINCE *stays downstage, turns and looks at her.*)

VINCE: I just inherited a house.

SHELLY: (*through hole, from porch*) You want to stay here?

VINCE: (*as he pushes* BRADLEY'S *leg out of reach*) I've gotta carry on the line. I've gotta see to it that things keep rolling.

(BRADLEY *looks up at him from floor, keeps pulling himself toward his leg.* VINCE *keeps moving it.*)

SHELLY: What happened to you Vince? You just disappeared.

VINCE: (*pause, delivers speech front*) I was gonna run last night. I was gonna run and keep right on running. I drove all night. Clear to the Iowa border. The old man's two bucks sitting right on the seat beside me. It never stopped raining the whole time. Never stopped once. I could see myself in the windshield. My face. My eyes. I studied my face. Studied everything about it. As though I was looking at another man. As though I could see his whole race behind him. Like a mummy's face. I saw him dead and alive at the same time. In the same breath. In the windshield, I watched him breathe as though he was frozen in time. And every breath marked him. Marked him forever without him knowing. And then his face changed. His face became his father's face. Same bones. Same eyes. Same nose. Same breath. And his father's face changed to his Grandfather's face. And it went on like that. Changing. Clear on back to faces I'd never seen before but still recognized. Still recognized the bones underneath. The eyes. The breath. The mouth. I followed my family clear into Iowa. Every last one. Straight into the Corn Belt and further. Straight back as far as they'd take me. Then it all dissolved. Everything dissolved.

(SHELLY *stares at him for a while then reaches through the hole in the screen and sets the saxophone case and* VINCE'S *overcoat on the sofa. She looks at* VINCE *again.*)

SHELLY: Bye Vince.

(*She exits left off the porch.* VINCE *watches her go.* BRADLEY *tries to make a lunge for his wooden leg.* VINCE *quickly picks it up and dangles it over* BRADLEY'S *head like a carrot.* BRADLEY *keeps making desperate grabs at the leg.* DEWIS *comes down the staircase and stops half way, staring at* VINCE *and* BRADLEY. VINCE *looks up at* DEWIS *and smiles. He keeps moving backwards with the leg toward upstage left as* BRADLEY *crawls after him.*)

VINCE: (*to* DEWIS *as he continues torturing* BRADLEY) Oh, excuse me Father. Just getting rid of some of the vermin in the house. This is my house now, ya' know? All mine. Everything. Except for the power tools and stuff. I'm gonna get all new equipment anyway. New plows, new tractor, everything. All brand new. (VINCE *teases* BRADLEY *closer to the up left corner of the stage.*) Start right off on the ground floor.

(VINCE *throws* BRADLEY'S *wooden leg far off stage left.* BRADLEY *follows his leg off stage, pulling himself along on the ground, whimpering. As* BRADLEY *exits* VINCE *pulls the blanket off him and throws it over his own shoulder. He crosses toward* DEWIS *with the blanket and smells the roses.* DEWIS *comes to the bottom of the stairs.*)

DEWIS: You'd better go up and see your Grandmother.

VINCE: (*looking up stairs, back to* DEWIS) My Grandmother? There's nobody else in this house. Except for you. And you're leaving aren't you?

(DEWIS *crosses toward stage right door. He turns back to* VINCE.)

DEWIS: She's going to need someone. I can't help her. I don't know what to do. I don't know what my position is. I just came in for some tea. I had no idea there was any trouble. No idea at all.

(VINCE *just stares at him.* DEWIS *goes out the door, crosses porch and exits left.* VINCE *listens to him leaving. He smells roses, looks up the staircase then smells roses again. He turns and looks upstage at* DODGE. *He crosses up to him and bends over looking at* DODGE'S *open eyes.* DODGE *is dead. His death should have come completely unnoticed. Vince lifts the blanket, then covers his head. He sits on the sofa, smelling roses and staring at* DODGE'S *body. Long pause.* VINCE *places the roses on* DODGE'S *chest then lays down on the sofa, arms folded behind his head, staring at the ceiling. His body is in the same relationship to* DODGE'S. *After a while* HALIE'S *voice is heard coming from above the staircase. The lights start to dim almost imperceptibly as* HALIE *speaks.* VINCE *keeps staring at the ceiling.*)

HALIE'S VOICE: Dodge? Is that you Dodge? Tilden was right about the corn you know. I've never seen such corn. Have you taken a look at it lately? Tall as a man already. This early in the year. Carrots too. Potatoes. Peas. It's like a paradise out there, Dodge. You oughta' take a look. A miracle. I've never seen it like this. Maybe the rain did something. Maybe it was the rain.

(*As* HALIE *keeps talking off stage,* TILDEN *appears from stage left, dripping with mud from the knees down. His arms and hands are covered with mud. In his hands he carries the corpse of a small child at chest level, staring down at it. The corpse mainly consists of bones wrapped in muddy, rotten cloth. He moves slowly downstage toward the staircase, ignoring* VINCE *on the sofa.* VINCE *keeps staring at the ceiling as though* TILDEN *wasn't there. As* HALIE'S VOICE *continues,* TILDEN *slowly makes his way up the stairs. His eyes never leave the corpse of the child. The lights keep fading.*)

HALIE'S VOICE: Good hard rain. Takes everything straight down deep to the roots. The rest takes care of itself. You can't force a thing to grow. You can't interfere with it. It's all hidden. It's all unseen. You just gotta wait til it pops up out of the ground. Tiny little shoot. Tiny little white shoot. All hairy and fragile. Strong though. Strong enough to break the earth even. It's a miracle, Dodge. I've never seen a crop like this in my whole life. Maybe it's the sun. Maybe that's it. Maybe it's the sun.

(TILDEN *disappears above. Silence. Lights go to black.*)

CURSE OF
THE STARVING CLASS

Curse of the Starving Class was first performed by the New York Shakespeare Festival on March 2, 1978, presented by Joseph Papp. The director was Robert Woodruff, and the cast was as follows:

WESLEY	Ebbe Roe Smith
ELLA	Olympia Dukakis
EMMA	Pamela Reed
TAYLOR	Kenneth Welsh
WESTON	James Gammon
ELLIS	Eddie Jones
MALCOLM	John Aquino
EMERSON	Michael J. Pollard
SLATER	Raymond J. Barry

ACT ONE

SCENE: *Upstage center is a very plain breakfast table with a red oilcloth covering it. Four mismatched metal chairs are set one at each side of the table. Suspended in midair to stage right and stage left are two ruffled, red-checked curtains, slightly faded. In the down left corner of the stage are a working refrigerator and a small gas stove, set right up next to each other. In the down right corner is a pile of wooden debris, torn screen, etc., which are the remains of a broken door. Lights come up on* WESLEY, *in sweatshirt, jeans and cowboy boots, who is picking up the pieces of the door and throwing them methodically into an old wheelbarrow. This goes on for a while. Then* WESLEY'S *mother,* ELLA, *enters slowly from down left. She is a small woman wearing a bathrobe, pink fuzzy slippers, hair in curlers. She is just waking up and winds an alarm clock in her hand as she watches* WESLEY *sleepily.* WESLEY *keeps cleaning up the debris, ignoring her.*

ELLA: (*after a while*) You shouldn't be doing that.
WESLEY: I'm doing it.
ELLA: Yes, but you shouldn't be. He should be doing it. He's the one who broke it down.
WESLEY: He's not here.
ELLA: He's not back yet?
WESLEY: Nope.
ELLA: Well, just leave it until he gets back.
WESLEY: In the meantime we gotta' live in it.
ELLA: He'll be back. He can clean it up then.

(WESLEY *goes on clearing the debris into the wheelbarrow.* ELLA *finishes winding the clock and then sets it on the stove.*)

ELLA: (*looking at clock*) I must've got to sleep at five in the morning.

135

WESLEY: Did you call the cops?

ELLA: Last night?

WESLEY: Yeah.

ELLA: Sure I called the cops. Are you kidding? I was in danger of my life. I was being threatened.

WESLEY: He wasn't threatening you.

ELLA: Are you kidding me? He broke the door down, didn't he?

WESLEY: He was just trying to get in.

ELLA: That's no way to get into a house. There's plenty of other ways to get into a house. He could've climbed through a window.

WESLEY: He was drunk.

ELLA: That's not my problem.

WESLEY: You locked the door.

ELLA: Sure I locked the door. I told him I was going to lock the door. I told him the next time that happened I was locking the door and he could sleep in a hotel.

WESLEY: Is that where he is now?

ELLA: How should I know?

WESLEY: He took the Packard I guess.

ELLA: If that's the one that's missing I guess that's the one he took.

WESLEY: How come you called the cops?

ELLA: I was scared.

WESLEY: You thought he was going to kill you?

ELLA: I thought— I thought, "I don't know who this is. I don't know who this is trying to break in here. Who is this? It could be anyone."

WESLEY: I heard you screaming at each other.

ELLA: Yes.

WESLEY: So you must've known who it was.

ELLA: I wasn't sure. That was the frightening part. I could smell him right through the door.

WESLEY: He was drinking that much?

ELLA: Not that. His skin.

WESLEY: Oh.

ELLA: (*suddenly cheerful*) You want some breakfast?

WESLEY: No thanks.

ELLA: (*going to refrigerator*) Well I'm going to have some.

WESLEY: (*still cleaning*) It's humiliating to have the cops come to your own house. Makes me feel like we're someone else.

ELLA: (*looking in refrigerator*) There's no eggs but there's bacon and bread.

WESLEY: Makes me feel lonely. Like we're in trouble or something.

ELLA: (*still looking in refrigerator*) We're not in trouble. He's in trouble, but we're not.

WESLEY: You didn't have to call the cops.

ELLA: (*slamming refrigerator door and holding bacon and bread*) I told you, he was trying to kill me!

(*They look at each other for a moment.* ELLA *breaks it by putting the bacon and bread down on top of the stove.* WESLEY *goes back to cleaning up the debris. He keeps talking as* ELLA *looks through the lower drawers of the stove and pulls out a frying pan. She lights one of the burners on the stove and starts cooking the bacon.*)

WESLEY: (*as he throws wood into wheelbarrow*) I was lying there on my back. I could smell the avocado blossoms. I could hear the coyotes. I could hear stock cars squealing down the street. I could feel myself in my bed in my room in this house in this town in this state in this country. I could feel this country close like it was part of my bones. I could feel the presence of all the people outside, at night, in the dark. Even sleeping people I could feel. Even all the sleeping animals. Dogs. Peacocks. Bulls. Even tractors sitting in the wetness, waiting for the sun to come up. I was looking straight up at the ceiling at all my model airplanes hanging by all their thin metal wires. Floating. Swaying very quietly like they were being blown by someone's breath. Cobwebs moving with them. Dust laying on their wings. Decals peeling off their wings. My P-39. My Messerschmitt. My Jap Zero. I could feel myself lying far below them on my bed like I was on the ocean and overhead they were on reconnaissance. Scouting me. Floating. Taking pictures of the enemy. Me, the enemy. I could feel the space around me like a big, black world. I listened like an animal. My listening was afraid. Afraid of sound. Tense. Like any second something could invade me. Some foreigner. Something undescribable. Then I heard the Packard coming up the hill. From a mile off I could tell it was the Packard by the sound of the valves. The lifters have a sound like nothing else. Then I could picture my Dad driving it. Shifting unconsciously. Downshifting into second for the last pull up the hill. I could feel the headlights closing in. Cutting through the orchard. I could see the trees being lit one after the other by the lights, then going back to black. My heart was pounding. Just from my Dad coming back. Then I heard him pull the brake. Lights go off. Key's turned off. Then a long silence. Him just sitting in the car. Just sitting. I picture him just sitting. What's he doing? Just sitting. Waiting to get out. Why's he waiting to get out? He's plastered and can't move. He's plastered and doesn't want to move. He's going to sleep there all night. He's slept there before. He's woken up with dew on the hood before. Freezing headache. Teeth covered with peanuts. Then I hear the door of the Packard open. A pop of metal. Dogs barking down the road. Door slams. Feet. Paper bag being tucked under one arm. Paper bag covering "Tiger Rose." Feet coming. Feet walking toward the door. Feet stopping. Heart pounding. Sound of door not opening. Foot kicking door. Man's voice. Dad's voice. Dad calling Mom. No answer. Foot kicking. Foot kicking harder. Wood splitting. Man's voice. In the night. Foot kicking hard through door. One foot right through door. Bottle crashing. Glass breaking. Fist through door. Man cursing. Man going insane. Feet and hands tearing. Head smashing. Man yelling. Shoulder smashing. Whole body crashing. Woman screaming. Mom screaming. Mom screaming for police. Man throwing wood. Man throwing up. Mom calling cops. Dad crashing away. Back down driveway. Car door slamming. Ignition grinding. Wheels screaming. First gear grinding. Wheels screaming off down hill. Packard disappearing. Sound disappearing. No sound. No sight. Planes still hanging. Heart still pounding. No sound. Mom crying soft. Soft crying. Then no sound. Then softly crying. Then moving around through house. Then no moving. Then crying softly. Then stopping. Then, far off the freeway could be heard.

(WESLEY *picks up one end of the wheelbarrow. He makes the sound of a car and pushes it off right, leaving* ELLA *alone at the stove watching the bacon. She speaks alone.*)

ELLA: Now I know the first thing you'll think is that you've hurt yourself. That's only natural. You'll think that something drastic has gone wrong with your insides and that's why you're bleeding. That's only a natural reaction. But I want you to know the truth. I want you to know all the facts before you go off and pick up a lot of lies. Now, the first thing is that you should never go swimming when that happens. It can cause you to bleed to death. The water draws it out of you.

(WESLEY's *sister*, EMMA, *enters from right. She is younger and dressed in a white and green 4-H Club uniform. She carries several hand-painted charts on the correct way to cut up a frying chicken. She sets the charts down on the table upstage and arranges them as* ELLA *talks to her as though she's just continuing the conversation.*)

EMMA: But what if I'm invited? The Thompsons have a new heated pool. You should see it, Ma. They even got blue lights around it at night. It's really beautiful. Like a fancy hotel.

ELLA: (*tending to the bacon*) I said no swimming and that's what I meant! This thing is no joke. Your whole life is changing. You don't want to live in ignorance do you?

EMMA: No, Ma.

ELLA: All right then. The next thing is sanitary napkins. You don't want to buy them out of any old machine in any old gas station bathroom. I know they say "sanitized" on the package but they're a far cry from "sanitized." They're filthy in fact. They've been sitting around in those places for months. You don't know whose quarters go into those machines. Those quarters carry germs. Those innocent looking silver quarters with Washington's head staring straight ahead. His handsome jaw jutting out. Spewing germs all over those napkins.

EMMA: (*still arranging charts*) How come they call them napkins?

ELLA: (*stopping for a second*) What?

EMMA: How come they call them napkins?

ELLA: (*back to the bacon*) Well, I don't know. I didn't make it up. Somebody called them napkins a long time ago and it just stuck.

EMMA: "Sanitary napkins."

ELLA: Yes.

EMMA: It's a funny sound. Like a hospital or something.

ELLA: Well that's what they should be like, but unfortunately they're not. They're not hospital clean that's for sure. And you should know that anything you stick up in there should be absolutely hospital clean.

EMMA: Stick up in where?

(ELLA *turns upstage toward* EMMA, *then changes the subject.*)

ELLA: What are those things?
EMMA: They're for my demonstration.
ELLA: What demonstration?
EMMA: How to cut up a frying chicken.
ELLA: (*back to bacon*) Oh.
EMMA: For 4-H. You know. I'm giving a demonstration at the fair. I told you before. I hope you haven't used up my last chicken.

(EMMA *goes to refrigerator and looks inside for a chicken.*)

ELLA: I forgot you were doing that. I thought that wasn't for months yet.
EMMA: I told you it was this month. The fair's always this month. Every year it's this month.
ELLA: I forgot.
EMMA: Where's my chicken?
ELLA: (*innocently*) What chicken?
EMMA: I had a fryer in here all ready to go. I killed it and dressed it and everything!
ELLA: It's not in there. All we got is bacon and bread.
EMMA: I just stuck it in here yesterday, Ma! You didn't use it did you?
ELLA: Why would I use it?
EMMA: For soup or something.
ELLA: Why should I use a fryer for soup. Don't be ridiculous.
EMMA: (*slamming refrigerator*) It's not in there!
ELLA: Don't start screaming in here! Go outside and scream if you're going to scream!

(EMMA *storms off stage right.* ELLA *takes the bacon off the stove. Slight pause, then* EMMA *can be heard yelling off stage.* ELLA *puts some bread in the frying pan and starts frying it.*)

EMMA'S VOICE: (*off*) That was my chicken and you fucking boiled it! YOU BOILED MY CHICKEN! I RAISED THAT CHICKEN FROM THE INCUBATOR TO THE GRAVE AND YOU BOILED IT LIKE IT WAS ANY OLD FROZEN HUNK OF FLESH! YOU USED IT WITH NO CONSIDERATION FOR THE LABOR INVOLVED! I HAD

TO FEED THAT CHICKEN CRUSHED CORN EVERY
MORNING FOR A YEAR! I HAD TO CHANGE ITS
WATER! I HAD TO KILL IT WITH AN AX! I HAD TO
SPILL ITS GUTS OUT! I HAD TO PLUCK EVERY
FEATHER ON ITS BODY! I HAD TO DO ALL THAT
WORK SO THAT YOU COULD TAKE IT AND BOIL
IT!

(WESLEY *enters from left and crosses to center.*)

WESLEY: What's all the screaming?
ELLA: Somebody stole her chicken.
WESLEY: Stole it?
ELLA: Boiled it.
WESLEY: You boiled it.
ELLA: I didn't know it was hers.
WESLEY: Did it have her name on it?
ELLA: No, of course not.
WESLEY: Then she's got nothing to scream about. (*yelling off stage*) SHUT UP OUT THERE! YOU SHOULD'VE PUT YOUR NAME ON IT IF YOU DIDN'T WANT ANY- BODY TO BOIL IT!
EMMA'S VOICE: (*off*) EAT MY SOCKS!
WESLEY: (*crossing up to table*) Great language. (*noticing charts on table*) What's all this stuff?
ELLA: Her charts. She's giving a demonstration.
WESLEY: (*holding one of the charts up*) A demonstration? On what?
ELLA: How to cut up a chicken. What else.

(ELLA *takes her bacon and bread on a plate and crosses up to table. She sits at the stage left end.*)

WESLEY: Anybody knows how to cut up a chicken.
ELLA: Well, there's special bones you have to crack. Special ways of doing it evidently.
WESLEY: (*turning downstage with chart held out in front of him*) What's so special about it.
ELLA: (*eating at table*) The anatomy is what's special. The anat- omy of a chicken. If you know the anatomy you're half-way home.
WESLEY: (*facing front, laying chart down on floor*) It's just bones.
EMMA'S VOICE: (*off*) THERE'S NO CONSIDERATION! IF I'D COME ACROSS A CHICKEN IN THE FREEZER I

WOULD'VE ASKED SOMEONE FIRST BEFORE I BOILED IT!

ELLA: (*yelling, still eating*) NOT IF YOU WERE STARVING!

(WESLEY *unzips his fly, takes out his pecker, and starts pissing all over the chart on the floor.* ELLA *just keeps eating at the table, not noticing.*)

EMMA'S VOICE: (*off*) NO ONE'S STARVING IN THIS HOUSE! YOU'RE FEEDING YOUR FACE RIGHT NOW!

ELLA: So what!

EMMA'S VOICE: (*off*) SO NO ONE'S STARVING! WE DON'T BELONG TO THE STARVING CLASS!

ELLA: Don't speak unless you know what you're speaking about! There's no such thing as a starving class!

EMMA'S VOICE: (*off*) THERE IS SO! THERE'S A STARVING CLASS OF PEOPLE, AND WE'RE NOT PART OF IT!

ELLA: WE'RE HUNGRY, AND THAT'S STARVING ENOUGH FOR ME!

EMMA'S VOICE: (*off*) YOU'RE A SPOILED BRAT!

ELLA: (*to* WESLEY) Did you hear what she called me? (*she notices what he's doing, she yells to* EMMA) EMMA!

EMMA'S VOICE: (*off*) WHAT!

ELLA: YOUR BROTHER'S PISSING ALL OVER YOUR CHARTS! (*goes back to eating*)

(EMMA *enters fast from right and watches* WESLEY *put his joint back in his pants and zip up. They stare at each other as* ELLA *goes on eating at the table.*)

EMMA: What kind of a family is this?

ELLA: (*not looking up*) I tried to stop him but he wouldn't listen.

EMMA: (*to* WESLEY) Do you know how long I worked on those charts? I had to do research. I went to the library. I took out books. I spent hours.

WESLEY: It's a stupid thing to spend your time on.

EMMA: I'm leaving this house! (*she exists right*)

ELLA: (*calling after her but staying at table*) YOU'RE TOO YOUNG! (*to* WESLEY) She's too young to leave. It's ridiculous. I can't say I blame her but she's way too young. She's only just now having her first period.

WESLEY: (*crossing to refrigerator*) Swell.

ELLA: Well, you don't know what it's like. It's very tough. You don't have to make things worse for her.

WESLEY: (*opening refrigerator and staring into it*) I'm not. I'm opening up new possibilities for her. Now she'll have to do something else. It could change her whole direction in life. She'll look back and remember the day her brother pissed all over her charts and see that day as a turning point in her life.

ELLA: How do you figure?

WESLEY: Well, she's already decided to leave home. That's a beginning.

ELLA: (*standing abruptly*) She's too young to leave! And get out of that refrigerator!

(*She crosses to refrigerator and slams the door shut.* WESLEY *crosses up to the table and sits at the stage right end.*)

ELLA: You're always in the refrigerator!

WESLEY: I'm hungry.

ELLA: How can you be hungry all the time? We're not poor. We're not rich but we're not poor.

WESLEY: What are we then?

ELLA: (*crossing back to table and sitting opposite* WESLEY) We're somewhere in between. (*pause as* ELLA *starts to eat again;* WESLEY *watches her*) We're going to be rich though.

WESLEY: What do you mean?

ELLA: We're going to have some money real soon.

WESLEY: What're you talking about?

ELLA: Never mind. You just wait though. You'll be very surprised.

WESLEY: I thought Dad got fired.

ELLA: He did. This has nothing to do with your father.

WESLEY: Well, you're not working are you?

ELLA: Just never mind. I'll let you know when the time comes. And then we'll get out of this place, once and for all.

WESLEY: Where are we going?

ELLA: Europe maybe. Wouldn't you like to go to Europe?

WESLEY: No.

ELLA: Why not?

WESLEY: What's in Europe?

ELLA: They have everything in Europe. High art. Paintings. Castles. Buildings. Fancy food.

WESLEY: They got all that here.

ELLA: Why aren't you sensitive like your Grandfather was? I

always thought you were just like him, but you're not, are you?

WESLEY: No.

ELLA: Why aren't you? You're circumcized just like him. It's almost identical in fact.

WESLEY: How do you know?

ELLA: I looked. I looked at them both and I could see the similarity.

WESLEY: He's dead.

ELLA: When he was alive is when I looked. Don't be ridiculous.

WESLEY: What'd you sneak into his room or something?

ELLA: We lived in a small house.

EMMA'S VOICE: (*off*) WHERE'S MY JODHPURS!

ELLA: (*to* WESLEY) What's she yelling about?

WESLEY: Her jodhpurs.

ELLA: (*yelling to* EMMA) What do you need your jodhpurs for?

EMMA'S VOICE: (*off*) I'M TAKING THE HORSE!

ELLA: DON'T BE RIDICULOUS! DO YOU KNOW HOW FAR YOU'LL GET ON THAT HORSE? NOT VERY FAR!

EMMA'S VOICE: (*off*) FAR ENOUGH!

ELLA: YOU'RE NOT TAKING THE HORSE! (*to* WESLEY) Go down and lock that horse in the stall.

WESLEY: Let her go.

ELLA: On a horse? Are you crazy? She'll get killed on the freeway.

WESLEY: She won't take him on the freeway.

ELLA: That horse spooks at its own shadow. (*yelling off to* EMMA) EMMA, YOU'RE NOT TAKING THAT HORSE! (*no answering from* EMMA) EMMA! (*to* WESLEY) Go see if she went down there. I don't want her taking off on that horse. It's dangerous.

WESLEY: She's a good rider.

ELLA: I don't care!

WESLEY: You go down there then.

(*Pause. She looks at him.*)

ELLA: Well, maybe she'll be all right.

WESLEY: Sure she will. She's been out on overnight trail rides before.

ELLA: What a temper she's got.

WESLEY: She's just spoiled.

ELLA: No, she's not. I never gave her a thing extra. Nothing. Bare minimums. That's all.

WESLEY: The old man spoils her.

ELLA: He's never around. How could he spoil her?

WESLEY: When he's around he spoils her.

ELLA: That horse is a killer. I wish you'd go down there and check.

WESLEY: She can handle him.

ELLA: I've seen that horse get a new set of shoes and he's an idiot! They have to throw him down every time.

WESLEY: Look, where's this money coming from?

ELLA: What money?

WESLEY: This money that's going to make us rich.

ELLA: I'm selling the house.

(*Long pause, as* WESLEY *stares at her. She turns away from him.*)

ELLA: I'm selling the house, the land, the orchard, the tractor, the stock. Everything. It all goes.

WESLEY: It's not yours.

ELLA: It's mine as much as his!

WESLEY: You're not telling him?

ELLA: No! I'm not telling him and I shouldn't have told you. So just keep it under your hat.

WESLEY: How can you sell the house? It's not legal even.

ELLA: I signed the deed, same as him. We both signed it.

WESLEY: Then he has to co-sign the sale. Fifty-fifty.

ELLA: I already checked with a lawyer, and it's legal.

WESLEY: What about the mortgages? It's not even paid off, and you've borrowed money on it.

ELLA: Don't start questioning me! I've gone through all the arrangements already.

WESLEY: With who!

ELLA: I HAVE A LAWYER FRIEND!

WESLEY: A lawyer friend?

ELLA: Yes. He's very successful. He's handling everything for me.

WESLEY: You hired a lawyer?

ELLA: I told you, he's a friend. He's doing it as a favor.

WESLEY: You're not paying him?

ELLA: He's taking a percentage. A small percentage.

WESLEY: And you're just going to split with the money without telling anybody?

ELLA: I told you. That's enough. You could come with me.

WESLEY: This is where I live.

ELLA: Some home. It doesn't even have a front door now. Rain's going to pour right through here.

WESLEY: You won't even make enough to take a trip to San Diego off this house. It's infested with termites.

ELLA: This land is valuable. Everybody wants a good lot these days.

WESLEY: A lot?

ELLA: This is wonderful property for development. Do you know what land is selling for these days? Have you got any idea?

WESLEY: No.

ELLA: A lot. Tons. Thousands and thousands are being spent every day by ordinary people just on this very thing. Banks are loaning money right and left. Small family loans. People are building. Everyone wants a piece of land. It's the only sure investment. It can never depreciate like a car or a washing machine. Land will double its value in ten years. In less than that. Land is going up every day.

WESLEY: You're crazy.

ELLA: Why? For not being a sucker? Who takes care of this place?

WESLEY: Me!

ELLA: Ha! Are you kidding? What do you do? Feed a few sheep. Disc the orchard once in a while. Irrigate. What else?

WESLEY: I take care of it.

ELLA: I'm not talking about maintenance. I'm talking about fixing it up. Making it look like somebody lives here. Do you do that?

WESLEY: Somebody does live here!

ELLA: Who! Not your father!

WESLEY: He works on it. He does the watering.

ELLA: When he can stand up. How often is that? He comes in here and passes out on the floor for three days then disappears for a week. You call that work? I can't run this place by myself.

WESLEY: Nobody's asking you to!

ELLA: Nobody's asking me period! I'm selling it, and that's all there is to it!

(*Long pause, as they sit there.* WESLEY *gets up fast.*)

ELLA: Where are you going?

WESLEY: I'm gonna' feed the sheep!

(*He exists left.* ELLA *calls after him.*)

ELLA: Check on Emma for me would you, Wesley? I don't like her being down there all alone. That horse is crazy.

WESLEY'S VOICE: (*off*) HE'S GOING TO KILL YOU WHEN HE FINDS OUT!

ELLA: (*standing, shouting off*) HE'S NOT GOING TO FIND OUT! (*pause, as she waits for a reply; nothing; she yells again*) THE ONLY PERSON HE'S GOING TO KILL IS HIMSELF!

(*Another pause, as she stands there waiting for* WESLEY *to reply. Nothing. She turns to the table and stares at the plate. She picks up the plate and carries it to the stove. She sets it on the stove. She stares at the stove. She turns toward refrigerator and looks at it. She crosses to refrigerator and opens it. She looks inside.*)

ELLA: Nothing.

(*She closes refrigerator door. She stares at refrigerator. She talks to herself.*)

ELLA: He's not going to kill me. I have every right to sell. Every right. He doesn't have a leg to stand on.

(*She stares at refrigerator, then opens it again and looks inside.* EMMA *enters from right, holding a rope halter in one hand, her white uniform covered in mud. She watches* ELLA *staring into refrigerator.*)

EMMA: That bastard almost killed me.

(ELLA *shuts refrigerator and turns toward* EMMA.)

ELLA: What happened to you?

EMMA: He dragged me clear across the corral.

ELLA: I told you not to play around with that fool horse. He's insane, that horse.

EMMA: How am I ever going to get out of here?

ELLA: You're not going to get out of here. You're too young. Now go and change your clothes.

EMMA: I'm not too young to have babies, right?

ELLA: What do you mean?

EMMA: That's what bleeding is, right? That's what bleeding's for.

ELLA: Don't talk silly, and go change your uniform.

EMMA: This is the only one I've got.

ELLA: Well, change into something else then.

EMMA: I can't stay here forever.

ELLA: Nobody's staying here forever. We're all leaving.

EMMA: We are?

ELLA: Yes. We're going to Europe.

EMMA: Who is?

ELLA: All of us.

EMMA: Pop too?

ELLA: No. Probably not.

EMMA: How come? He'd like it in Europe wouldn't he?

ELLA: I don't know.

EMMA: You mean just you, me, and Wes are going to Europe? That sounds awful.

ELLA: Why? What's so awful about that? It could be a vacation.

EMMA: It'd be the same as it is here.

ELLA: No, it wouldn't! We'd be in Europe. A whole new place.

EMMA: But we'd all be the same people.

ELLA: What's the matter with you? Why do you say things like that?

EMMA: Well, we would be.

ELLA: I do my best to try to make things right. To try to change things. To bring a little adventure into our lives and you go and reduce the whole thing to smithereens.

EMMA: We don't have any money to go to Europe anyway.

ELLA: Go change your clothes!

EMMA: No. (*she crosses to table and sits stage right end.*)

ELLA: If your father was here you'd go change your clothes.

EMMA: He's not.

ELLA: Why can't you just cooperate?

EMMA: Because it's deadly. It leads to dying.

ELLA: You're not old enough to talk like that.

EMMA: I was down there in the mud being dragged along.

ELLA: It's your own fault. I told you not to go down there.

EMMA: Suddenly everything changed. I wasn't the same person anymore. I was just a hunk of meat tied to a big animal. Being pulled.

ELLA: Maybe you'll understand the danger now.

EMMA: I had the whole trip planned out in my head. I was going to head for Baja California.

ELLA: Mexico?

EMMA: I was going to work on fishing boats. Deep sea fishing. Helping businessmen haul in huge swordfish and barracuda. I was going to work my way along the coast, stopping at all the little towns, speaking Spanish. I was going to learn to be a mechanic and work on four-wheel-drive vehicles that broke down. Transmissions. I could've learned to fix anything. Then I'd learn how to be a short-order cook and write novels on the side. In the kitchen. Kitchen novels. Then I'd get published and disappear into the heart of Mexico. Just like that guy.

ELLA: What guy?

EMMA: That guy who wrote *Treasure of Sierra Madre*.

ELLA: When did you see that?

EMMA: He had initials for a name. And he disappeared. Nobody knew where to send his royalties. He escaped.

ELLA: Snap out of it, Emma. You don't have that kind of a background to do jobs like that. That's not for you, that stuff. You can do beautiful embroidery; why do you want to be a mechanic?

EMMA: I like cars. I like travel. I like the idea of people breaking down and I'm the only one who can help them get on the road again. It would be like being a magician. Just open up the hood and cast your magic spell.

ELLA: What are you dreaming for?

EMMA: I'm not dreaming now. I was dreaming then. Right up to the point when I got the halter on. Then as soon as he took off I stopped. I stopped dreaming and saw myself being dragged through the mud.

ELLA: Go change your clothes.

EMMA: Stop saying that over and over as though by saying it you relieve yourself of responsibility.

ELLA: I can't even follow the way you talk to me anymore.

EMMA: That's good.

ELLA: Why is that good?

EMMA: Because if you could then that would mean that you understood me.

(*Pause.* ELLA *turns and opens the refrigerator again and stares into it.*)

EMMA: Hungry?

ELLA: No.

EMMA: Just habit?

ELLA: What?

EMMA: Opening and closing?

(ELLA *closes refrigerator and turns toward* EMMA.)

ELLA: Christ, Emma, what am I going to do with you?

EMMA: Let me go.

ELLA: (*after pause*) You're too young.

(ELLA *exits left.* EMMA *stays sitting at table. She looks around the space, then gets up slowly and crosses to the refrigerator. She pauses in front of it, then opens the door slowly and looks in. She speaks into refrigerator.*)

EMMA: Hello? Anything in there? We're not broke you know, so you don't have to hide! I don't know where the money goes to but we're not broke! We're not part of the starving class!

(TAYLOR, *the lawyer, enters from down right and watches* EMMA *as she speaks into refrigerator. He is dressed in a smart suit, middle-aged, with a briefcase. He just stands there watching her.*)

EMMA: (*into refrigerator*) Any corn muffins in there? Hello! Any produce? Any rutabagas? Any root vegetables? Nothing? It's all right. You don't have to be ashamed. I've had worse. I've had to take my lunch to school wrapped up in a Weber's bread wrapper. That's the worst. Worse than no lunch. So don't feel bad! You'll get some company before you know it! You'll get some little eggs tucked into your sides and some yellow margarine tucked into your little drawers and some frozen chicken tucked into your—(*pauses*) You haven't seen my chicken have you? You motherfucker!

(*She slams the door to refrigerator and turns around. She sees* TAYLOR *standing there. They stare at each other.* TAYLOR *smiles.*)

TAYLOR: Your mother home?

EMMA: I don't know.

TAYLOR: I saw her car out there so I thought she might be.

EMMA: That's not her car.

TAYLOR: Oh. I thought it was.

EMMA: It's my Dad's car.

TAYLOR: She drives it, doesn't she?

EMMA: He bought it.

TAYLOR: Oh. I see.

EMMA: It's a Kaiser-Fraser.

TAYLOR: Oh.

EMMA: He goes in for odd-ball cars. He's got a Packard, too.

TAYLOR: I see.

EMMA: Says they're the only ones made out of steel.

TAYLOR: Oh.

EMMA: He totaled that car but you'd never know it.

TAYLOR: The Packard?

EMMA: No, the other one.

TAYLOR: I see.

EMMA: Who are you anyway?

TAYLOR: My name's Taylor. I'm your mother's lawyer.

EMMA: Is she in trouble or something?

TAYLOR: No. Not at all.

EMMA: Then what are you doing here?

TAYLOR: Well, I've got some business with your mother.

EMMA: You're creepy.

TAYLOR: Oh, really?

EMMA: Yeah, really. You give me the creeps. There's something about you that's weird.

TAYLOR: Well, I did come to speak to your mother.

EMMA: I know, but you're speaking to me now.

TAYLOR: Yes. (*pause, as he looks around awkwardly*) Did someone break your door down?

EMMA: My Dad.

TAYLOR: Accident?

EMMA: No, he did it on purpose. He was pissed off.

TAYLOR: I see. He must have a terrible temper.

EMMA: What do you want?

TAYLOR: I told you—

EMMA: Yeah, but what do you want my mother for?

TAYLOR: We have some business.

EMMA: She's not a business woman. She's terrible at business.

TAYLOR: Why is that?

EMMA: She's a sucker. She'll believe anything.

TAYLOR: She seems level-headed enough to me.

EMMA: Depends on what you're using her for.

(*Pause, as* TAYLOR *looks at her.*)

TAYLOR: You don't have to be insulting.

EMMA: I got nothing to lose.

TAYLOR: You *are* her daughter, aren't you?

EMMA: What line of business are you in?

TAYLOR: Do you mind if I sit down?

EMMA: I don't mind. My Dad might mind, though.

TAYLOR: He's not home, is he?

EMMA: He might come home any second now.

TAYLOR: (*crossing to chair at table*) Well, I'll just wait for your mother.

EMMA: He's got a terrible temper. He almost killed one guy he caught her with.

TAYLOR: (*sitting in stage right chair*) You misunderstand me. I'm here on business.

EMMA: A short fuse they call it. Runs in the family. His father was just like him. And his father before him. Wesley is just like Pop, too. Like liquid dynamite.

TAYLOR: (*setting attaché case on table*) Liquid dynamite?

EMMA: Yeah. What's that stuff called?

TAYLOR: I don't know.

EMMA: It's chemical. It's the same thing that makes him drink. Something in the blood. Hereditary. Highly explosive.

TAYLOR: Sounds dangerous.

EMMA: Yeah.

TAYLOR: Don't you get afraid living in an environment like this?

EMMA: No. The fear lies with the ones who carry the stuff in their blood, not the ones who don't. I don't have it in me.

TAYLOR: I see.

EMMA: Nitroglycerine. That's what it's called. Nitroglycerine.

TAYLOR: What do you mean?

EMMA: In the blood. Nitroglycerine.

TAYLOR: Do you think you could call your mother for me?

EMMA: (*yelling but looking straight at* TAYLOR) MOM!!!!

TAYLOR: (*after pause*) Thank you.

EMMA: What do you want my mother for?

TAYLOR: (*getting irritated*) I've already told you!

EMMA: Does she bleed?

TAYLOR: What?

EMMA: You know. Does she have blood coming out of her?

TAYLOR: I don't think I want to talk anymore.
EMMA: All right.

(EMMA *crosses to table and sits opposite* TAYLOR *at the stage left end. She stares at him. They sit silently for a while.* TAYLOR *squirms nervously, taps on his attaché case.* EMMA *just watches him.*)

TAYLOR: Marvelous house this is. (*pause, as she just looks at him*) The location I mean. The land is full of potential. (*pause*) Of course it's a shame to see agriculture being slowly pushed into the background in deference to low-cost housing, but that's simply a product of the times we live in. There's simply more people on the planet these days. That's all there is to it. Simple mathematics. More people demand more shelter. More shelter demands more land. It's an equation. We have to provide for the people some way. The new people. We're lucky to live in a country where that provision is possible. In some countries, like India for instance, it's simply not possible. People live under banana leaves.

(WESLEY *enters from right carrying a small collapsible fence structure. He sets it up center stage to form a small rectangular enclosure. He turns and looks at* TAYLOR, *then turns to* EMMA.)

WESLEY: (*to* EMMA) Who's he?
EMMA: He's a lawyer.

(TAYLOR *stands, smiling broadly at* WESLEY *and extending his hand.* WESLEY *doesn't shake but just looks at him.*)

TAYLOR: Taylor. You must be the son.
WESLEY: Yeah, I'm the son.

(WESLEY *exits right.* TAYLOR *sits down again. He smiles nervously at* EMMA, *who just stares at him.*)

TAYLOR: It's a funny sensation.
EMMA: What?
TAYLOR: I feel like I'm on enemy territory.
EMMA: You are.
TAYLOR: I haven't felt this way since the war.
EMMA: What war?

(TAYLOR *just looks at her.* WESLEY *enters again from right carrying a small live lamb. He sets the lamb down inside the fenced area. He watches the lamb as it moves around inside the fence.*)

EMMA: (*to* WESLEY) What's the matter with him?

WESLEY: (*watching lamb*) Maggots.

EMMA: Can't you keep him outside? He'll spread germs in here.

WESLEY: (*watching lamb*) You picked that up from Mom.

EMMA: Picked what up?

WESLEY: Germs. The idea of germs. Invisible germs mysteriously floating around in the air. Anything's a potential carrier.

TAYLOR: (*to* WESLEY) Well, it does seem that if the animal has maggots it shouldn't be in the kitchen. Near the food.

WESLEY: We haven't got any food.

TAYLOR: Oh. Well, when you do have food you prepare it in here, don't you?

EMMA: That's nothing. My brother pisses on the floor in here.

TAYLOR: Do you always talk this way to strangers?

EMMA: Look, that's his piss right there on the floor. Right on my chart.

WESLEY: (*turning to* TAYLOR) What're you doing here anyway?

TAYLOR: I don't feel I have to keep justifying myself all the time. I'm here to meet your mother.

WESLEY: Are you the one who's trying to sell the house?

TAYLOR: We're negotiating, yes.

EMMA: (*standing*) What? Trying to sell what house? This house?

TAYLOR: (*to* EMMA) Didn't she tell you?

WESLEY: She told me.

EMMA: Where are we going to live?

WESLEY: (*to* EMMA) You're leaving home anyway. What do you care?

EMMA: (*yelling off stage*) MOM!!!

TAYLOR: (*to* WESLEY) I didn't mean to shock her or anything.

WESLEY: (*to* TAYLOR) Aren't you going to talk to my old man?

TAYLOR: That's not necessary right now.

WESLEY: He'll never sell you know.

TAYLOR: Well, he may have to. According to your mother he owes a great deal of money.

EMMA: To who? Who does he owe money to?

TAYLOR: To everyone. He's in hock up to his ears.

EMMA: He doesn't owe a cent! Everything's paid for!

WESLEY: Emma, shut up! Go change your clothes.

EMMA: You shut up! This guy's a creep, and he's trying to sell us all down the river. He's a total meatball!

WESLEY: I know he's a meatball! Just shut up, will you?

EMMA: (*to* TAYLOR) My Dad doesn't owe money to anyone!

TAYLOR: (*to* WESLEY) I'm really sorry. I thought your mother told her.

(ELLA *enters from left in a dress and handbag with white gloves.* TAYLOR *stands when he sees her.*)

ELLA: What's all the shouting going on for? Oh, Mr. Taylor. I wasn't expecting you for another half-hour.

TAYLOR: Yes, I know. I saw the car out in front so I thought I'd stop in early.

ELLA: Well, I'm glad you did. Did you meet everyone?

TAYLOR: Yes, I did.

ELLA: (*noticing lamb*) What's that animal doing in here, Wesley?

WESLEY: It's got maggots.

ELLA: Well, get him out of the kitchen.

WESLEY: It's the warmest part of the house.

ELLA: Get him out!

EMMA: Mom, are you selling this house?

ELLA: Who told her?

TAYLOR: Well, I'm afraid it slipped out.

ELLA: Emma, I'm not going to discuss it now. Go change your clothes.

EMMA: (*coldly*) If you sell this house, I'm never going to see you again.

(EMMA *exits left.* TAYLOR *smiles, embarrassed.*)

TAYLOR: I'm very sorry. I assumed that she knew.

ELLA: It doesn't matter. She's leaving anyway. Now, Wes, I'm going out with Mr. Taylor for a little lunch and to discuss our business. When I come back I want that lamb out of the kitchen.

TAYLOR: (*to* WESLEY, *extending his hand again*) It was very nice to have met you.

(WESLEY *ignores the gesture and just stares at him.*)

ELLA: (*to* TAYLOR) He's sullen by nature. Picks it up from his father.

TAYLOR: I see. (*to* WESLEY) Nitroglycerine, too, I suppose? (*chuckles*)

(ELLA *and* TAYLOR *start to exit off right.* ELLA *turns to* WESLEY.)

ELLA: Keep an eye out for Emma, Wes. She's got the curse. You know what that's like for a girl, the first time around.

(TAYLOR *and* ELLA *exit.* WESLEY *stands there for a while. He turns and looks at the lamb.*)

WESLEY: (*staring at lamb*) "Eat American Lamb. Twenty million coyotes can't be wrong."

(*He crosses to refrigerator and opens it. He stares into it.*)

WESLEY: You're out of luck. Santa Claus hasn't come yet.

(*He slams refrigerator door and turns to lamb. He stares at lamb.*)

WESLEY: (*to lamb*) You're lucky I'm not really starving. You're lucky this is a civilized household. You're lucky it's not Korea and the rains are pouring through the cardboard walls and you're tied to a log in the mud and you're drenched to the bone and you're skinny and starving, but it makes no difference because someone's starving more than you. Someone's hungry. And his hunger takes him outside with a knife and slits your throat and eats you raw. His hunger eats you, and you're starving.

(*Loud crash of garbage cans being knocked over off stage right. Sound of* WESTON, WESLEY'S *father, off right.*)

WESTON'S VOICE: (*off right*) WHO PUT THE GODDAMN GAR-BAGE CANS RIGHT IN FRONT OF THE GODDAMN DOOR?

(WESLEY *listens for a second, then bolts off stage left. More crashing is heard off right. General cursing from* WESTON, *then he enters from right with a large duffel bag full of laundry and a large bag full of groceries. He's a very big man, middle-aged, wearing a dark overcoat which looks like it's been slept in, a blue baseball cap, baggy pants, and tennis shoes. He's unshaven and slightly drunk. He takes a few steps and stops cold when he sees the lamb. He just stares at the lamb for a minute, then crosses to the table and sets the bag of groceries and the laundry on the table. He crosses back to center and looks at the lamb inside the fence.*)

WESTON: (*to lamb*) What in the hell are you doin' in here? (*he looks around the space, to himself*) Is this inside or outside? This is inside, right? This is the inside of the house. Even with the door out it's still the inside. (*to lamb*) Right? (*to himself*) Right. (*to lamb*) So what the hell are you doing in here if this is the inside? (*he chuckles to himself*) That's not funny.

(*He crosses to the refrigerator and opens it.*)

WESTON: Perfect! ZERO! ABSOLUTELY ZERO! NADA! GOOSE EGGS! (*he yells at the house in general*) WE'VE DONE IT AGAIN! WE'VE GONE AND LEFT EVERYTHING UP TO THE OLD MAN AGAIN! ALL THE UPKEEP! THE MAINTENANCE! PERFECT!

(*He slams the refrigerator door and crosses back to the table.*)

WESTON: I don't even know why we keep a refrigerator in this house. All it's good for is slamming.

(*He picks up the bag of groceries and crosses back to the refrigerator, talking to himself.*)

WESTON: Slams all day long and through the night. SLAM! SLAM! SLAM! What's everybody hoping for, a miracle! IS EVERYBODY HOPING FOR A MIRACLE?

(*He opens refrigerator as* WESLEY *enters from stage right and stops.* WESTON'S *back is to him.* WESTON *starts taking artichokes out of the bag and putting them in the refrigerator.*)

WESTON: (*to house*) THERE'S NO MORE MIRACLES! NO MIRACLES TODAY! THEY'VE BEEN ALL USED UP! IT'S ONLY ME! MR. SLAVE LABOR HIMSELF COME HOME TO REPLENISH THE EMPTY LARDER!

WESLEY: What're you yelling for? There's nobody here.

(WESTON *wheels around facing* WESLEY. WESLEY *stays still.*)

WESTON: What the hell are you sneakin' up like that for? You coulda' got yourself killed!

WESLEY: What's in the bag?

WESTON: Groceries! What else. Somebody's gotta' feed this house.

(WESTON *turns back to refrigerator and goes on putting more artichokes into it.*)

WESLEY: What kind of groceries?

WESTON: Artichokes! What do you think?

WESLEY: (*coming closer*) Artichokes?

WESTON: Yeah. Good desert artichokes. Picked 'em up for half-price out in Hot Springs.

WESLEY: You went all the way out there for artichokes?

WESTON: 'Course not! What do you think I am, an idiot or something? I went out there to check on my land.

WESLEY: What land?

WESTON: My desert land! Now stop talking! Everything was all right until you came in. I was talking to myself and everything was all right.

(WESTON *empties the bag into the refrigerator, then slams the door shut. He crunches up the bag and crosses back to the table. He opens up his bag of laundry and starts taking dirty clothes out and stacking them in piles on the table.* WESLEY *crosses to refrigerator and opens it, looks in at artichokes. He takes one out and looks at it closely, then puts it back in. They keep talking through all this.*)

WESLEY: I didn't know you had land in the desert.

WESTON: 'Course I do. I got an acre and a half out there.

WESLEY: You never told me.

WESTON: Why should I tell you? I told your mother.

WESLEY: She never told me.

WESTON: Aw, shut up, will ya'?

WESLEY: What kind of land is it?

WESTON: It's not what I expected, that's for sure.

WESLEY: What is it, then?

WESTON: It's just not what I expected. Some guy came to the door selling land. So I bought some.

WESLEY: What guy?

WESTON: Some guy. Looked respectable. Talked a real good line. Said it was an investment for the future. All kinds of great things were going to be developed. Golf courses, shopping centers, banks, sauna baths. All that kinda' stuff. So I bought it.

WESLEY: How much did you pay?

WESTON: Well, I didn't pay the whole thing. I put something down on it. I'm not stupid.

WESLEY: How much?

WESTON: Why should I tell you? I borrowed it, so it's none of your goddamn business how much it was!

WESLEY: But it turned out to be a hoax, huh?

WESTON: A real piece of shit. Just a bunch of strings on sticks, with the lizards blowing across it.

WESLEY: Nothing around it?

WESTON: Not a thing. Just desert. No way to even get water to the goddamn place. No way to even set a trailer on it.

WESLEY: Where's the guy now?

WESTON: How should I know! Where's your mother anyway?

WESLEY: (*shutting refrigerator*) She went out.

WESTON: Yeah, I know she went out. The car's gone. Where'd she go to?

WESLEY: Don't know.

WESTON: (*bundling up empty duffel bag under his arm*) Well, when she gets back tell her to do this laundry for me. Tell her not to put bleach in anything but the socks and no starch in the collars. Can you remember that?

WESLEY: Yeah, I think so. No bleach and no starch.

WESTON: That's it. You got it. Now don't forget. (*he heads for stage right*)

WESLEY: Where are you going?

WESTON: Just never mind where I'm going! I can take care of myself. (*he stops and looks at the lamb*) What's the matter with the lamb?

WESLEY: Maggots.

WESTON: Poor little bugger. Put some a' that blue shit on it. That'll fix him up. You know that blue stuff in the bottle?

WESLEY: Yeah.

WESTON: Put some a' that on it. (*pauses a second, looks around*) You know I was even thinkin' a' sellin' this place.

WESLEY: You were?

WESTON: Yeah. Don't tell your mother though.

WESLEY: I won't.

WESTON: Bank probably won't let me, but I was thinkin' I could sell it and buy some land down in Mexico.

WESLEY: Why down there?

WESTON: I like it down there. (*looks at lamb again*) Don't forget about that blue stuff. Can't afford to lose any lambs. Only had but two sets a' twins this year, didn't we?

WESLEY: Three.

WESTON: Well, three then. It's not much.

(WESTON *exits stage right*. WESLEY *looks at lamb. Lights fade to black.*)

ACT TWO

SCENE: *Same set. Loud hammering and sawing heard in darkness. Lights come up slowly on* WESLEY *building a new door center stage. Hammers, nails, saw, and wood lying around, sawdust on floor. The fence enclosure and the lamb are gone. A big pot of artichokes is boiling away on the stove.* WESTON'S *dirty laundry is still in piles on the table.* EMMA *sits at the stage left end of the table making a new set of charts for her demonstration with magic markers and big sheets of cardboard. She is dressed in jodhpurs, riding boots, and a western shirt. Lights up full. They each continue working at their separate tasks in silence, each of them totally concentrated.* WESLEY *measures wood with a tape measure and then cuts it on one of the chairs with the saw. He nails pieces together. After a while they begin talking but still concentrate on their work.*

EMMA: Do you think she's making it with that guy?

WESLEY: Who, Taylor? How should I know?

EMMA: I think she is. She's after him for his money.

WESLEY: He's after our money. Why should she be after his?

EMMA: What money?

WESLEY: Our potential money.

EMMA: This place couldn't be that valuable.

WESLEY: Not the way it is now, but they'll divide it up. Make lots out of it.

EMMA: She's after more than that.

WESLEY: More than what?

EMMA: Money. She's after esteem.

WESLEY: With Taylor?

EMMA: Yeah. She sees him as an easy ticket. She doesn't want to be stuck out here in the boonies all her life.

WESLEY: She shoulda' thought of that a long time ago.

EMMA: She couldn't. Not with Pop. He wouldn't let her think. She just went along with things.

WESLEY: She can't think. He can't either.

EMMA: Don't be too harsh.

WESLEY: How can they think when they're behind the eight ball all the time. They don't have time to think.

EMMA: How come you didn't tell me when Pop came in last night?

WESLEY: I don't know.

EMMA: You could've told me.

WESLEY: He just brought his dirty laundry and then left.

EMMA: He brought food, too.

WESLEY: Artichokes.

EMMA: Better than nothing. (*pause, as they work*) They're probably half way to Mexico by now.

WESLEY: Who?

EMMA: She's snuggling up to him and giggling and turning the dial on the radio. He's feeling proud of himself. He's buying her hot dogs and bragging about his business.

WESLEY: She'll be back.

EMMA: She's telling him all about us and about how Dad's crazy and trying to kill her all the time. She's happy to be on the road. To see new places go flashing by. They cross the border and gamble on the jai alai games. They head for Baja and swim along the beaches. They build campfires and roast fish at night. In the morning they take off again. But they break down somewhere outside a little place called Los Cerritos. They have to hike five miles into town. They come to a small beat-up gas station with one pump and a dog with three legs. There's only one mechanic in the whole town, and that's me. They don't recognize me though. They ask if I can fix their "carro," and I speak only Spanish. I've lost the knack for English by now. I understand them though and give them a lift back up the road in my rebuilt four-wheel-drive International. I jump out and look inside the hood. I see that it's only the rotor inside the distributor that's broken, but I tell them that it needs an entire new generator, a new coil, points and plugs, and some slight adjustments to the carburetor. It's an overnight job, and I'll have to charge them for labor. So I set a cot up for them in the garage, and after they've fallen asleep I take out the entire engine and put in a rebuilt Volkswagen block. In the morning I charge them double for labor, see them on their way, and then resell their engine for a small mint.

WESLEY: If you're not doing anything, would you check the artichokes?

EMMA: I am doing something.

WESLEY: What?

EMMA: I'm remaking my charts.

WESLEY: What do you spend your time on that stuff for? You should be doing more important stuff.

EMMA: Like checking artichokes?

WESLEY: Yeah!

EMMA: You check the artichokes. I'm busy.

WESLEY: You're on the rag.

EMMA: Don't get personal. It's not nice. You should have more consideration.

WESLEY: Just put some water in them, would you? Before they burn.

(EMMA *throws down her magic marker and crosses to the pot of artichokes. She looks in the pot and then crosses back to her chair and goes on working on her charts.*)

WESLEY: Are they all right?

EMMA: Perfect. Just like a little boiling paradise in a pot. What're you making anyway?

WESLEY: A new door. What's it look like?

EMMA: Looks like a bunch of sawed-up wood to me.

WESLEY: At least it's practical.

EMMA: We're doing okay without a front door. Besides it might turn off potential buyers. Makes the place look like a chicken shack. (*remembers her chicken*) Oh, my chicken! I could've killed her right then.

WESLEY: You don't understand what's happening yet, do you?

EMMA: With what?

WESLEY: The house. You think it's Mr. and Mrs. America who're gonna' buy this place, but it's not. It's Taylor.

EMMA: He's a lawyer.

WESLEY: He works for an agency. Land development.

EMMA: So what?

WESLEY: So it means more than losing a house. It means losing a country.

EMMA: You make it sound like an invasion.

WESLEY: It is. It's a zombie invasion. Taylor is the head zombie. He's the scout for the other zombies. He's only a sign that more zombies are on their way. They'll be filing through the door pretty soon.

EMMA: Once you get it built.

WESLEY: There'll be bulldozers crashing through the orchard. There'll be giant steel balls crashing through the walls. There'll be foremen with their sleeves rolled up and blueprints under their arms. There'll be steel girders spanning acres of land. Cement pilings. Prefab walls. Zombie architecture, owned by invisible zombies, built by zombies for the use and convenience of all other zombies. A zombie city! Right here! Right where we're living now.

EMMA: We could occupy it. Dad's got a gun.

WESLEY: It's a Jap gun.

EMMA: It works. I saw him shoot a peacock with it once.

WESLEY: A peacock?

EMMA: Blasted it to smithereens. It was sitting right out there in the sycamore tree. It was screaming all night long.

WESLEY: Probably mating season.

EMMA: (*after long pause*) You think they'll come back?

WESLEY: Who?

EMMA: Our parents.

WESLEY: You mean ever?

EMMA: Yeah. Maybe they'll never come back, and we'll have the whole place to ourselves. We could do a lot with this place.

WESLEY: I'm not staying here forever.

EMMA: Where are you going?

WESLEY: I don't know. Alaska, maybe.

EMMA: Alaska?

WESLEY: Sure. Why not?

EMMA: What's in Alaska?

WESLEY: The frontier.

EMMA: Are you crazy? It's all frozen and full of rapers.

WESLEY: It's full of possibilities. It's undiscovered.

EMMA: Who wants to discover a bunch of ice?

(WESTON *suddenly stumbles on from stage right. He's considerably drunker than the last time.* EMMA *stands at the table, not knowing whether to stay or leave.* WESTON *looks at her.*)

WESTON: (*to* EMMA) Just relax. Relax! It's only your old man. Sit down!

(EMMA *sits again.* WESLEY *stands by awkwardly.* WESTON *looks at the wood on the floor.*)

WESTON: (*to* WESLEY) What the hell's all this? You building a barn in here or something?

WESLEY: New door.

WESTON: What! Don't talk with your voice in the back of your throat like a worm! Talk with your teeth! Talk!

WESLEY: I am talking.

WESTON: All right. Now I asked you what all this is. What is all this?

WESLEY: It's a new door.

WESTON: What's a new door? What's the matter with the old door?

WESLEY: It's gone.

(WESTON *turns around, weaving slightly, and looks off stage right.*)

WESTON: Oh. (*he turns back to* WESLEY) Where'd it go?

WESLEY: You broke it down.

WESTON: Oh. (*he looks toward table*) My laundry done yet?

EMMA: She didn't come back yet.

WESTON: Who didn't?

EMMA: Mom.

WESTON: She didn't come back yet? It's been all night. Hasn't it been all night?

EMMA: Yes.

WESTON: Hasn't the sun rised and falled on this miserable planet?

EMMA: Yes.

WESTON: (*turning to* WESLEY) So where's she been?

WESLEY: Don't know.

WESTON: Don't pull that one! Don't pull that one on me!

(*He starts to come after* WESLEY. WESLEY *backs off fast.* WESTON *stops. He stands there weaving in place.*)

WESLEY: I don't know. Really.

WESTON: Don't try protecting her! There's no protection! Understand! None! She's had it!

WESLEY: I don't know where she went.

EMMA: She went with a lawyer.

(WESTON *turns to* EMMA *slowly*.)

WESTON: A what?

EMMA: A lawyer.

WESTON: What's a lawyer? A law man? A person of the law? (*suddenly yelling*) WHAT'S A LAWYER?

EMMA: A guy named Taylor.

(*Long pause, as* WESTON *stares at her drunkenly, trying to fathom it. Then he turns to* WESLEY.)

WESTON: (*to* WESLEY) Taylor? You knew?

WESLEY: I thought she'd be back by now. She said she was going out for a business lunch.

WESTON: You knew!

EMMA: Maybe they had an accident.

WESTON: (*to* EMMA) In my car! In my Kaiser-Fraser! I'll break his fucking back!

WESLEY: Maybe they did have an accident. I'll call the hospitals.

WESTON: DON'T CALL ANYBODY! (*quieter*) Don't call anybody. (*pause*) That car was an antique. Worth a fortune.

EMMA: (*after long pause*) You wanna' sit down, Pop?

WESTON: I'm standing. What's that smell in here? What's that smell!

WESLEY: Artichokes.

WESTON: They smell like that?

WESLEY: They're boiling.

WESTON: Stop them from boiling! They might boil over.

(WESLEY *goes to stove and turns it off*.)

WESTON: Where's that goddamn sheep you had in here? Is that what you're building? A barn for that sheep?

WESLEY: A door.

WESTON: (*staggering*) I gotta sit down.

(*He stumbles toward table and sits at stage right end.* EMMA *stands*.)

WESTON: (*to* EMMA) Sit down! Sit back down! Turn off those artichokes!

WESLEY: I did.

WESTON: (*pushing laundry to one side*) She didn't do any of this. It's the same as when I brought it. None of it!

EMMA: I'll do it.

WESTON: No, you won't do it! You let her do it! It's her job! What does she do around here anyway? Do you know? What does she do all day long? What does a woman do?

EMMA: I don't know.

WESTON: You should be in school.

EMMA: It's all right if I do it. I don't mind doing it.

WESTON: YOU'RE NOT DOING IT! (*long silence*) What do you think of this place?

EMMA: The house?

WESTON: The whole thing. The whole fandango! The orchard! The air! The night sky!

EMMA: It's all right.

WESTON: (*to* WESLEY) What do you think of it?

WESLEY: I wouldn't sell it.

WESTON: You wouldn't sell it. You couldn't sell it! It's not yours!

WESLEY: I know. But I wouldn't if it was.

WESTON: How come? What good is it? What good's it doing?

WESLEY: It's just here. And we're on it. And we wouldn't be if it got sold.

WESTON: Very sound reasoning. Very sound. (*turns to* EMMA) Your brother never was much in the brain department, was he? You're the one who's such a smart-ass. You're the straight-A student, aren't you?

EMMA: Yes.

WESTON: Straight-A's and you're moldering around this dump. What're you going to do with yourself?

EMMA: I don't know.

WESTON: You don't know. Well you better think of something fast, because I've found a buyer. (*silence*) I've found someone to give me cash. Cash on the line! (*he slams table with his hand. Long silence, then* EMMA *gets up and exits off left.*)

WESTON: What's the matter with her?

WESLEY: I don't know. She's got her first period.

WESTON: Her what? She's too young for that. That's not supposed to happen when they're that age. It's premature.

WESLEY: She's got it.

WESTON: What happens when I'm gone, you all sit around and talk about your periods? You're not supposed to know when your sister has her period! That's confidential between women. They keep it a secret that means.

WESLEY: I know what "confidential" means.

WESTON: Good.

WESLEY: Why don't you go to bed or something, so I can finish this door.

WESTON: What for? I told ya' I'm selling the joint. Why build a new door? No point in putting money into it.

WESLEY: I'm still living here. I'm living here right up to the point when I leave.

WESTON: Very brave. Very courageous outlook. I envy it in fact.

WESLEY: You do?

WESTON: Sure! Of course! What else is there to envy but an outlook? Look at mine! Look at my outlook. You don't envy it, right?

WESLEY: No.

WESTON: That's because it's full of poison. Infected. And you recognize poison, right? You recognize it when you see it?

WESLEY: Yes.

WESTON: Yes, you do. I can see that you do. My poison scares you.

WESLEY: Doesn't scare me.

WESTON: No?

WESLEY: No.

WESTON: Good. You're growing up. I never saw my old man's poison until I was much older than you. Much older. And then you know how I recognized it?

WESLEY: How?

WESTON: Because I saw myself infected with it. That's how. I saw me carrying it around. His poison in my body. You think that's fair?

WESLEY: I don't know.

WESTON: Well, what do you think? You think I asked for it?

WESLEY: No.

WESTON: So it's unfair, right?

WESLEY: It's just the way it happened.

WESTON: I didn't ask for it, but I got it.

WESLEY: What is it anyway?

WESTON: What do you mean, what is it? You can see it for yourself!

WESLEY: I know it's there, but I don't know what it is.

WESTON: You'll find out.

WESLEY: How?

WESTON: How do you poison coyotes?

WESLEY: Strychnine.

WESTON: How! Not what!

WESLEY: You put it in the belly of a dead lamb.

WESTON: Right. Now do you see?

WESLEY: (*after pause*) No.

WESTON: You're thick! You're really thick. (*pause*) You know I watched my old man move around. I watched him move through rooms. I watched him drive tractors, watched him watching baseball, watched him keeping out of the way of things. Out of the way of my mother. Away from my brothers. Watched him on the sidelines. Nobody saw him but me. Everybody was right here, but nobody saw him but me. He lived apart. Right in the midst of things and he lived apart. Nobody saw that.

(*Long pause.*)

WESLEY: You want an artichoke?

WESTON: No.

WESLEY: Who's the buyer?

WESTON: Some guy. Owns the "Alibi Club" downtown. Said he'll give me cash.

WESLEY: How much?

WESTON: Enough to get to Mexico. They can't touch me down there.

WESLEY: Who?

WESTON: None of your goddamn business! Why is it you always drive yourself under my skin when I'm around? Why is that?

WESLEY: We don't get along.

WESTON: Very smart! Very observant! What's the matter with you anyway? What're you doing around here?

WESLEY: I'm part of your offspring.

WESTON: Jesus, you're enough to drive a sane man crazy! You're like having an espionage spy around. Why are you watching me all the time?

(WESTON *looks at him. They stare at each other for a moment.*)

WESTON: You can watch me all you want to. You won't find out
a thing.

WESLEY: Mom's trying to sell the place, too.

(WESTON *looks at him hard.*)

WESLEY: That's who the lawyer guy was. She's selling it
through him.

(WESTON *stands and almost topples over.*)

WESTON: I'LL KILL HER! I'LL KILL BOTH OF THEM!
Where's my gun? I had a gun here! A captured gun!

WESLEY: Take it easy.

WESTON: No, you take it easy! This whole thing has gone far
enough! It's like living in a den of vipers! Spies! Conspiracies
behind my back! I'M BEING TAKEN FOR A RIDE BY
EVERY ONE OF YOU! I'm the one who works! I'm the one
who brings home food! THIS IS MY HOUSE! I BOUGHT
THIS HOUSE! AND I'M SELLING THIS HOUSE! AND
I'M TAKING ALL THE MONEY BECAUSE IT'S OWED
ME! YOU ALL OWE IT TO ME! EVERY LAST ONE OF
YOU! SHE CAN'T STEAL THIS HOUSE AWAY FROM
ME! IT'S MINE!

(*He falls into table and collapses on it. He tries to keep himself from
falling to the floor.* WESLEY *moves toward him.*)

WESTON: JUST KEEP BACK! I'M NOT DYING, SO JUST
KEEP BACK!

(*He struggles to pull himself up on the table, knocking off dirty
laundry and* EMMA'S *charts.*)

WESTON: I don't need a bed. I don't need anything from you!
I'll stay right here. DON'T ANYONE TRY TO MOVE ME!
NOBODY! I'm staying right here.

(*He finally gets on table so that he's lying flat out on it. He slowly
goes unconscious.* WESLEY *watches him from a safe distance.*)

WESLEY: (*still standing there watching* WESTON) EMMA! (*no answer*)
Oh, shit. Don't go out on me. Pop?

(*He moves toward* WESTON *cautiously.* WESTON *comes to suddenly. Still lying on table.*)

WESTON: DON'T GET TOO CLOSE!

(WESLEY *jumps back.*)

WESLEY: Wouldn't you rather be on the bed?

WESTON: I'm all right here. I'm numb. Don't feel a thing. Feels good to be numb.

WESLEY: We don't have to sell, you know. We could fix the place up.

WESTON: It's too late for that. I owe money.

WESLEY: I could get a job.

WESTON: You're gonna' have to.

WESLEY: I will. We could work this place by ourselves.

WESTON: Don't be stupid. There's not enough trees to make a living.

WESLEY: We could join the California Avocado Association. We could make a living that way.

WESTON: Get out of here! Get away from me!

WESLEY: Taylor can't buy this place without your signature.

WESTON: I'll kill him! If I have to, I'll kill myself along with him. I'll crash into him. I'll crash the Packard right into him. What's he look like? (*no answer from* WESLEY) WHAT'S HE LOOK LIKE?

WESLEY: Ordinary. Like a crook.

WESTON: (*still lying on table*) I'll find him. Then I'll find that punk who sold me that phony desert land. I'll track them all down. Every last one of them. Your mother too. I'll track her down and shoot them in their bed. In their hotel bed. I'll splatter their brains all over the vibrating bed. I'll drag him into the hotel lobby and slit his throat. I was in the war. I know how to kill. I was over there. I know how to do it. I've done it before. It's no big deal. You just make an adjustment. You convince yourself it's all right. That's all. It's easy. You just slaughter them. Easy.

WESLEY: You don't have to kill him. It's illegal, what he's doing.

WESTON: HE'S WITH MY WIFE! THAT'S ILLEGAL!

WESLEY: She'll come back.

WESTON: He doesn't know what he's dealing with. He thinks I'm just like him. Cowardly. Sniveling. Sneaking around.

He's not counting on what's in my blood. He doesn't realize the explosiveness. We don't belong to the same class. He doesn't realize that. He's not counting on that. He's counting on me to use my reason. To talk things out. To have a conversation. To go out and have a business lunch and talk things over. He's not counting on murder. Murder's the farthest thing from his mind.

WESLEY: Just take it easy, Pop. Try to get some sleep.

WESTON: I am sleeping! I'm sleeping right here. I'm falling away. I was a flyer you know.

WESLEY: I know.

WESTON: I flew giant machines in the air. Giants! Bombers. What a sight. Over Italy. The Pacific. Islands. Giants. Oceans. Blue oceans.

(*Slowly* WESTON *goes unconscious again as* WESLEY *watches him lying on table.* WESLEY *moves toward him slightly.*)

WESLEY: Pop? (*he moves in a little closer*) You asleep?

(*He turns downstage and looks at the wood and tools. He looks toward the refrigerator.* ELLA *enters from down right carrying a bag of groceries. She stops when she sees* WESLEY. WESLEY *turns toward her.* ELLA *looks at* WESTON *lying on the table.*)

ELLA: How long's he been here?

WESLEY: Just got here. Where have you been?

ELLA: (*crossing to refrigerator*) Out.

WESLEY: Where's your boyfriend?

ELLA: (*opening refrigerator*) Don't get insulting. Who put all these artichokes in here? What's going on?

WESLEY: Dad. He brought them back from the desert.

ELLA: What desert?

WESLEY: Hot Springs.

ELLA: Oh. He went down to look at his pathetic piece of property, I guess.

(ELLA *sets the bag of groceries on the stove, then starts throwing the artichokes out onto the floor from the refrigerator.*)

WESLEY: What are you doing?

ELLA: Throwing these out. It's a joke bringing artichokes back here when we're out of food.

WESLEY: How do you know about his desert property?

ELLA: I just know, that's all.

WESLEY: He told you? He never told me about it.

ELLA: I just happen to know he was screwed out of five hundred bucks. Let's leave it at that. Another shrewd business deal.

WESLEY: Taylor.

ELLA: (*turning to* WESLEY) What?

WESLEY: Taylor sold it to him right?

ELLA: Don't be ridiculous. (*turns back to refrigerator*)

WESLEY: How else would you know?

ELLA: He's not the only person in the world involved in real estate, you know.

WESLEY: He's been sneaking around here for months.

ELLA: Sneaking? He doesn't sneak. He comes right to the front door every time. He's very polite.

WESLEY: He's venomous.

ELLA: You're just jealous of him, that's all.

WESLEY: Don't give me that shit! It was him, wasn't it? I remember seeing him with his briefcase, wandering around the property.

ELLA: He's a speculator. That's his job. It's very important in this day and age to have someone who can accurately assess the value of land. To see its potential for the future.

(*She starts putting all the groceries from her bag into the refrigerator.*)

WESLEY: What exactly is he anyway? You told me he was a lawyer.

ELLA: I don't delve into his private affairs.

WESLEY: You don't, huh?

ELLA: Why are you so bitter all of a sudden?

WESLEY: It's not all of a sudden.

ELLA: I should think you'd be very happy to leave this place. To travel. To see other parts of the world.

WESLEY: I'm not leaving!

ELLA: Oh, yes you are. We all are. I've sealed the deal. It just needs one last little signature from me and it's finished. Everything. The beat-up cars, the rusted out tractor, the moldy avocados, the insane horse, the demented sheep, the chickens, the whole entire shooting match. The whole collection. Over.

WESLEY: Then you're free I suppose?

ELLA: Exactly.

WESLEY: Are you going off with him?

ELLA: I wish you'd get your mind out of the garbage. I'm on my own.

WESLEY: Where'd you get the groceries?

ELLA: I picked them up.

WESLEY: (*after pause*) You know, you're too late. All your wheeling and dealing and you've missed the boat.

ELLA: (*closing refrigerator, turning to* WESLEY) What do you mean?

WESLEY: Dad's already sold it.

ELLA: You must be crazy! He couldn't sell a shoestring! Look at him! Look at him lying there! Does that look like a man who could sell something as valuable as a piece of property? Does that look like competence to you? Take a look at him! He's pathetic!

WESLEY: I wouldn't wake him up if I were you.

ELLA: He can't hurt me now! I've got protection! If he lays a hand on me, I'll have him cut to ribbons! He's finished!

WESLEY: He's beat you to the punch and he doesn't even know it.

ELLA: Don't talk stupid! And get this junk out of here! I'm tired of looking at broken doors every time I come in here.

WESLEY: That's a new door.

ELLA: GET IT OUT OF HERE!

WESLEY: (*quietly*) I told you, you better not wake him up.

ELLA: I'm not tiptoeing around anymore. I'm finished with feeling like a foreigner in my own house. I'm not afraid of him anymore.

WESLEY: You should be. He's going to kill Taylor, you know.

ELLA: He's always going to kill somebody! Every day he's going to kill somebody!

WESLEY: He means it this time. He's got nothing to lose.

ELLA: That's for sure!

WESLEY: He's going to kill you, too.

(ELLA *is silent for a while. They look at each other.*)

ELLA: Do you know what this is? It's a curse. I can feel it. It's invisible but it's there. It's always there. It comes onto us like nighttime. Every day I can feel it. Every day I can see it coming. And it always comes. Repeats itself. It comes even when you do everything to stop it from coming. Even when you try to change it. And it goes back. Deep. It goes back and back to tiny little cells and genes. To atoms. To tiny little swimming things making up their minds without us. Plotting in the womb. Before that even. In the air. We're surrounded with it. It's bigger than government even. It goes forward too. We spread it. We pass it on. We inherit it and pass it down, and then pass it down again. It goes on and on like that without us.

(ELLIS, *the owner of the "Alibi Club," enters from right and smiles at them. He is wearing a shiny yellow shirt, open at the collar, with a gold cross on a chain hanging from his neck. He's very burly, with tattooes all over his arms, tight-fitting pants, shiny shoes, lots of rings. He looks around and notices* WESTON *still lying on the table.*)

ELLIS: A few too many "boiler-makers," huh? I keep telling him to go light, but it's like fartin' in the wind. (*laughs at his own joke*) You must be the wife and kids. Name's Ellis, I run the "Alibi Club," down in town. You must know it, huh?

(*No reaction from* ELLA *and* WESLEY.)

ELLIS: Well, the old man knows it, that's for sure. Down there pretty near every night. Regular steady. Always wondered where he slept. What's that smell in here?

WESLEY: Artichokes.

ELLIS: Artichokes, huh? Smells like stale piss. (*bursts out laughing; no reaction from others*) Never was big on vegetables myself. I'm a steak man. "Meat and blood," that's my motto. Keeps your bones hard as ivory.

ELLA: I know it may be asking a little bit too much to knock when there's no door to knock on, but do you always make a habit of just wandering into people's houses like you own them?

ELLIS: I do own it. (*pause*) That's right. Signed, sealed, and delivered. Got the cash right here.

(*He pulls out two big stacks of bills from his belt and waves them in the air.*)

ELLIS: Fifteen hundred in hard core mean green.

WESLEY: Fifteen hundred dollars! (*looks at* ELLA)

ELLIS: That's what he owes. That's the price we agreed on. Look, buddy, I didn't even have to show up here with it.

Your old man's such a sap he signed the whole thing over to me without a dime even crossing the bar. I coulda' stung him easy. Just happens that I'm a man of honor.

ELLA: (*to* WESLEY) Get him out of here!

ELLIS: (*coldly to* WESLEY) I wouldn't try it, buddy boy.

(ELLIS *and* WESLEY *stare at each other.* ELLIS *smiles.*)

ELLIS: I've broken too many backs in my time, buddy. I'm not a hard man, but I'm strong as a bull calf, and I don't realize my own strength. It's terrible when that happens. You know? Before you know it, someone's hurt. Someone's lying there.

ELLA: This is a joke! You can't buy a piece of property from an alcoholic! He's not responsible for his actions!

ELLIS: He owns it, doesn't he?

ELLA: I OWN IT!

ELLIS: That's not what he told me.

ELLA: I own it and it's already been sold, so just get the hell out!

ELLIS: Well, I've got the deed right here. (*he pulls deed out*) Right here. Signed, sealed, and delivered. How do you explain that?

ELLA: It's not legal!

WESLEY: Who does he owe money to?

ELLIS: Oh, well, now I don't stick my nose where it doesn't belong. I just happen to know that he owes to some pretty hard fellas.

WESLEY: Fifteen hundred bucks?

ELLIS: That's about the size of it.

ELLA: Wake him up! We'll get to the bottom of this.

WESLEY: (*to* ELLA) Are you crazy? If he sees you here he'll go off the deep end.

ELLA: (*going to* WESTON *and shaking him*) I'll wake him up, then!

WESLEY: Oh, Jesus!

(WESTON *remains unconscious.* ELLA *keeps shaking him violently.*)

ELLA: Weston! Weston get up! Weston!

ELLIS: I've seen some hard cases in my time, but he's dedicated. That's for sure. Drinks like a Canadian. Flat out.

WESLEY: You say these guys are tough? What does he owe them for?

ELLIS: Look, buddy, he borrows all the time. He's a borrowing fool. It could be anything. Payments on a car. Land in the desert. He's always got some fool scheme going. He's just let it slide too long this time, that's all.

WESLEY: What'll they do to him?

ELLIS: Nothing now. I've saved his hide. You should be kissing my feet.

ELLA: WESTON! GET UP!

(*She is tiring from shaking him.* WESTON *remains unconscious.*)

WESLEY: They'd kill him for fifteen hundred bucks?

ELLIS: Who said anything about killing? Did I say anything about killing?

WESLEY: No.

ELLIS: Then don't jump to conclusions. You can get in trouble that way.

WESLEY: Maybe you should deliver it to them.

ELLIS: Look, I've carried the ball this far, now he's gonna' have to do the rest. I'm not his bodyguard.

WESLEY: What if he takes off with it?

ELLIS: That's his problem.

WESLEY: Give it to me.

ELLIS: What?

WESLEY: The money. I'll deliver it.

ELLA: (*leaving* WESTON) Wesley, don't you touch that money! It's tainted! Don't you touch it!

(ELLIS *and* WESLEY *look at each other.*)

WESLEY: You've got the deed. I'm his oldest son.

ELLA: You're his only son!

WESLEY: Just give it to me. I'll take care of it.

ELLIS: (*handing money to* WESLEY) All right, buddy. Just don't go off half-cocked. That's a lot a' spendin' change for a young man.

(WESLEY *takes it.*)

ELLA: Wesley, it's illegal! You'll be an accomplice!

WESLEY: (*to* ELLIS) Where do I find them?

ELLIS: That's your business, buddy. I'm just the buyer.

(ELLIS *walks around, looking over the place.* ELLA *crosses to* WESLEY *as* WESLEY *counts the money.*)

ELLA: Wesley, you give me that money! It doesn't belong to you! Give it to me!

WESLEY: (*looking at her coldly*) There's not enough here to go to Europe on, Mom.

ELLIS: I was thinkin' of turning this place into a steak house. What do you think? Make a nice little steak house, don't you think?

WESLEY: (*still counting money*) Sure.

ELLIS: People stop in off the highway, have a steak, a martini, afternoon cocktail, look out over the valley. Nice and peaceful. Might even put in a Japanese garden out front. Have a few goldfish swimming around. Maybe an eight-hole pitch-and-putt course right out there, too. Place is full of potential.

ELLA: Wesley!

(TAYLOR *appears with attaché case stage right.* ELLA *turns and sees him.* WESLEY *keeps counting money.*)

TAYLOR: Oh. I'm sorry. I didn't realize you had company. (*to* ELLA) I've got the final draft drawn up.

(TAYLOR *crosses toward table, sees* WESTON *lying on it, stops, looks for a place to set down his attaché case.*)

ELLA: (*to* TAYLOR) It's too late.

TAYLOR: Excuse me? What's too late?

ELLA: The whole thing. Weston's sold it.

TAYLOR: That's silly. I've got the final draft right here in my case. All it needs is your signature.

ELLIS: Who's this character?

ELLA: (*to* TAYLOR) He sold it for fifteen hundred dollars.

TAYLOR: (*laughs*) That's impossible.

ELLA: There it is right there! Wesley's got it in his hands! Wesley's taking it!

TAYLOR: He can't sell this piece of property. He's incompetent. We've already been through that.

ELLIS: (*crossing to* TAYLOR) Hey, listen, buddy. I don't know what your story is, but I suggest you get the fuck outa' here because this is my deal here. Understand? This is my little package.

TAYLOR: (*to* ELLA) Who's this?

ELLA: He's the buyer.

WESLEY: (*to* TAYLOR) Too slow on the trigger, Taylor. Took it right out from under you, didn't he?

TAYLOR: Well, it's simply a matter of going to court then. He doesn't have a leg to stand on. Legally he's a ward of the state. He can't sell land.

ELLIS: (*waving deed*) Look, I checked this deed out at city hall, and everything's above board.

TAYLOR: The deed has nothing to do with it. I'm speaking of psychological responsibility.

WESLEY: Does that apply to buying the same as selling?

TAYLOR: (*to* EMMA) What's he talking about?

ELLA: Nothing. Wesley, you give that money back!

WESLEY: Does that apply to buying dried up land in the middle of the desert with no water and a hundred miles from the nearest gas pump?

TAYLOR: (*to* WESLEY) I think you're trying to divert the focus of the situation here. The point is that your father's psychologically and emotionally unfit to be responsible for his own actions, and, therefore, any legal negotiations issuing from him cannot be held binding. This can be easily proven in a court of law. We have first-hand evidence that he's prone to fits of violence. His license for driving has been revoked, and yet he still keeps driving. He's unable to get insurance. He's unable to hold a steady job. He's absent from his home ninety percent of the time. He has a jail record. It's an open and shut case.

ELLIS: (*to* TAYLOR) What are you anyway? A lawyer or something? Where do you get off talkin' like that in my house!

ELLA: IT'S NOT YOUR HOUSE! THAT'S WHAT HE'S SAYING! CAN'T YOU LISTEN? DON'T YOU HAVE A BRAIN IN YOUR HEAD?

ELLIS: Listen, lady, I sell booze. You know what I mean? A lot a' weird stuff goes on in my bar, but I never seen anything as weird as this character. I never seen anything I couldn't handle.

WESLEY: You best take off, Taylor, before it all catches up to you.

TAYLOR: I refuse to be intimidated any further! I put myself out on a limb for this project and all I'm met with is resistance!

ELLA: I'm not resisting.

TAYLOR: (*to* WESLEY) You may not realize it, but there's corporations behind me! Executive management! People of influence. People with ambition who realize the importance of investing in the future. Of building this country up, not tearing it down. You people carry on as though the whole world revolved around your petty little existence. As though everything was holding its breath, waiting for your next move. Well, it's not like that! Nobody's waiting! Everything's going forward! Everything's going ahead without you! The wheels are in motion. There's nothing you can do to turn it back. The only thing you can do is cooperate. To play ball. To become part of us. To invest in the future of this great land. Because if you don't, you'll all be left behind. Every last one of you. Left high and dry. And there'll be nothing to save you. Nothing and nobody.

(*A policeman appears stage right in highway patrol gear.*)

SERGEANT MALCOLM: Uh—excuse me. Mrs. Tate?

ELLA: Yes.

MALCOLM: Are you Mrs. Tate?

ELLA: Yes, I am.

MALCOLM: I'm sorry. I would have knocked but there's no door.

ELLA: That's all right.

(TAYLOR *begins to move to stage left nervously.* WESLEY *watches him.*)

MALCOLM: I'm Sergeant Malcolm, Highway Patrol.

ELLA: Well, what is it?

MALCOLM: You have a daughter, Emma Tate?

ELLA: Yes. What's wrong?

MALCOLM: She's been apprehended.

ELLA: What for?

MALCOLM: It seems she rode her horse through a bar downtown and shot the place full of holes with a rifle.

ELLA: What?

ELLIS: What bar?

MALCOLM: Place called the "Alibi Club." I wasn't there at the time, but they picked her up.

ELLIS: That's my club!

MALCOLM: (*to* ELLIS) Are you the owner?

ELLIS: THAT'S MY CLUB!

MALCOLM: Are you Mr. Ellis?

ELLIS: What kind of damages?

MALCOLM: Well, we'll have to get an estimate, but it's pretty severe. Shot the whole place up. Just lucky there was no one in it at the time.

ELLIS: (*to* WESLEY) Give me that money back!

(ELLIS *grabs money out of* WESLEY's *hands.* TAYLOR *sneaks off stage left.*)

WESLEY: (*to cop*) Hey! He's getting away! That guy's a crook!

MALCOLM: What guy?

WESLEY: (*moving toward stage left*) That guy! That guy who just ran out of here! He's an embezzler! A confidence man! Whatever you call it. He sold my old man phony land!

MALCOLM: That's not within my jurisdiction.

ELLIS: (*to* ELLA) I know he sent her down there. I wasn't born yesterday, ya' know! He's crazy if he thinks he can put that kind of muscle on me! What does he think he is anyway? I'm gonna' sue him blind for this! I'm gonna' take the shirt right off his back! I was trying to do him a favor! I was stickin' my neck out for him! You just tell him when he wakes up out of his stupor that he's in bigger trouble than he thinks! He ain't seen nothin' yet! You tell him. (*starts to leave*) And just remember that I own this place. It's mine! So don't try any more funny stuff. I got friends in high places, too. I deal directly with them all the time. Ain't that right, Sarge?

MALCOLM: I don't know about that. I'm here on other business.

ELLIS: (*to* ELLA) You just tell him! I'll teach him to mess around with me!

(ELLIS *exits. Right.*)

ELLA: (*to cop*) He's taking our money!

MALCOLM: Look, lady, your daughter's in jail. I don't know about any of this other stuff. I'm here about your daughter.

(WESLEY *runs off right.* ELLA *yells after him.*)

ELLA: WESLEY! WHERE ARE YOU GOING?

WESLEY'S VOICE: (*off*) I'M GONNA' GET THAT MONEY BACK!

ELLA: IT'S NOT YOUR MONEY! COME BACK HERE! WESLEY! (*she stops and looks at* MALCOLM) Everybody's running off. Even Mr. Taylor. Did you hear the way he was talking to me? He was talking to me all different. All different than before. He wasn't nice at all.

MALCOLM: Mrs. Tate, what are we going to do about your daughter?

ELLA: I don't know. What should we do?

MALCOLM: Well, she has to stay in overnight, and if you don't want her back home she can be arraigned in juvenile court.

ELLA: We're all leaving here though. Everyone has to leave. She can't come home. There wouldn't be anyone here.

MALCOLM: You'll have to sign a statement then.

ELLA: What statement?

MALCOLM: Giving permission for the arraignment.

ELLA: All right.

MALCOLM: You'll have to come down with me unless you have a car.

ELLA: I have a car. (*pause*) Everyone's run away.

MALCOLM: Will you be all right by yourself?

ELLA: I am by myself.

MALCOLM: Yes, I know. Will you be all right or do you want to come with me in the patrol car?

ELLA: I'll be all right.

MALCOLM: I'll wait for you down at the station then.

(MALCOLM *exits.* ELLA *just stands there.*)

ELLA: (*to herself*) Everybody ran away.

(WESTON *sits up with a jolt on the table.* ELLA *jumps. They look at each other for a moment, then* ELLA *runs off stage.* WESTON *just stays sitting up on the table. He looks around the stage. He gets to his feet and tries to steady himself. He walks toward the refrigerator and kicks the artichokes out of his way. He opens refrigerator and looks in. Lights slowly fade to black with* WESTON *standing there looking into refrigerator.*)

ACT THREE

SCENE: *Same set. Stage is cleared of wood and tools and artichokes. Fence enclosure with the lamb inside is back, center stage. Pot of fresh coffee heating on the stove. All the laundry has been washed and* WESTON *is at the table to stage left folding it and stacking it in neat piles. He's minus his overcoat, baseball cap, and tennis shoes and wears a fresh clean shirt, new pants, shined shoes, and has had a shave. He seems sober now and in high spirits compared to before. The lamb is heard "baaing" in the dark as the lights slowly come up on* WESTON *at the table.*

WESTON: (*to lamb as he folds clothes*) There's worse things than maggots ya' know. Much worse. Maggots go away if they're properly attended to. If you got someone around who can take the time. Who can recognize the signs. Who brings ya' in out of the cold, wet pasture and sets ya' up in a cushy situation like this. No lamb ever had it better. It's warm. It's free of draft, now that I got the new door up. There's no varmints. No coyotes. No eagles. No—(*looks over at lamb*) Should I tell ya' something about eagles? This is a true story. This is a true account. One time I was out in the fields doing the castrating, which is a thing that has to be done. It's not my favorite job, but it's something that just has to be done. I'd set myself up right beside the lean-to out there. Just a little roof-shelter thing out there with my best knife, some boiling water, and a hot iron to cauterize with. It's a bloody job on all accounts. Well, I had maybe a dozen spring ram lambs to do out there. I had 'em all gathered up away from the ewes in much the same kinda' set up as you got right there. Similar fence structure like that. It was a crisp, bright

182

type a' morning. Air was real thin and you could see all the way out across the pasture land. Frost was still well bit down on the stems, right close to the ground. Maybe a couple a' crows and the ewes carrying on about their babies, and that was the only sound. Well, I was working away out there when I feel this shadow cross over me. I could feel it even before I saw it take shape on the ground. Felt like the way it does when the clouds move across the sun. Huge and black and cold like. So I look up, half expecting a buzzard or maybe a red-tail, but what hits me across the eyes is this giant eagle. Now I'm a flyer and I'm used to aeronautics, but this sucker was doin' some downright suicidal antics. Real low down like he's coming in for a landing or something, then changing his mind and pulling straight up again and sailing out away from me. So I watch him going small for a while, then turn back to my work. I do a couple more lambs maybe, and the same thing happens. Except this time he's even lower yet. Like I could almost feel his feathers on my back. I could hear his sound real clear. A giant bird. His wings made a kind of cracking noise. Then up he went again. I watched him longer this time, trying to figure out his intentions. Then I put the whole thing together. He was after those testes. Those fresh little remnants of manlihood. So I decided to oblige him this time and threw a few a' them on top a' the shed roof. Then I just went back to work again, pretending to be preoccupied. I was waitin' for him this time though. I was listening hard for him, knowing he'd be coming in from behind me. I was watchin' the ground for any sign of blackness. Nothing happened for about three more lambs, when all of a sudden he comes. Just like a thunder clap. Blam! He's down on that shed roof with his talons taking half the tar paper with him, wings whippin' the air, screaming like a bred mare then climbing straight back up into the sky again. I had to stand up on that one. Somethin' brought me straight up off the ground and I started yellin' my head off. I don't know why it was comin' outa' me but I was standing there with this icy feeling up my backbone and just yelling my fool head off. Cheerin' for that eagle. I'd never felt like that since the first day I went up in a B-49. After a while I sat down again and went on workin'. And every time I cut a lamb I'd throw those balls up on top a' the

shed roof. And every time he'd come down like the Cannon-
ball Express on that roof. And every time I got that feeling.

(WESLEY *appears stage right with his face and hands bloody.*)

WESLEY: Then what?

WESTON: Were you listening to me?

WESLEY: What happens next?

WESTON: I was tellin' it to the lamb!

WESLEY: Tell it to me.

WESTON: You've already heard it. What happened to your face
anyway?

WESLEY: Ran into a brick wall.

WESTON: Why don't ya' go clean up.

WESLEY: What happens next?

WESTON: I ain't tellin' it again!

WESLEY: Then I ain't cleaning up!

WESTON: What's the matter with you anyway? Are you drunk or
something?

WESLEY: I was trying to get your money back.

WESTON: What money?

WESLEY: From Ellis.

WESTON: That punk. Don't waste your time. He's a punk
crook.

WESLEY: He ran off with your money. And he's got the house
too.

WESTON: I've got the house! I've decided to stay.

WESLEY: What?

WESTON: I'm stayin'. I finished the new door. Did you notice?

WESLEY: No.

WESTON: Well, you shoulda' noticed. You walked right through
it. What's the matter with you? I'm fixin' the whole place up.
I decided.

WESLEY: You're fixing it up?

WESTON: Yeah. That's what I said. What's so unusual about
that? This could be a great place if somebody'd take some
interest in it. Why don't you have some coffee and clean
yourself up a little. You look like forty miles a' rough road.
Go ahead. There's fresh coffee on the stove.

(WESLEY *crosses slowly to the stove and looks at the coffee.*)

WESTON: I got up and took a walk around the place. Bright

and early. Don't think I've walked around the whole place for a couple a' years. I walked around and a funny thing started happening to me.

WESLEY: (*looking at coffee*) What?

WESTON: I started wondering who this was walking around in the orchard at six-thirty in the morning. It didn't feel like me. It was some character in a dark overcoat and tennis shoes and a baseball cap and stickers comin' out of his face. It didn't feel like the owner of a piece a' property as nice as this. Then I started to wonder who the owner was. I mean if I didn't feel like the owner, then who was the owner? I started wondering if the real owner was gonna' pop up out of nowhere and blast my brains out for trespassing. I started feeling like I should be running or hiding or something. Like I shouldn't be there in this kind of a neighborhood. Not that it's fancy or anything, but it's peaceful. It's real peaceful up here. Especially at that time a' the morning. Then it struck me that I actually was the owner. That somehow it was me and I was actually the one walking on my own piece of land. And that gave me a great feeling.

WESLEY: (*staring at coffee*) It did?

WESTON: Yeah. So I came back in here, and the first thing I did was I took all my old clothes off and walked around here naked. Just walked through the whole damn house in my birthday suit. Tried to get the feeling of it really being me in my own house. It was like peeling off a whole person. A whole stranger. Then I walked straight in and made myself a hot bath. Hot as I could stand it. Just sank down into it and let it sink deep into the skin. Let it fog up all the windows and the glass on the medicine cabinet. Then I let all the water drain out, and then I filled the whole tub up again but this time with ice cold water. Just sat there and let it creep up on me until I was in up to my neck. Then I got out and took a shave and found myself some clean clothes. Then I came in here and fixed myself a big old breakfast of ham and eggs.

WESLEY: Ham and eggs?

WESTON: Yeah. Somebody left a whole mess a' groceries in the ice box. Surprised the hell outa' me. Just like Christmas. Just like somebody knew I was gonna' be reborn this morning or something. Couldn't believe my eyes.

(WESLEY *goes to refrigerator and looks in.*)

WESTON: Then I started makin' coffee and found myself doing all this stuff I used to do. Like I was coming back to my life after a long time a' being away.

WESLEY: (*staring in refrigerator*) Mom brought this stuff.

WESTON: Then I started doing the laundry. All the laundry. I went around the house and found all the piles of dirty clothes I could get my hands on. Emma's, Ella's, even some a' yours. Some a' your socks. Found everybody's clothes. And every time I bent down to pick up somebody's clothes I could feel that person like they were right there in the room. Like the clothes were still attached to the person they belonged to. And I felt like I knew every single one of you. Every one. Like I knew you through the flesh and blood. Like our bodies were connected and we could never escape that. But I didn't feel like escaping. I felt like it was a good thing. It was good to be connected by blood like that. That a family wasn't just a social thing. It was an animal thing. It was a reason of nature that we were all together under the same roof. Not that we had to be but that we were supposed to be. And I started feeling glad about it. I started feeling full of hope.

WESLEY: (*staring in refrigerator*) I'm starving.

WESTON: (*crossing to* WESLEY) Look, go take a bath and get that crap off your face, and I'll make ya' some ham and eggs. What is that crap anyway?

WESLEY: Blood.

WESTON: He took a few swipes at ya', huh? Well go wash it off and come back in here. Go on!

WESLEY: (*turning to* WESTON) He wouldn't give me the money, you know.

WESTON: So what. The guy's a knuckle-head. Don't have the brains God gave a chicken. Now go in there and clean up before *I* start swingin' on you.

(WESLEY *exits off left.* WESTON *starts taking ham and eggs out of refrigerator and fixing a breakfast at the stove. He yells off stage to* WESLEY *as he cooks.*)

WESTON: (*yelling*) So I was thinkin' about that avocado deal you were talkin' about before! You know, joining up with the

"Growers Association" and everything! And I was thinkin' it might not be such a bad deal after all! I mean we don't have to hire Chicanos or nothin'! We could pick 'em ourselves and sell 'em direct to the company! How 'bout that idea! Cut down on the overhead! That tractor's still workin', isn't it? I mean the motor's not seized up or nothin', and we got plenty a' good pressure in the irrigation! I checked it this morning! Water's blastin' right through those pipes! Wouldn't take much to get the whole operation goin' full-tilt again! I'll resell that piece a' land out there! That'll give us somethin' to get us started! Somebody somewhere's gonna' want a good piece a' desert land! It's prime location even if it isn't being developed! Only a three-hour drive from Palm Springs, and you know what that's like! You know the kinda' people who frequent that place! One of 'em's bound to have some extra cash!

(ELLA *enters from stage right. She looks haggard and tired. She stands there looking at* WESTON, *who keeps cooking the eggs. Then she looks at the lamb.* WESTON *knows she's there but doesn't look at her.*)

ELLA: (*after pause*) What's that lamb doing back in here?
WESTON: I got him back on his feet. It was nip and tuck there for a while. Didn't think he'd pull through. Maggots clear up into the small intestine.
ELLA: (*crossing to table*) Spare me the details.

(*She pulls off her white gloves and sits exhausted into the chair at stage right. She looks at the piles of clean laundry.*)

WESTON: (*still cooking*) Where you been anyway?
ELLA: Jail.
WESTON: Oh, they finally caught ya', huh? (*chuckles*)
ELLA: Very humorous.
WESTON: You want some breakfast? I was just fixin' something up for Wes, here.
ELLA: You're cooking?
WESTON: Yeah. What's it look like?
ELLA: Who did all this laundry?
WESTON: Yours truly.
ELLA: Are you having a nervous breakdown or what?
WESTON: Can't a man do his own laundry?

ELLA: As far as I know he can.

WESTON: Even did some a' yours too.

ELLA: Gee, thanks.

WESTON: Well, I coulda' just left it. I was doin' a load of my own, so I thought I'd throw everybody else's in to boot.

ELLA: I'm very grateful.

WESTON: So where you been? Off with that fancy lawyer?

ELLA: I've been to jail, like I said.

WESTON: Come on. What, on a visit? They throw you in the drunk tank? Out with it.

ELLA: I was visiting your daughter.

WESTON: Oh, yeah? What'd they nab her for?

ELLA: Possession of firearms. Malicious vandalism. Breaking and entering. Assault. Violation of equestrian regulations. You name it.

WESTON: Well, she always was a fireball.

ELLA: Part of the inheritance, right?

WESTON: Right. Direct descendant.

ELLA: Well, I'm glad you've found a way of turning shame into a source of pride.

WESTON: What's shameful about it? Takes courage to get charged with all that stuff. It's not everyone her age who can run up a list of credits like that.

ELLA: That's for sure.

WESTON: Could you?

ELLA: Don't be ridiculous! I'm not self-destructive. Doesn't run in my family line.

WESTON: That's right. I never thought about it like that. You're the only one who doesn't have it. Only us.

ELLA: Oh, so now I'm the outsider.

WESTON: Well, it's true. You come from a different class of people. Gentle. Artists. They were all artists, weren't they?

ELLA: My grandfather was a pharmacist.

WESTON: Well, scientists then. Members of the professions. Professionals. Nobody raised their voice.

ELLA: That's bad?

WESTON: No. Just different. That's all. Just different.

ELLA: Are we waxing philosophical over our eggs now? Is that the idea? Sobered up over night, have we? Awoken to a brand-new morning? What is this crap! I've been down there all night trying to pull Emma back together again and I come

back to Mr. Hyde! Mr. "Goody Two-Shoes"! Mister Mia
Copa himself! Well, you can kiss off with that crap because
I'm not buying it!

WESTON: Would you like some coffee?

ELLA: NO, I DON'T WANT ANY GODDAMN COFFEE!
AND GET THAT SON-OF-A-BITCHING SHEEP OUT
OF MY KITCHEN!!

WESTON: (*staying cool*) You've picked up on the language okay,
but your inflection's off.

ELLA: There's nothing wrong with my inflection!

WESTON: Something doesn't ring true about it. Something deep
in the voice. At the heart of things.

ELLA: Oh, you are really something. How can you accuse me of
not measuring up to your standards! You're a complete washout!

WESTON: It's got nothing to do with standards. It's more like
fate.

ELLA: Oh, knock it off, would you? I'm exhausted.

WESTON: Try the table. Nice and hard. It'll do wonders for you.

ELLA: (*suddenly soft*) The table?

WESTON: Yeah. Just stretch yourself out. You'll be amazed.
Better than any bed.

(ELLA *looks at the table for a second, then starts pushing all the
clean laundry off it onto the floor. She pulls herself up onto it and
stretches out on it.* WESTON *goes on cooking with his back to her. She
watches him as she lies there.*)

WESTON: And when you wake up I'll have a great big breakfast of ham and eggs, ready and waiting. You'll feel like a
million bucks. You'll wonder why you spent all those years in
bed, once you feel that table. That table will deliver you.

(WESLEY *wanders on stage from stage left, completely naked, his
hair wet. He looks dazed.* WESTON *pays no attention but goes on
preparing the breakfast and talking as* WESLEY *wanders upstage and
stares at* ELLA. *She looks at him but doesn't react. He turns
downstage and looks at* WESTON. *He looks at lamb and crosses
down to it. He bends over and picks it up, then carries it off stage
right.* WESTON *goes on cooking and talking.* ELLA *stays on table.*)

WESTON: That's the trouble with too much comfort, you
know? Makes you forget where you come from. Makes you
lose touch. You think you're making headway but you're

losing all the time. You're falling behind more and more.
You're going into a trance that you'll never come back from.
You're being hypnotized. Your body's being mesmerized.
You go into a coma. That's why you need a hard table once
in a while to bring you back. A good hard table to bring you
back to life.

ELLA: (*still on table, sleepily*) You should have been a preacher.

WESTON: You think so?

ELLA: Great voice you have. Deep. Resonates.

WESTON: (*putting eggs on plate*) I'm not a public person.

ELLA: I'm so exhausted.

WESTON: You just sleep.

ELLA: You should have seen that jail, Weston.

WESTON: I have.

ELLA: Oh, that's right. How could you ever sleep in a place like
that?

WESTON: If you're numb enough you don't feel a thing. (*he yells
off stage to* WESLEY) WES! YOUR BREAKFAST'S READY!

ELLA: He just went out.

WESTON: What?

ELLA: He just walked out stark naked with that sheep under his
arm.

(WESTON *looks at fence enclosure, sees lamb gone. He's still holding
plate.*)

WESTON: Where'd he go?

ELLA: Outside.

WESTON: (*crossing right, carrying plate*) WES! GODDAMNIT,
YOUR BREAKFAST'S READY!

(WESTON *exits carrying plate off stage right.* ELLA *tries to keep her
eyes open, still on table.*)

ELLA: (*to herself*) Nothing surprises me anymore.

(*She slowly falls asleep on table. Nothing happens for a while. Then*
WESTON *comes back on from right still carrying plate.* ELLA *stays
asleep on table.*)

WESTON: (*crossing to stove*) He's not out there. Wouldn't ya'
know it? Just when it's ready, he walks out. (*turning to* ELLA)
Why'd he take the lamb? That lamb needs to be kept warm.
(*sees that* ELLA'S *sound asleep*) Great. (*turns and sets plate down on*

stove; looks at food) Might as well eat it myself. A double breakfast. Why not? (*he starts eating off the plate, talks to himself*) Can't expect the thing to get well if it's not kept warm. (*he turns upstage again and looks at* ELLA *sleeping, then turns back to the plate of food*) Always was best at talkin' to myself. Always was the best thing. Nothing like it. Keeps ya' company at least.

(WESLEY *enters from right dressed in* WESTON'S *baseball cap, overcoat, and tennis shoes. He stands there.* WESTON *looks at him.* ELLA *sleeps.*)

WESTON: What in the hell's goin' on with you? I was yellin' for you just now. Didn't you hear me?

WESLEY: (*staring at* WESTON) No.

WESTON: Your breakfast was all ready. Now it's cold. I've eaten half of it already. Almost half gone.

WESLEY: (*blankly*) You can have it.

WESTON: What're you doin' in those clothes anyway?

WESLEY: I found them.

WESTON: I threw them out! What's got into you? You go take a bath and then put on some old bum's clothes that've been thrown-up in, pissed in, and God knows what all in?

WESLEY: They fit me.

WESTON: I can't fathom you, that's for sure. What'd you do with that lamb?

WESLEY: Butchered it.

WESTON: (*turning away from him, disgusted*) I swear to God. (*pause, then turning to* WESLEY) WHAT'D YA' BUTCHER THE DUMB THING FOR!

WESLEY: We need some food.

WESTON: THE ICE BOX IS CRAMMED FULL A' FOOD!

(WESLEY *crosses quickly to refrigerator, opens it, and starts pulling all kinds of food out and eating it ravenously.* WESTON *watches him, a little afraid of* WESLEY'S *state.*)

WESTON: WHAT'D YA' GO AND BUTCHER IT FOR? HE WAS GETTING BETTER! (*watches* WESLEY *eating hungrily*) What's a' matter with you, boy? I made ya' a big breakfast. Why didn't ya' eat that? What's the matter with you?

(WESTON *moves cautiously, away from* WESLEY *to stage right.* WESLEY *keeps eating, throwing half-eaten food to one side and then digging into more. He groans slightly as he eats.*)

WESTON: (*to* WESLEY) Look, I know I ignored some a' the chores around the place and you had to do it instead a' me. But I brought you some artichokes back, didn't I? Didn't I do that? I didn't have to do that. I went outa' my way. I saw the sign on the highway and drove two miles outa' my way just to bring you back some artichokes. (*pause, as he looks at* WESLEY *eating; he glances nervously up at* ELLA, *then back to* WESLEY) You couldn't be all that starving! We're not that bad off, goddamnit! I've seen starving people in my time, and we're not that bad off! (*pause, no reaction from* WESLEY, *who continues to eat ravenously*) You just been spoiled, that's all! This is a paradise for a young person! There's kids your age who'd give their eyeteeth to have an environment like this to grow up in! You've got everything! Everything! Opportunity is glaring you in the teeth here! (*turns toward* ELLA) ELLA! ELLA, WAKE UP! (*no reaction from* ELLA; *turns back to* WESLEY, *still eating*) If this is supposed to make me feel guilty, it's not working! It's not working because I don't have to pay for my past now! Not now! Not after this morning! All that's behind me now! YOU UNDERSTAND ME? IT'S ALL OVER WITH BECAUSE I'VE BEEN REBORN! I'M A WHOLE NEW PERSON NOW! I'm a whole new person.

(WESLEY *stops eating suddenly and turns to* WESTON.)

WESLEY: (*coldly*) They're going to kill you.
WESTON: (*pause*) Who's going to kill me! What're you talking about! Nobody's going to kill me!
WESLEY: I couldn't get the money.
WESTON: What money?
WESLEY: Ellis.
WESTON: So what?
WESLEY: You owe it to them.
WESTON: Owe it to who? I don't remember anything. All that's over with now.
WESLEY: No, it's not. It's still there. Maybe you've changed, but you still owe them.
WESTON: I can't remember. Must've borrowed some for the car payment. Can't remember it.

WESLEY: They remember it.

WESTON: So, I'll get it to them. It's not that drastic.

WESLEY: How? Ellis has the house and everything now.

WESTON: How does he have the house? This is my house!

WESLEY: You signed it over.

WESTON: I never signed anything!

WESLEY: You were drunk.

WESTON: SHUT UP!

WESLEY: How're you going to pay them?

WESTON: (*pause*) I can sell that land.

WESLEY: It's phony land. The guy's run off to Mexico.

WESTON: What guy?

WESLEY: Taylor. The lawyer. The lawyer friend of Mom's.

WESTON: (*pause, looks at* ELLA *sleeping, then back to* WESLEY) Same guy?

WESLEY: Same guy. Ripped us all off.

WESTON: This isn't right. I was on a whole new track. I was getting right up on top of it all.

WESLEY: They've got it worked out so you can't.

WESTON: I was ready for a whole new attack. This isn't right!

WESLEY: They've moved in on us like a creeping disease. We didn't even notice.

WESTON: I just built a whole new door and everything. I washed all the laundry. I cleaned up all the artichokes. I started over.

WESLEY: You better run.

WESTON: Run? What do you mean, run? I can't run!

WESLEY: Take the Packard and get out of here.

WESTON: I can't run out on everything.

WESLEY: Why not?

WESTON: 'CAUSE THIS IS WHERE I SETTLED DOWN! THIS IS WHERE THE LINE ENDED! RIGHT HERE! I MIGRATED TO THIS SPOT! I GOT NOWHERE TO GO TO! THIS IS IT!

WESLEY: Take the Packard.

(WESTON *stands there for a while. He looks around, trying to figure a way out.*)

WESTON: (*after pause*) I remember now. I was in hock. I was in hock up to my elbows. See, I always figured on the future. I banked on it. I was banking on it getting better. It couldn't get worse, so I figured it'd just get better. I figured that's why everyone wants you to buy things. Buy refrigerators. Buy cars, houses, lots, invest. They wouldn't be so generous if they didn't figure you had it comin' in. At some point it had to be comin' in. So I went along with it. Why not borrow if you know it's coming in. Why not make a touch here and there. They all want you to borrow anyhow. Banks, car lots, investors. The whole thing's geared to invisible money. You never hear the sound of change anymore. It's all plastic shuffling back and forth. It's all in everybody's heads. So I figured if that's the case, why not take advantage of it? Why not go in debt for a few grand if all it is is numbers? If it's all an idea and nothing's really there, why not take advantage? So I just went along with it, that's all. I just played ball.

WESLEY: You better go.

(*Pause, as* WESTON *looks at* ELLA *sleeping.*)

WESTON: Same guy, huh? She musta' known about it, too. She musta' thought I left her.

(WESTON *turns and looks at* WESLEY. *Silence.*)

WESLEY: You did.

WESTON: I just went off for a little while. Now and then. I couldn't stand it here. I couldn't stand the idea that everything would stay the same. That every morning it would be the same. I kept looking for it out there somewhere. I kept trying to piece it together. The jumps. I couldn't figure out the jumps. From being born, to growing up, to droppin' bombs, to having kids, to hittin' bars, to this. It all turned on me somehow. It all turned around on me. I kept looking for it out there somewhere. And all the time it was right inside this house.

WESLEY: They'll be coming for you here. They know where you live now.

WESTON: Where should I go?

WESLEY: How 'bout Mexico?

WESTON: Mexico? Yeah. That's where everyone escapes to, right? It's full of escape artists down there. I could go down there and get lost. I could disappear. I could start a whole new life down there.

WESLEY: Maybe.

WESTON: I could find that guy and get my money back. That real estate guy. What's his name?

WESLEY: Taylor.

WESTON: Yeah, Taylor. He's down there too, right? I could find him.

WESLEY: Maybe.

WESTON: (*looking over at* ELLA *again*) I can't believe she knew and still went off with him. She musta' thought I was dead or something. She musta' thought I was never coming back.

(WESTON *moves toward* ELLA, *then stops. He looks at* WESLEY, *then turns and exits off right.* WESLEY *just stands there.* WESLEY *bends down and picks some scraps of food up off the floor and eats them very slowly. He looks at the empty lamb pen.* EMMA *enters from left, dressed as she was in Act 2. She crosses into center, looking in the direction of where* WESTON *went.* WESLEY *seems dazed as he slowly chews the food.* ELLA *stays asleep on table.* EMMA *carries a riding crop. She taps her leg with it as she looks off right.*)

EMMA: Mexico, huh? He won't last a day down there. They'll find him easy. Stupid going to Mexico. That's the first place they'll look. (*to* WESLEY) What're you eating?

WESLEY: Food.

EMMA: Off the floor? You'll wind up just like him. Diseased!

WESLEY: (*dazed*) I'm hungry.

EMMA: You're sick! What're you doing with his clothes on? Are you supposed to be the head of the family now or something? The Big Cheese? Daddy Bear?

WESLEY: I tried his remedy, but it didn't work.

EMMA: He's got a remedy?

WESLEY: (*half to himself*) I tried taking a hot bath. Hot as I could stand it. Then freezing cold. Then walking around naked. But it didn't work. Nothing happened. I was waiting for something to happen. I went outside. I was freezing cold out there and I looked for something to put over me. I started digging around in the garbage and I found his clothes.

EMMA: Digging around in the garbage?

WESLEY: I had the lamb's blood dripping down my arms. I thought it was me for a second. I thought it was me bleeding.

EMMA: You're disgusting. You're even more disgusting than him. And that's pretty disgusting. (*looking at* ELLA, *still asleep*) What's she doing?

WESLEY: I started putting all his clothes on. His baseball cap, his tennis shoes, his overcoat. And every time I put one thing on it seemed like a part of him was growing on me. I could feel him taking over me.

EMMA: (*crossing up to table, tapping crop on her leg*) What is she, asleep or something? (*she whacks* ELLA *across the butt with the riding crop*) WAKE UP! (ELLA *stays sleeping*)

WESLEY: I could feel myself retreating. I could feel him coming in and me going out. Just like the change of the guards.

EMMA: Well, don't eat your heart out about it. You did the best you could.

WESLEY: I didn't do a thing.

EMMA: That's what I mean.

WESLEY: I just grew up here.

EMMA: (*crossing down to* WESLEY) Have you got any money?

(WESLEY *starts digging around in the pockets of the overcoat.*)

EMMA: What're you fishing around in there for? That's *his* coat.

WESLEY: I thought you were supposed to be in jail?

EMMA: (*crossing back up to table*) I was.

WESLEY: What happened?

EMMA: (*picking up* ELLA'S *handbag and going through it*) I used my ingenuity. I made use of my innate criminal intelligence.

(EMMA *throws things onto the floor from* ELLA'S *pocket book as she searches through it.*)

WESLEY: What'd you do?

EMMA: I got out.

WESLEY: I know, but how?

EMMA: I made sexual overtures to the sergeant. That's how. Easy.

(*She takes a big wad of money out of pocket book and a set of car keys, then throws the bag away. She holds up the money.*)

EMMA: I'm going into crime. It's the only thing that pays these days.

WESLEY: (*looking at roll of bills in* EMMA'S *hand*) Where'd she get that?

EMMA: Where do you think?

WESLEY: You're taking her car?

EMMA: It's the perfect self-employment. Crime. No credentials. No diplomas. No overhead. No upkeep. Just straight profit. Right off the top.

WESLEY: How come I'm going backwards?

EMMA: (*moving in toward* WESLEY) Because you don't look ahead. That's why. You don't see the writing on the wall. You gotta learn how to read these things, Wes. It's deadly otherwise. You can't believe people when they look you in the eyes. You gotta' look behind them. See what they're standing in front of. What they're hiding. Everybody's hiding, Wes. Everybody. Nobody looks like what they are.

WESLEY: What are you?

EMMA: (*moving away*) I'm gone. I'm gone! Never to return.

(ELLA *suddenly wakes up on the table. She sits up straight.*)

ELLA: (*as though waking from a bad dream*) EMMA!!

(EMMA *looks at her, then runs off stage left.* ELLA *sits there on table staring in horror at* WESLEY. *She doesn't recognize him.*)

ELLA: (*to* WESLEY) Weston! Was that Emma?

WESLEY: It's me, Mom.

ELLA: (*yelling off stage but still on table*) EMMA!! (*she jumps off table and looks for a coat*) We've got to catch her! She can't run off like that! That horse will kill her! Where's my coat? (*to* WESLEY) WHERE'S MY COAT?

WESLEY: You weren't wearing one.

ELLA: (*to* WESLEY) Go catch her, Weston! She's your daughter! She's trying to run away!

WESLEY: Let her go.

ELLA: I can't let her go! I'm responsible!

(*Huge explosion off stage. Flash of light, then silence.* WESLEY *and* ELLA *just stand there staring.* EMERSON *enters from right, giggling. He's a small man in a suit.*)

EMERSON: Jeeezus! Did you ever hear a thing like that? What a wallop! Jeezus Christ! (*giggles*)

(WESLEY *and* ELLA *look at him.*)

EMERSON: Old Slater musta' packed it brim full. I never heard such a godalmighty bang in my whole career.

(SLATER, *his partner, enters from right, holding out the skinned lamb carcass. He's taller than* EMERSON, *also in a suit. They both giggle as though they'd pulled off a halloween stunt.*)

SLATER: Emerson, get a load a'this! (*giggling*) Did you see this thing? (*to* WESLEY) What is this, a skinned goat?
WESLEY: (*blank*) Lamb.
SLATER: Oh, it's a lamb! (*they laugh*) Looks like somebody's afterbirth to me! (*they laugh hysterically*)
WESLEY: What was that bang?

(*They stop laughing and look at* WESLEY. *They laugh again, then stop.*)

EMERSON: Bang? What bang?
WESLEY: That explosion.
EMERSON: Oh that! That was just a little reminder. A kind of a post-hypnotic suggestion. (*they laugh*)
ELLA: Who are these men, Weston?
EMERSON: (*to* WESLEY) Weston? You're Weston?
WESLEY: My father.
EMERSON: (*to* SLATER) Looks a little young, don't ya' think?
SLATER: (*dropping lamb carcass into fence enclosure*) Well, if she says he's Weston, he must be Weston.
ELLA: What are these men doing here? (*she moves away from them*)
EMERSON: (*to* WESLEY) So you're Weston? We had a different picture in mind. We had someone altogether different in mind.
WESLEY: What was it that blew up out there?
EMERSON: Something that wasn't paid for. Something past due.
SLATER: Long overdue.
WESLEY: The car. You blew up the car.
EMERSON: Bingo!

(*They crack up.* WESLEY *moves upstage and looks out as though trying to see outside.*)

ELLA: Get these men out of here, Weston! They're in my kitchen.
SLATER: (*looking around*) Some mess in here, boy. I couldn't live like this if you paid me.
EMERSON: Well, that's what comes from not paying your bills.

You let one thing slide; first thing you know you let everything slide. You let everything go downhill until you wind up
in a dungheap like this.

WESLEY: (*looking out, upstage*) There's a fire out there.

SLATER: It'll go out. It's just a gelignite-nitro mixture. Doesn't
burn for long. May leave a few scars on the lawn but nothin'
permanent.

WESLEY: (*without emotion, still looking out*) Nothing left of the car.

SLATER: That's right. Very thorough. The Irish developed it.
Beautiful stuff. Never know what hit ya'.

EMERSON: (*to* WESLEY) Well, we gotta' run, Weston. But you can
get the general drift. (*they start to leave;* EMERSON *stops*) Oh,
and if you see your old man, you might pass on the info. We
hate to keep repeating ourselves. The first time is great, but
after that it gets pretty boring.

SLATER: (*to* WESLEY) Don't forget to give that lamb some milk.
He looks pretty bad off.

(*They both laugh loudly, then exit.* ELLA *is facing downstage now,
staring at the lamb carcass in the pen.* WESLEY *has his back to her
upstage. He looks out. Pause.*)

ELLA: (*staring at dead lamb*) I must've slept right through the day.
How long did I sleep?

(*They stay in these positions facing away from each other.*)

WESLEY: Not so long.

ELLA: And Emma left. She really left on that horse. I didn't think
she'd do it. I had a dream she was leaving. That's what woke
me up.

WESLEY: She was right here in the kitchen.

ELLA: I must've slept right through it. (*pause, as she stares at lamb
carcass*) Oh! You know what, Wes?

WESLEY: What?

ELLA: Something just went right through me. Just from looking
at this lamb.

WESLEY: What?

ELLA: That story your father used to tell about that eagle. You
remember that?

WESLEY: Yeah.

ELLA: You remember the whole thing?

WESLEY: Yeah.

ELLA: I don't. I remember something about it. But it just went right through me.

WESLEY: Oh.

ELLA: (*after pause*) I remember he keeps coming back and swooping down on the shed roof and then flying off.

WESLEY: Yeah.

ELLA: What else?

WESLEY: I don't know.

ELLA: You remember. What happens next?

WESLEY: A cat comes.

ELLA: That's right. A big tom cat comes. Right out in the fields. And he jumps up on top of that roof to sniff around in all the entrails or whatever it was.

WESLEY: (*still with back to her*) And that eagle comes down and picks up the cat in his talons and carries him screaming off into the sky.

ELLA: (*staring at lamb*) That's right. And they fight. They fight like crazy in the middle of the sky. That cat's tearing his chest out, and the eagle's trying to drop him, but the cat won't let go because he knows if he falls he'll die.

WESLEY: And the eagle's being torn apart in midair. The eagle's trying to free himself from the cat, and the cat won't let go.

ELLA: And they come crashing down to the earth. Both of them come crashing down. Like one whole thing.

(*They stay like that with* WESLEY *looking off upstage, his back to* ELLA, *and* ELLA *downstage, looking at the lamb. Lights fade very slowly to black.*)

THE TOOTH OF CRIME

A play with music in two acts

The Tooth of Crime was first performed at the Open Space, London, on July 17, 1972. The cast was as follows:

HOSS	Malcolm Storry
BECKY LOU	Petronella Ford
STAR-MAN	Michael Weller
GALACTIC JACK	Tony Milner
REFEREE	
CHEYENNE	Tony Sibbalt
DOC	John Grillo
CROW	David Schofield

Directed by Charles Marowitz, assisted by Walter Donohue. Designed by Robin Don. Music composed by Sam Shepard, and arranged and played by Blunderpuss.

ACT ONE

SCENE: *A bare stage except for an evil-looking black chair with silver studs and a very high back, something like an Egyptian Pharaoh's throne but simple, centre stage. In the dark, heavy lurking Rock and Roll starts low and builds as the lights come up. The band should be hidden. The sound should be like "Heroin" by the Velvet Underground. When the lights are up full,* HOSS *enters in black rocker gear with silver studs and black kid gloves. He holds a microphone. He should look like a mean Rip Torn but a little younger. He takes the stage and sings "The Way Things Are." The words of the song should be understood so the band has to back off on volume when he starts singing.*

"The Way Things Are"

HOSS: You may think every picture you see is a true history of
    the way things used to be or the way things are
While you're ridin' in your radio or walkin' through the late
    late show ain't it a drag to know you just don't know
you just don't know
So here's another illusion to add to your confusion
Of the way things are
Everybody's doin' time for everybody else's crime and
I can't swim for the waves in the ocean
All the heroes is dyin' like flies they say it's a sign a' the
    times
And everybody's walkin' asleep eyes open—eyes open

So here's another sleep-walkin' dream
A livin' talkin' show of the way things seem
I used to believe in rhythm and blues
Always wore my blue suede shoes
Now everything I do goes down in doubt

But sometimes in the blackest night I can see a little light
That's the only thing that keeps me rockin'—keeps me
   rockin'

So here's another fantasy
About the way things seem to be to me.

(*He finishes the song and throws down the microphone and yells off
stage.*)

Becky Lou!

(BECKY *comes on in black rock and roll gear. She's very tall and
blonde. She holds two black satchels, one in each hand. They should
look like old country-doctor bags.*)

BECKY: Ready just about.
HOSS: Let's have a look at the gear.

(BECKY *sets the bags down on the floor and opens them. She pulls out
a black velvet piece of cloth and lays it carefully on the floor then
begins to take out pearl-handled revolvers, pistols, derringers and
rifles with scopes, shotguns broken down. All the weapons should
look really beautiful and clean. She sets them carefully on the velvet
cloth.* HOSS *picks up the rifles and handles them like a pro, cocking
them and looking down the barrel through the scope, checking out the
chambers on the pistols and running his hands over them as though
they were alive.*)

How's the Maserati?
BECKY: Clean. Greased like a bullet. Cheyenne took it up to 180
   on the Ventura Freeway then backed her right down. Said
   she didn't bark once.
HOSS: Good. About time he stopped them quarter-mile orgasms.
   They were rippin' her up. Gotta let the gas flow in a machine
   like that. She's Italian. Likes a full-tilt feel.
BECKY: Cheyenne's hungry for long distance now. Couldn't hold
   him back with nails. Got lead in his gas foot.
HOSS: These look nice and blue. Did the Jeweler check 'em out?
BECKY: Yeah, Hoss. Everything's taken care of.
HOSS: Good. Now we can boogie.
BECKY: What's the moon chart say?
HOSS: Don't ask me! I hired a fucking star-man. A gazer. What
   the fuck's he been doin' up there.

BECKY: I don't know. Last I knew it was the next first quarter moon. That's when he said things'd be right.

HOSS: Get that fucker down here! I wanna see him. I gave him thirteen grand to get this chart in line. Tell him to get his ass down here!

BECKY: O.K., O.K.

(*She exits,* HOSS *caresses the guns.*)

HOSS: That fuckin' Scorpion's gonna crawl if this gets turned around now. Now is right. I can feel it's right. I need the points! Can't they see that! I'm winning in three fucking States! I'm controlling more borders than any a' them punk Markers. The El Camino Boys. Bunch a' fuckin' punks. GET THAT FUCKER DOWN HERE!!!

(STAR-MAN *enters with* BECKY. *He's dressed in silver but shouldn't look like Star Trek, more contemporary silver.*)

O.K., slick face, what's the scoop. Can we move now?

STAR-MAN: Pretty risky, Hoss.

HOSS: I knew it! I knew it! You fuckin' creep! Every time we get hot to trot you throw on the ice water. Whatsa matter now.

STAR-MAN: Venus is entering Scorpio.

HOSS: I don't give a shit if it's entering Brigitte Bardot. I'm ready for a kill!

STAR-MAN: You'll blow it.

HOSS: I'll blow it. What do you know. I've always moved on a sixth sense. I don't need you, meatball.

BECKY: Hoss, you never went against the charts before.

HOSS: Fuck before. This time I feel it. I can smell blood. It's right. The time is right! I'm fallin' behind. Maybe you don't understand that.

STAR-MAN: Not true, Hoss. The El Caminos are about six points off the pace. Mojo Root Force is the only one close enough to even worry about.

HOSS: Mojo? That fruit? What'd he knock over?

STAR-MAN: Vegas, Hoss. He rolled the big one.

HOSS: Vegas! He can't take Vegas, that's my mark! That's against the code!

STAR-MAN: He took it.

HOSS: I don't believe it.

BECKY: We picked it up on the bleeper.

HOSS: When? How come I'm the last to find out?

STAR-MAN: We thought it'd rattle you too much.

HOSS: When did it happen!

STAR-MAN: This morning from what the teleprompters read.

HOSS: I'm gonna get that chump. I'm gonna have him. He can't do that. He knew Vegas was on my ticket. He's trying to shake me. He thinks I'll just jump borders and try suburban shots. Well he's fuckin' crazy. I'm gonna roll him good.

BECKY: You can't go against the code, Hoss. Once a Marker strikes and sets up colors, that's his turf. You can't strike claimed turf. They'll throw you out of the game.

HOSS: *He* did it! He took my mark. It was on my ticket, goddamnit!

STAR-MAN: He can just claim his wave system blew and he didn't find out till too late.

HOSS: Well he's gonna find out now. I'll get a fleet together and wipe him out.

BECKY: But, Hoss, you'll be forced to change class. You won't have solo rights no more. You'll be a gang man. A punk.

HOSS: I don't care. I want that fuckin' gold record and nobody's gonna stop me. Nobody!

STAR-MAN: You gotta hold steady, Hoss. This is a tender time. The wrong move'll throw you back a year or more. You can't afford that now. The charts are moving too fast. Every week there's a new star. You don't wanna be a fly-by-night mug in the crowd. You want something durable, something lasting. How're you gonna cop an immortal shot if you give up soloing and go into a gang war. They'll rip you up in a night. Sure you'll have a few moments of global glow, maybe even an interplanetary flash. But it won't last, Hoss, it won't last.

BECKY: He's right, Hoss.

HOSS: O.K., O.K. I'm just gettin' hungry that's all. I need a kill. I haven't had a kill for months now. You know what that's like. I gotta kill. It's my whole life. If I don't kill I get crazy. I start eating away at myself. It's not good. I was born to kill.

STAR-MAN: Nobody knows that better than us, Hoss. But you gotta listen to management. That's what we're here for. To advise and direct. Without us you'd be just like a mad dog again. Can't you remember what that was like.

HOSS: Yeah, yeah! Go away now. Go on! I wanna be alone with Becky.

STAR-MAN: O.K. Just try and take it easy. I know you were wired for a big kill but your time is coming. Don't forget that.

HOSS: Yeah, all right. Beat it!

(STAR-MAN *exits leaving* HOSS *alone with* BECKY. *He looks around the stage dejected. He kicks at the guns and pulls off his gloves.*)

I'm too old fashioned. That's it. Gotta kick out the scruples. Go against the code. That's what they used to do. The big ones. Dylan, Jagger, Townsend. All them cats broke codes. Time can't change that.

BECKY: But they were playin' pussy, Hoss. They weren't killers . . . You're a killer, man. You're in the big time.

HOSS: So were they. My Pa told me what it was like. They were killers in their day too. Cold killers.

BECKY: Come on. You're talkin' treason against the game. You could get the slammer for less than that.

HOSS: Fuck 'em. I know my power. I can go on Gypsy Kill and still gain status. There's a whole underground movement going on. There's a lot of Gypsy Markers comin' up.

BECKY: Why do you wanna throw everything away. You were always suicidal like that. Right from the start.

HOSS: It's part of my nature.

BECKY: That's what we saved you from, your nature. Maybe you forgot that. When we first landed you, you were a complete beast of nature. A sideways killer. Then we molded and shaped you and sharpened you down to perfection because we saw in you a true genius killer. A killer to end them all. A killer's killer.

HOSS: Aw fuck off. I don't believe that shit no more. That stuff is for schoolies. Sure I'm good. I might even be great but I ain't no genius. Genius is something outside the game. The game can't contain a true genius. It's too small. The next genius is gonna be a Gypsy Killer. I can feel it. I know it's goin' down right now. We don't have the whole picture. We're too successful . . . We're insulated from what's really happening by our own fame.

BECKY: You're really trying to self-destruct aren't you? Whatsa matter, you can't take fame no more? You can't hold down the pressure circuits? Maybe you need a good lay or two.

HOSS: Your ass. I can handle the image like a fuckin' jockey. It's just that I don't trust the race no more. I dropped the blinkers.

BECKY: You're not gettin' buck fever are ya'?

HOSS: Get outa' here!

BECKY: Come on. Put it in fourth for a while, Hoss. Cruise it. You can afford to take it easy.

HOSS: GET THE FUCK OUTA' HERE!!!

BECKY: O.K., O.K. I'm your friend. Remember?

HOSS: Yeah, sure.

BECKY: I am. You're in a tough racket. The toughest. But now ain't the time to crack. You're knockin' at the door, Hoss. You gotta hold on. Once you get the gold then you can back off. But not now.

HOSS: I'm not backin' off. I'm just havin' a doubt dose.

BECKY: Maybe I should call a D.J. One a' the big ones. Then you could sit down with him and he could lay the charts out right in front of you. Show you exactly where you stand.

HOSS: That's a good idea. Good. Go get one. Get Galactic Jack and his Railroad Track. Tell him to bring his latest charts. Go on!

BECKY: O.K. I'll be back.

(*She exits.* HOSS *stalks around the stage building up his confidence.*)

HOSS: She's right! She's right goddamnit! I'm so fucking close. Knockin' at the door. I can't chicken out of it now. This is my last chance. I'm gettin' old. I can't do a Lee Marvin in the late sixties. I can't pull that number off. I've stomped too many heads. I'm past shitkicker class now. Past the rumble. I'm in the big time. Really big. It's now or never. Come on, Hoss, be a killer, man. Be a killer!

(*Music starts. He sings "Cold Killer."*)

"Cold Killer"
I'm a cold killer Mama—I got blood on my jeans
I got a Scorpion star hangin' over me
I got snakes in my pockets and a razor in my boot
You better watch it don't get you—It's faster'n you can
    shoot
I got the fastest action in East L.A.

I got the fastest action in San Berdoo
And if you don't believe it lemme shoot it to you

Now watch me slide into power glide—supercharged down
    the line
There ain't no way for you to hide from the killer's eye
My silver studs, my black kid gloves make you cry inside
But there ain't no way for you to hide from the killer's eye

I'm a cold killer Mama—and I've earned my tattoo
I got a Pachooko cross hangin' over you
I got whiplash magic and a rattlesnake tongue
My John the Conqueroot says I'm the cold gun

Now watch me slide into power glide supercharged down
    the line
There ain't no way for you to hide from the killer's eye
My silver studs, my black kid gloves make you cry inside
But there ain't no way for you to hide from the killer's eye.

(*The song ends.* BECKY *enters with* GALACTIC JACK *the disc jockey.
He's white and dressed like a 42nd Street pimp, pink shirt, black
tie, black patent leather shoes, white panama straw hat and a flash
suit. He talks like Wolfman Jack and carries a bundle of huge
charts.*)

Ah! The man. Galactic Jack and his Railroad Track.

GALACTIC JACK: That's me, Jim. Heavy duty and on the whim.
    Back flappin', side trackin', finger poppin', reelin' rockin'
    with the tips on the picks in the g at killer race. All tricks,
    no sale, no avail. It's in the can and on the lam. Grease it,
    daddyo!

(*He holds out his hand palm up for* HOSS *to give him five.* HOSS
holds back.)

HOSS: Back down, Jack. Just give it to me straight. Am I risin' or
    fallin'.

GALACTIC JACK: A shootin' star, baby. High flyin' and no jivin'.
    You is off to number nine.

HOSS: Show me what you got. Just lay it out on the floor.

BECKY: Shall I get ya'll some drinks?

HOSS: Yeah. Tequila Gold. What do you take, Jack?

GALACTIC JACK: Not me, baby. I'm runnin' reds all down the
    spine. Feelin' fine and mixin's a crime.

BECKY: Right.

(*She exits.* JACK *lays his chart on the floor.* HOSS *and* JACK *crouch down to get a close inspection.*)

GALACTIC JACK: O.K. Here's the stand on the national band. The game's clean now. Solo is the word. Gang war is takin' a back seat. The Low Riders are outa' the picture and you is in, Jim. In like a stone winner.

HOSS: Don't type it up, Jack. Just show me how it's movin'. I was ready to take Nevada clean and that meathead Mojo Root Force rolled Vegas.

GALACTIC JACK: Yeah I heard that. Supposed to be on your ticket too. Bad news.

HOSS: He can't get away with that can he?

GALACTIC JACK: I can't dope them sheets, Hoss. You'll have to consult a Ref for the rules or go straight to the Keepers.

HOSS: I can't go to the game Keepers. They'll ask for an itinerary and question past kills. I can't afford a penalty now. I need every point.

GALACTIC JACK: Well lookee here. There's movement all around but no numero uno. That's what they're backin' their chips on you for, boy. The bookies got you two to one.

HOSS: That close?

GALACTIC JACK: All of 'em runnin' it down to you. There's Little Willard from the East in his formula Lotus. Fast machine. Doin' O.K. with a stainless steel Baretta.

HOSS: Willard's solo now?

GALACTIC JACK: Yeah but no threat. Just a front runner. Lots a' early speed but can't go the distance. Here's one outa Tupalo called Studie Willcock. Drivin' a hot Merc, dual cams, Chrysler through and through. Fast but not deadly. He's offered four in a week and almost had Arkansas wrapped up but he's fadin' fast. You're it, Jim. You is the coldest on the circuit.

HOSS: What about this mark? (*pointing at the charts*)

GALACTIC JACK: Oh yeah, that's Grease Jam. Got a supercharged Mini Cooper. Takes the corners. Tried a hit on St. Paul and almost had Minnesota to its knees when he blew a head gasket. Some say he's even been offed by the El Caminos.

HOSS: Those guys are pressin' it pretty hard. They're gonna get blown off sooner or later.

GALACTIC JACK: No doubt. No need to pout. The course is clear.

Maybe a few Gypsy Killers comin' into the picture but nothin' to fret your set.

HOSS: Gypsies? Where? I knew it. I got a feeling.

GALACTIC JACK: Just some side bets. They go anonymous 'cause a' the code. One slip and they is pissed. You can dig it. They's playin' with the king fire.

HOSS: But they got a following right? They're growing in the poles?

GALACTIC JACK: Hard to suss it yet, man. Some poles don't even mention their kills for fear of the Keepers comin' down on 'em. I could maybe sound some flies for ya'. See if I could whiff some sniff on that action.

HOSS: Yeah, do.

GALACTIC JACK: What's the keen to the Gypsy scene. These boys are losin' to the cruisin' baby.

HOSS: They've got time on their side. Can't you see that. The youth's goin' to 'em. The kids are flocking to Gypsy Kills. It's a market opening up, Jack. I got a feeling. I know they're on their way in and we're going out. We're gettin' old, Jack.

GALACTIC JACK: You just got the buggered blues, man. You been talkin' to the wrong visions. You gotta get a head set. Put yer ears on straight. Zoot yerself down, boy. These Gypsies is committin' suicide. We got the power. We got the game. If the Keepers whimsy it all they do is scratch 'em out. Simple. They're losers, man. The bookies don't even look past their left shoulder at a Gypsy Mark. They won't last, man. Believe me.

HOSS: I don't know. There's power there. Full blown.

GALACTIC JACK: They don't know the ropes, man. Rules is out. They're into slaughter straight off. Not a clean kill in the bunch.

HOSS: But they got balls. They're on their own.

GALACTIC JACK: So are you. Solo's the payolo.

HOSS: But I'm inside and they're out. They could unseat us all.

GALACTIC JACK: Not a King. The crown sticks where it fits and right now it looks about your size.

HOSS: What if they turned the game against us. What if they started marking us!

GALACTIC JACK: That's revolution, man.

HOSS: You hit it.

GALACTIC JACK: Old time shuffle. Don't stand a chance at this dance.

HOSS: But that's how we started ain't it. We went up against the Dudes. Wiped 'em out.

GALACTIC JACK: The Dudes weren't pros, man. You gotta see where you stand. I do believe you is tastin' fear. Runnin' scared. These Gypsies is just muckrakers. Second hand, one night stand. They ain't worth shit on shinola in your league. Dig yourself on the flip side. You're number one with a bullet and you ain't even got the needle in the groove.

HOSS: We'll see. Somethin's goin' down big out there. The shit's gonna hit the fan before we can get to the bank.

GALACTIC JACK: Take a deep knee bend, Hoss. It's just the pre-victory shakes. Tomorrow you'll have the gold in your hand. The bigee. Don't be shy, I tell no lie. Catch ya' on the re-bop. Say bye and keep the slide greased down.

HOSS: Yeah. Thanks.

(JACK *collects his charts and exits.* HOSS *paces and talks to himself.*)

(*to himself*) Come on, come on. Confidence, man. Confidence. Don't go on the skids now. Keep it together. Tighten down. Talk it out. Quit jumpin' at shadows. They got you goose bumped and they ain't even present. Put yourself in their place. They got nothin'. You got it all. All the chips. Come on dice! Come on dice! That's it. Roll 'em sweet. The sweet machine. Candy in the gas tank. Floor it. Now you got the wheel. Take it. Take it!

(BECKY *enters with the drink.* HOSS *catches himself.*)

BECKY: What happened to Jack?

HOSS: We ran the session.

BECKY: Here's your drink.

HOSS: Thanks. Listen, Becky, is Cheyenne ready to roll?

BECKY: Yeah. He's hot. Why?

HOSS: Maybe we could just do a cruise. No action. Just some scouting. I'm really feelin' cooped up in here. This place is drivin' me nuts.

BECKY: Too dangerous, Hoss. We just got word that Eyes sussed somebody's marked you.

HOSS: What! Marked *me*? Who?

BECKY: One a' the Gypsies.

HOSS: It's all comin' down like I said. I must be top gun then.

BECKY: That's it.

HOSS: They gotta be fools, man. A Gypsy's marked *me*?

BECKY: That's the word from Eyes.

HOSS: Where is he?

BECKY: Vegas.

HOSS: Vegas? Oh now I get it. Mojo. He's hired a Gypsy to off me clean. That's it. That fuckin' chicken shit. I'm gonna blast him good. Doesn't have the balls to come down to me. Gotta hire a Gypsy.

BECKY: Might be just a renegade solo, Hoss. They're all lookin' to put you under. You're the main trigger. The word's out.

HOSS: Don't you get it? The Root Force is slip-streamin' my time. Takin' my marks and hirin' amateurs to rub me out. It's a gang shot. They're workin' doubles. I gotta team up now. It's down to that. I gotta get ahold a' Little Willard. Get him on the line.

BECKY: Hoss, don't fly off, man. You're safe here.

HOSS: Safe! Safe and amputated from the neck down! I'm a Marker man, not a desk clerk. Get fucking Willard to the phone! And tell Cheyenne to come in here!

(BECKY *exits*)

O.K. Now the picture brightens. I can play for high stakes now. I can draw to the straight, outside or in. I'm ready to take on any a' these flash heads. Vegas is mine, man. It belongs in my pocket. The West is mine. I could even take on the Keepers. That's it. I'll live outside the fucking law altogether. Outside the whole shot. That's it. Why didn't I think a' that before!

(CHEYENNE *enters in green velvet with silver boots and racing gloves.*)

CHEYENNE: You want me, Hoss?

HOSS: Yeah! Yeah I want you! You're my main man.

(*He gives* CHEYENNE *a bear hug.*)

Listen, Cheyenne, we done a lotta' marks in our time. Right?

CHEYENNE: Yeah.

HOSS: Good clean kills. Honest kills. But now the times are changin'. The race is deadly. Mojo Root Force is movin' in on turf marks and tryin' to put me out with a Gypsy.

CHEYENNE: A Gypsy?

HOSS: Yeah.

CHEYENNE: They can't do that. It's against the code.

HOSS: Fuck the code. Nobody's playin' by the rules no more. We been suckers to the code for too long now. Now we move outside. You remember Little Willard?

CHEYENNE: East Coast. Drove a Galaxie. Into Remington over and unders.

HOSS: Yeah. He's changed his style now. Got himself a Lotus Formula 2 and a Baretta.

CHEYENNE: Sounds mean.

HOSS: He is, man. And I trust him. He was right with me when we took off the Dudes. Becky's on the phone to him now. He's our man. Just him and us.

CHEYENNE: But Root Force has probably got Vegas locked up, Hoss. It's gonna be hard penetration.

HOSS: We rolled Phoenix didn't we?

CHEYENNE: Yeah.

HOSS: Tucson?

CHEYENNE: Yeah.

HOSS: San Berdoo?

CHEYENNE: Yeah.

HOSS: So Vegas ain't no Fort Knox.

CHEYENNE: So it's back to the rumble?

HOSS: Temporary. Just temporary. We can't sit back and let the good times roll when the game's breakin' down.

CHEYENNE: I don't know. I love the game, Hoss. I ain't hot to go back to gang war.

HOSS: We got to now! Otherwise we're down the tubes.

CHEYENNE: What about the Keepers?

HOSS: Fuck them too. We'll take 'em all on.

CHEYENNE: The critics won't like it.

HOSS: The critics! They're outside, man. They don't know what's goin' on.

CHEYENNE: What about our reputation. We worked hard to get where we are. I'm not ready to throw that away. I want a taste a' that gold.

HOSS: I'm surrounded by assholes! Can't you see what's happened to us. We ain't Markers no more. We ain't even Rockers. We're punk chumps cowering under the Keepers and the Refs and the critics and the public eye. We ain't free no more! Goddamnit! We ain't flyin' in the eye of contempt. We've become respectable and safe. Soft, mushy chewable ass lickers. What's happened to our killer heart. What's happened to our blind fucking courage! Cheyenne, we ain't got much time, man. We were warriors once.

CHEYENNE: That was a long time ago.

HOSS: Then you're backing down?

CHEYENNE: No. I'm just playin' the game.

(CHEYENNE *exits*)

HOSS: God! Goddamnit! This is gettin' weird now. Solo ain't the word for it. It's gettin' lonely as an ocean in here. My driver's gone against me and my time's runnin' thin. Little Willard's my last chance. Him and me. He's runnin' without a driver, so can I. The two of us. Just the two of us. That's enough against the Root Force. He's East Coast though. Maybe he don't know the Western Ropes. He could learn it. We'll cruise the action. He'll pick up the streets. Cheyenne knows the West though. Born and raised like me. Backyard schoolin'. Goddamn! Why's he have to go soft now! Why now!

(BECKY *enters*)

You get Willard?

BECKY: No.

HOSS: How come! I need him bad. Keep tryin'!!

BECKY: He's dead, Hoss. Shot himself in the mouth.

HOSS: Who told you?

BECKY: His Rep. They just found him in New Haven slumped over an intersection. They say his car was still runnin'.

HOSS: Why'd he go and do that? He was in the top ten and risin'.

BECKY: Couldn't take it I guess. Too vulnerable. They found a pound of Meth in the back seat.

HOSS: Becky, I'm marked. What the fuck am I gonna do? I can't just sit here and wait for him to come.

BECKY: Least you'll know he's comin'. If you go out cruisin' he's liable to strike anywhere, any time. A Gypsy's got the jump on you that way.

HOSS: What if I busted into Vegas myself? Just me. They'd never expect somethin' like that. I could take off Mojo and split before they knew what happened.

BECKY: You're dealin' with a pack now, man. It ain't one against one no more.

HOSS: Well what am I gonna do!

BECKY: Wait him out. Meet him on a singles match and bounce him hard. Challenge him.

HOSS: What if he snipes me?

BECKY: We got the watch out. We'll give him the usher routine. Say that you've been expecting him. That'll challenge his pride. Then fight him with shivs.

HOSS: Shivs! I ain't used a blade for over ten years. I'm out of practice.

BECKY: Practice up. I'll get you a set and a dummy.

HOSS: O.K. And call in the Doc. I need a good shot.

BECKY: Good.

(*She exits.* HOSS *stalks the stage.*)

HOSS: Backed into a fucking box. I can't believe it. Things have changed that much. They don't even apprentice no more. Just mark for the big one. No respect no more. When I was that age I'd sell my leathers to get a crack at a good teacher. I would. And I had some a' the best. There's no sense of tradition in the game no more. There's no game. It's just back to how it was. Rolling night clubs, strip joints. Bustin' up poker games. Zip guns in the junk yard. Rock fights, dirt clods, bustin' windows. Vandals, juvies, West Side Story. Can't they see where they're goin'! Without a code it's just crime. No art involved. No technique, finesse. No sense of mastery. The touch is gone.

(BECKY *enters with* DOC *who is dressed in red*. BECKY *has two knives and a dummy which she sets up centre stage right*. HOSS *sits in his chair*. DOC *has a syringe and a vial of dope and a rubber surgical hose*. HOSS *rolls his sleeve up and* DOC *goes about shooting him up*.)

Oh, Doc, it's good to see ya'. I'm in need. I'm under the gun, Doc.

DOC: Yeah. Things are tough now. This'll cool you out.

HOSS: Good. Doc, what do you think about Gypsy Kills. Do you think it's ethical?

DOC: Haven't thought too much about it actually. I suppose it was bound to happen. Once I remember this early Gypsy. I guess you'd call him a Gypsy now but at the time he was just a hard luck fella name a' Doc Carter. Little got to be known of the man on account a' the fact that he was ridin' a certain William F. Cody's shirttail all through the West, and, for that matter, half around the planet. Anyhow, ole Doc came to be known as the "Spirit Gun of the West" and a well-deserved title it was, too. That boy could shoot the hump off a buffalo on the backside of a nickel at a hundred paces. To this very day his saddle is settin' in some musty ole Wyoming museum decorated with a hundred silver coins. Each one shot through and through with his Colt .45. And all surroundin' this saddle is pictures tall as a man of this William F. Cody fella pallin' it up with the Indians. Ole Doc never got out from behind the shadow a' that Cody. But I suppose nowadays he'd just take over the whole show. Don't rightly know what made me think a' that. Just popped into my mind.

HOSS: Yeah. It's just funny finding myself on the other side.

BECKY: It ain't revolution, man. This Gypsy's a hired trigger from Mojo. He ain't a martyr.

HOSS: But he works outside the code.

BECKY: Fuck it. All you gotta worry about is gettin' him before he gets you.

HOSS: You were one of the ones who taught me the code. Now you can throw it away like that.

BECKY: It's back down to survival, Hoss. Temporary suspension. That's all.

HOSS: I don't think so. I think the whole system's gettin' shot to shit. I think the code's going down the tubes. These are gonna be the last days of honor. I can see it comin'.

DOC: There. That oughta' do you for a while.

HOSS: Thanks, Doc.

DOC: If you need any crystal later just call me down.

HOSS: Thanks, man.

(DOC *exits*)

BECKY: You wanna try these out?

(*She offers the knives to* HOSS. *He goes limp and relaxed in the chair.*)

HOSS: Not now. Just come and sit with me for a while.

(BECKY *sits at his feet. He strokes her hair.*)

Becky?

BECKY: Yeah?

HOSS: You remember the El Monte Legion Stadium?

BECKY: Yeah?

HOSS: Ripple Wine?

BECKY: Yeah.

HOSS: The Coasters?

BECKY (*she sings a snatch*): "Take out the papers and the trash or you don't get no spendin' cash."

HOSS: (*sings*) "Just tell your hoodlum friend outside. You ain't got time to take a ride."

BECKY: "Yackety yack."

HOSS: "Don't talk back."

(*They laugh.* HOSS *stops himself.*)

Don't let me go too soft.

BECKY: Why not. You've earned it.

HOSS: Earned it? I ain't earned nothin'. Everything just happened. Just fell like cards. I never made a choice.

BECKY: But you're here now. A hero. All those losers out there barkin' at the moon.

HOSS: But where am I goin'? The future's just like the past.

BECKY: You gotta believe, Hoss.

HOSS: In what?

BECKY: Power. That's all there is. The power of the machine. The killer Machine. That's what you live and die for. That's what you wake up for. Every breath you take you breathe the power. You live the power. You are the power.

HOSS: Then why do I feel so weak!

BECKY: The knife's gotta be pulled out before you can stab again. The gun's gotta be cocked. The energy's gotta be stored. You're just gettin' a trickle charge now. The ignition's gotta turn yet.

HOSS: Yeah. It's just hard to wait.

BECKY: It's harder for movers. You're a mover, Hoss. Some people, all they do is wait.

HOSS: Maybe I should take a ramble.

BECKY: Where to?

HOSS: Anywhere. Just to get out for a while.

BECKY: You carry your gun wherever you go.

HOSS: Listen, maybe I should go on the lam.

BECKY: Are you crazy?

HOSS: No, I'm serious. I'm gettin' too old for this. I need some peace.

BECKY: Do you know what it's like out there, outside the game? You wouldn't recognize it.

HOSS: What about New York? Second Avenue.

BECKY: What Second Avenue? There ain't no Second Avenue. They're all zoned out. You wouldn't stand a snowball's chance in hell of makin' it outside the game. You're too professional. It'd be like keepin' a wild animal as a pet then turnin' him back loose again. You couldn't cope, Hoss.

HOSS: I did it once. I was good on the streets. I was a true hustler.

BECKY: The streets are controlled by the packs. They got it locked up. The packs are controlled by the gangs. The gangs and the Low Riders. They're controlled by cross syndicates. The next step is the Keepers.

HOSS: What about the country. Ain't there any farmers left, ranchers, cowboys, open space? Nobody just livin' their life.

BECKY: You ain't playin' with a full deck, Hoss. All that's gone. That's old time boogie. The only way to be an individual is in the game. You're it. You're on top. You're free.

HOSS: What free! How free! I'm tearin' myself inside out from this fuckin' sport. That's free? That's being alive? Fuck it. I just wanna have some fun. I wanna be a fuck off again. I don't wanna compete no more.

BECKY: And what about the kill? You don't need that?

HOSS: I don't know, maybe not. Maybe I could live without it.

BECKY: You're talkin' loser now, baby.

HOSS: Maybe so. Maybe I am a loser. Maybe we're all fuckin' losers. I don't care no more.

BECKY: What about the gold record. You don't need that?

HOSS: I don't know! I just wanna back off for a while. I can't think straight. I need a change. A vacation or something.

BECKY: Maybe so. I heard about a place, an island where they don't play the game. Everybody's on downers all day.

HOSS: That sounds good. What about that. Maybe you could find out for me. All I need is a week or two. Just to rest and think things out.

BECKY: I'll see what I can do.

HOSS: Jesus. How'd I get like this?

BECKY: It'll pass.

HOSS: Sing me a song or somethin', would ya? Somethin' to cool me off.

BECKY: O.K.

(*She sings*)

"Becky's Song"
Lemme take you for a ride down the road
Lean back in the tuck and roll
The radio's broken and I got no beer
But I can ease your load

> Listen to the song that the V-8 sings
> Watch the rhythm of the line
> Isn't it some magic that the night-time brings
> Ain't the highway fine

Tell me where ya' wanna go just take yer pick
All I'm really doin' is cruisin'
Take ya' down to Baton Rouge—New Orleans
Pick us up a Louisiana trick

> Listen to the song that the V-8 sings
> Watch the rhythm of the line
> Isn't it some magic that the night-time brings
> Ain't the highway fine

You could tell me stories of your yesterdays
I could break out a few a' mine
Roll down the window and kiss the wind
Anyway ya' want to ease the time

> Listen to the song that the V-8 sings
> Watch the rhythm of the line
> Isn't it some magic that the night-time brings
> Ain't the highway fine

(*The song ends and* CHEYENNE *enters.*)

CHEYENNE: Say, Hoss. We just got tapped that the Gypsy's made it through zone five. He's headed this way.

HOSS: Already? What's he drivin'?

CHEYENNE: You won't believe this. A '58 black Impala, fuel injected, bored and stroked, full blown Vet underneath.

HOSS: I'm gonna like this dude. O.K. let him through.

CHEYENNE: All the way?

HOSS: Yeah. Stop him at the mote and sound him on a shiv duel.

CHEYENNE: Shivs? You ain't in shape for blades, Hoss.

HOSS: I can handle it. Walk on.

CHEYENNE: O.K. (*he exits*)

BECKY: Good. He's finally comin'. This'll get ya' back on your feet, Hoss. Your waitin' time is over.

HOSS: Go tell the Doc I want some snow.

BECKY: You want the fit or snort?

HOSS: Snort. Hurry up.

BECKY: Right.

(BECKY *exits*. HOSS *picks up the knives and stalks the dummy. He circles it and talks to the dummy and himself. As he talks he stabs the dummy with sudden violent lunges then backs away again. Blood pours from the dummy onto the floor.*)

HOSS: O.K. Gypsy King, where's your true heart. Let's get down now. Let's get down. You talk a good story. You got the true flash but where's yer heart. That's the whole secret. The heart of a Gypsy must be there!

(*He stabs at the heart of the dummy then backs off.*)

Maybe not. Maybe yer colder than that. Maybe in the neck. Maybe it pumps from the neck down. Maybe there!

(*He stabs at the neck then backs off. Blood gushes out.*)

All right. All right. A secret's a secret. I can give you that much. But it comes from this end too. I'm your mystery. Figure me. Run me down to your experience. Go ahead. Make a move. Put me in a place. An inch is fatal. Just an inch. The wrong move'll leave you murdered. Come on. Lemme see it. Where's the action? That's not good enough for the back lot even. Here's one!

(*He makes a quick move and stabs the dummy in the stomach.*)

Now I get it. There ain't no heart to a Gypsy. Just bone. Just blind raging courage. Well that won't do you, boy. That won't take you the full length. Yer up against a pro, kid. A true champion Marker. Yer outclassed before the bell rings.

Now you've stepped across the line, boy. No goin' back.
Dead on yer feet. (*to himself*) What am I gettin' so wired
about? This kid is a punk. It ain't even a contest. He's still
ridin' in the fifties. Beach Boys behind the eyeballs. A blonde
boy. A fair head. Gang bangs, cheap wine and bonfires. I
could take him in my sleep. I could. I could—

(BECKY *enters with* DOC. DOC *has a large sheet of foil with mounds of
cocaine on it. He sets it down on the chair.*)

BECKY: How's it goin'?
HOSS: Something's lacking. I can't seem to get it up like the
other kills. My heart's not in it.
DOC: Have some a' this.

(*He holds out a rolled up hundred dollar bill.* HOSS *takes it and goes
to the coke.*)

HOSS: Yeah. Maybe that'll help.

(*He takes the bill and snorts the coke as he talks.*)

You know, I been thinkin'. What if the neutral field state
failed. One time. Just once.
BECKY: Like this time for instance?
HOSS: Yeah. Like this time.
BECKY: Then you're a gonner.
DOC: It shouldn't fail, Hoss. You've been trained.
HOSS: I know, but what if an emotional field came through
stronger.
BECKY: Like love or hate?
HOSS: Not that gross, not that simple. Something subtle like the
sound of his voice or a gesture or his timing. Something like
that could throw me off.
BECKY: You're really worried about this Gypsy.
HOSS: Not worried. Intrigued. His style is copping my patterns.
I can feel it already and he's not even here yet. He's got a
presence. Maybe even star quality. His movements have an
aura. Even his short. I mean nobody rides a '58 Impala to do
battle with a star Marker.
BECKY: He's just a fool.
DOC: You gotta stay disengaged, Hoss. The other way is fatal.
HOSS: Maybe not. Maybe there's an opening. A ground wire.
BECKY: For what. He's come to knock you over, man.

HOSS: O.K. but I can play in his key. Find his tuning. Jam a little before the big kill. I don't have to off him soon's he walks in the door.

DOC: You'd be better off. He's probably got eyes to work that on you.

HOSS: I don't think so. He's got more class than that. I can feel him coming. We might even be in the same stream. He's got respect.

BECKY: Respect! He's a killer, man.

HOSS: So am I. There's another code in focus here. An outside code. Once I knew this cat in High School who was a Creole. His name was Moose. He was real light skinned and big, curly blond hair, blue eyes. He could pass easy as a jock. Good musician. Tough in football but kinda dumb. Dumb in that way—that people put you down for in High School. Dumb in class. He passed as white until his sister started hangin' around with the black chicks. Then the white kids figured it out. He was black to them even though he looked white. He was a nigger, a coon, a jungle bunny. A Rock Town boy from that day on. We ran together, Moose and me and another cat from Canada who dressed and wore his hair like Elvis. They put him down too because he was too smart. His name was Cruise and he got straight A's without readin' none a' the books. Slept in a garage with his aunt. Built himself a cot right over an old Studebaker. His mother was killed by his father who drove skidders for a lumber company up near Vancouver. Got drunk and busted her in the head with a tire iron. The three of us had a brotherhood, a trust. Something unspoken. Then one day it came to the test. I was sorta' ridin' between 'em. I'd shift my personality from one to the other but they dug me 'cause I'd go crazy drunk all the time. We all went out to Bob's Big Boy in Pasadena to cruise the chicks and this time we got spotted by some jocks from our High School. Our own High School. There were eight of 'em, all crew cut and hot for blood. This was the old days ya' know. So they started in on Cruise 'cause he was the skinniest. Smackin' him around and pushin' him into the car. We was right in the parking lot there. Moose told 'em to ease off but they kept it up. They were really out to choose Moose. He was their mark. They wanted him bad. Girls and dates started gathering around until we was right in the center of a

huge crowd a' kids. Then I saw it. This was a class war.
These were rich white kids from Arcadia who got T-birds
and deuce coups for Xmas from Mommy and Daddy. All
them cardigan sweaters and chicks with ponytails and pedal
pushers and bubble hairdo's. Soon as I saw that I flipped out.
I found my strength. I started kickin'shit, man. Hard and
fast. Three of 'em went down screamin' and holdin' their
balls. Moose and Cruise went right into action. It was like
John Wayne, Robert Mitchum and Kirk Douglas all in one
movie. Those chumps must a' swung on us three times and
that was all she wrote. We had all eight of 'em bleedin' and
cryin' for Ma right there in the parking lot at Bob's Big Boy.
I'll never forget that. The courage we had. The look in all
them rich kids' faces. The way they stepped aside just like
they did for "Big John." The three of us had a silent pride.
We just walked strong, straight into that fuckin' burger palace
and ordered three cherry cokes with lemon and a order a'
fries.

DOC: Those were the old days.

HOSS: Yeah. Look at me now. Impotent. Can't strike a kill
unless the charts are right. Stuck in my image. Stuck in a
mansion. Waiting. Waiting for a kid who's probably just like
me. Just like I was then. A young blood. And I gotta off him.
I gotta roll him or he'll roll me. We're fightin' ourselves. Just
like turnin' the blade on ourselves. Suicide, man. Maybe
Little Willard was right. Blow your fuckin' brains out. The
whole thing's a joke. Stick a gun in your fuckin' mouth and
pull the trigger. That's what it's all about. That's what we're
doin'. He's my brother and I gotta kill him. He's gotta kill
me. Jimmy Dean was right. Drive the fuckin' Spider till it
stings ya' to death. Crack up your soul! Jackson Pollock!
Duane Allman! Break it open! Pull the trigger! Trigger me!
Trigger you! Drive it off the cliff! It's all an open highway.
Long and clean and deadly beautiful. Deadly and lonesome
as a jukebox.

DOC: Come on, Becky, let's leave him alone.

HOSS: Yeah. Right. Alone. That's me. Alone. That's us. All
fucking alone. All of us. So don't go off in your private rooms
with pity in mind. Your day is comin'. The mark'll come
down to you one way or the other.

BECKY: You better rest, Hoss.

HOSS: Ya' know, you'd be O.K., Becky, if you had a self. So would I. Something to fall back on in a moment of doubt or terror or even surprise. Nothin' surprises me no more. I'm ready to take it all on. The whole shot. The big one. Look at the Doc. A slave. An educated slave. Look at me. A trained slave. We're all so pathetic it's downright pathetic. And confidence is just a hype to keep away the open-ended shakes. Ain't that the truth, Doc?

DOC: I don't know.

HOSS: Right. Right. "I don't know" is exactly right. Now beat it, both of ya' before I rip your fuckin' teeth out a' yer heads!! GO ON BEAT IT!!!

(BECKY *and* DOC *exit.* HOSS *sits in his chair and stares out in front of him. He talks to himself, sometimes shifting voices from his own into an older man's.*)

(*old*) All right, Hoss, this is me talkin'. Yer old Dad. Yer old fishin' buddy. We used to catch eels side by side down by the dump. The full moon lit up the stream and the junk. The rusty chrome flashin' across the marsh. The fireflies dancin' like a faraway city. They'd swallow the hook all the way down. You remember that? (*himself*) Yeah. Sure. (*old*) O.K. You're not so bad off. It's good to change. Good to feel your blood pump. (*himself*) But where to? Where am I going? (*old*) It don't matter. The road's what counts. Just look at the road. Don't worry about where it's goin'. (*himself*) I feel so trapped. So fucking unsure. Everything's a mystery. I had it all in the palm of my hand. The gold, the silver. I knew. I was sure. How could it slip away like that? (*old*) It'll come back. (*himself*) But I'm not a true Marker no more. Not really. They're all countin' on me. The bookies, the agents, the Keepers. I'm a fucking industry. I even affect the stocks and bonds. (*old*) You're just a man, Hoss. Just a man. (*himself*) Yeah, maybe you're right. I'm just a man.

(CHEYENNE *enters.*)

CHEYENNE: Hoss. He's here.

(HOSS *stays seated, relaxed. He has an air of complete acceptance.*)

HOSS: Good. He's here. That's good. What's his name?

CHEYENNE: He calls himself Crow.

HOSS: Crow. That's a good name. Did you sound him on the duel?

CHEYENNE: Yeah. He's game. He looks tougher than I thought, Hoss.

HOSS: Tough. Tough? (*he laughs*) Good. A tough Crow.

CHEYENNE: What'll I tell him?

HOSS: Tell him I like his style. Tell him I'm very tired right now and I'm gonna cop some z's. He can take a swim, have a sauna and a massage, some drinks, watch a movie, have a girl, dope, whatever he wants. Tell him to relax. I'll see him when I come to.

CHEYENNE: O.K. You all right, Hoss?

HOSS: Yeah. Just tired. Just a little tired.

CHEYENNE: O.K.

HOSS: Thanks, man.

CHEYENNE: Sure.

(CHEYENNE *exits*. HOSS *stays seated looking out*.)

HOSS: Maybe the night'll roll in. A New Mexico night. All gold and red and blue. That would be nice. A long slow New Mexico night. Put that in your dream, Hoss, and sleep tight. Tomorrow you live or die.

ACT TWO

SCENE: *The stage is the same. The lights come up on* CROW. *He looks just like Keith Richard. He wears high-heeled green rock and roll boots, tight greasy blue jeans, a tight yellow t-shirt, a green velvet coat, a shark tooth earring, a silver swastika hanging from his neck and a black eye-patch covering the left eye. He holds a short piece of silver chain in his hand and twirls it constantly, tossing it from hand to hand. He chews a stick of gum with violent chomps. He exudes violent arrogance and cruises the stage with true contempt. Sometimes he stops to examine the guns on the floor, or check out the knives and the dummy. Finally he winds up sitting in* HOSS'S *chair. A pause as he chews gum at the audience.* HOSS *enters dressed the same as in Act One.* CROW *doesn't move or behave any different than when he was alone. They just stare at each other for a while.*

HOSS: My sleuth tells me you're drivin' a '58 Impala with a Vet underneath.

CROW: Razor, Leathers. Very razor.

HOSS: Did you rest up?

CROW: Got the molar chomps. Eyes stitched. You can vision what's sittin'. Very razor to cop z's sussin' me to be on the far end of the spectrum.

HOSS: It wasn't strategy man. I was really tired. You steal a lotta' energy from a distance.

CROW: No shrewd from this end either. We both bow to bigger fields.

HOSS: You wanna drink or somethin'?

CROW: (*he laughs with a cackle*) Lush in sun time gotta smell of lettuce or turn of the century. Sure Leathers, squeeze on the grape vine one time.

227

HOSS: White or red?
CROW: Blood.
HOSS: Be right back.
CROW: No slaves in this crib?
HOSS: They're all in the pool watchin' a movie.
CROW: Very Greek.
HOSS: Yeah. Just relax, I'll be right back.

(HOSS *exits.* CROW *gets up and walks around thinking out loud.*)

CROW: Very razor. Polished. A gleam to the movements. Weighs
out in the eighties from first to third. Keen on the left side
even though he's born on the right. Maybe forced his hand to
change. Butched some instincts down. Work them through
his high range. Cut at the gait. Heel-toe action rhythms of
New Orleans. Can't suss that particular. That's well covered.
Meshing patterns. Easy mistakes here. Suss the bounce.

(CROW *tries to copy* HOSS'S *walk. He goes back and forth across the
stage practising different styles until he gets the exact one. It's
important that he gets inside the feeling of* HOSS'S *walk and not just
the outer form.*)

Too heavy on the toe. Maybe work the shoulders down.
Here's a mode. Three-four cut time copped from Keith
Moon. Early. Very early. Now. Where's that pattern. Gotta
be in the "Happy Jack" album. Right around there. Triplets.
Six-eight. Here it comes. Battery. Double bass talk. Fresh
Cream influence. Where's that? Which track. Yeah. The old
Skip James tunes. Question there. Right there. (*sings it*) "I'm
so glad, I'm so glad, I'm glad, I'm glad, I'm glad." Yeah.
Ancient. Inborn. Has to be a surgery. Grind down.

(*He hears* HOSS *coming and darts back to the chair and sits as
though he'd never moved.* HOSS *enters with a bottle of red wine and
two glasses. He hands one to* CROW *and then he pours himself one
and sets the bottle down.*)

HOSS: Ya know I had a feeling you were comin' this way. A
sense. I was onto a Gypsy pattern early yesterday. Even
conjured going that way myself.
CROW: Cold, Leathers. Very icy. Back seat nights. Tuck and
roll pillow time. You got fur on the skin in this trunk.
HOSS: Yeah, yeah. I'm just gettin' bored I guess. I want out.

CROW: I pattern a conflict to that line. The animal says no. The blood won't go the route. Re-do me right or wrong?

HOSS: Right I guess. Can't you back the language up, man. I'm too old to follow the flash.

CROW: Choose an argot Leathers. Singles or LPs. 45, 78, 33⅓.

HOSS: I musta' misfed my data somehow. I thought you were raw, unschooled. Ya' know? I mean, maybe the training's changed since my time. Look, I wanna just sound you for a while before we get down to the cut. O.K.? You don't know how lonely it's been. I can talk to Cheyenne but we mostly reminisce on old kills. Ya' know. I don't get new information. I'm starving for new food. Ya' know? That don't mean I won't be game to mark you when the time comes. I don't sleep standin' up. Ya' know what I mean? It's just that I wanna find out what's going on. None of us knows. I'm surrounded by boobs who're still playin' in the sixties. That's where I figured you were. Earlier. I figured you for Beach Boys in fact.

CROW: That sand stayed on the beach with me. You can suss me in detail Leathers. What's your key?

HOSS: This is really weird, me learnin' from you. I mean I can't believe myself admitting it. Ya' know? I thought I could teach you somethin'. I thought you were playin' to the inside. Choosin' me off just to get in the door. I mean I know you must be Mojo's trigger, right?

CROW: De-rail Leathers. You're smokin' the track.

HOSS: Eyes traced a Nevada route. It don't matter. If you ain't from the Root Force you're on the Killin' floor Jack. Anyway you cut it you're a corpse. So let's lay that one on the rack for now. Let's just suspend and stretch it out.

CROW: We can breathe thin or thick. The air is your genius.

HOSS: Good. Now, first I wanna find out how the Gypsy Killers feature the stars. Like me. How do I come off. Are we playin' to a packed house like the Keepers all say?

CROW: (*he cackles*) Image shots are blown, man. No fuse to match the hole. Only power forces weigh the points in our match.

HOSS: You mean we're just ignored? Nobody's payin' attention?

CROW: We catch debris beams from your set. We scope it to our action then send it back to garbage game.

HOSS: Listen chump, a lotta' cats take this game serious. There's a lotta' good Markers in this league.

CROW: You chose ears against tongue Leathers. Not me, I can switch to suit. You wanna patter on my screen for a while?

HOSS: Sorry. It's just hard to take. If it's true. I don't believe we could be that cut off. How did it happen? We're playing in a vacuum? All these years. All the kills and no one's watching?

CROW: Watching takes a side seat. Outside. The Game hammered the outside.

HOSS: And now you hammer us with fucking indifference! This is incredible. It's just like I thought. The Outside is the Inside now.

CROW: (*he cackles*) Harrison, Beatle did that ancient. It cuts a thinner slice with us. Roles fall to birth blood. We're star marked and playing inter-galactic modes. Some travel past earthbound and score on Venus, Neptune, Mars.

HOSS: How do you get to fucking Neptune in a '58 Impala!

CROW: How did you get to earth in a Maserati?

HOSS: There! Why'd you slip just then? Why'd you suddenly talk like a person? You're into a wider scope than I thought. You're playin' my time Gypsy but it ain't gonna work. And get the fuck outa' my chair!!

(CROW *slides out of the chair and starts walking around, twirling his chain and chomping his gum.* HOSS *sits down. He sips his wine. Slowly through the dialogue* CROW *starts to get into* HOSS'S *walk until he's doing it perfect.*)

CROW: Your tappets are knockin' rock-man. I sense an internal smokin' at the seams.

HOSS: Yeah, so this is how you play the game. A style match. I'm beginning to suss the mode. Very deadly but no show. Time is still down to the mark, kid. How's your feel for shivs anyway?

CROW: Breakdown lane. Side a' the road days.

HOSS: Yeah, well that's the way it's gonna be. I ain't used a blade myself for over ten years. I reckon it's even longer for you. Maybe never.

(HOSS *begins to switch into a kind of Cowboy-Western image.*)

I reckon you ain't never even seen a knife. A pup like you. Up in Utah we'd use yer kind fer skunk bait and throw away the skunk.

CROW: Throwin' to snake-eyes now Leathers.

HOSS: So you gambled your measly grub stake for a showdown with the champ. Ain't that pathetic. I said that before and I'll say it again. Pathetic.

(CROW *is getting nervous. He feels he's losing the match. He tries to force himself into the walk. He chews more desperately and twirls the chain faster.*)

You young guns comin' up outa' prairie stock and readin' dime novels over breakfast. Drippin' hot chocolate down yer zipper. Pathetic.

CROW: Time warps don't shift the purpose, just the style. You're clickin' door handles now. There'll be more paint on your side than mine.

HOSS: We'd drag you through the street fer a nickel. Naw. Wouldn't even waste the horse. Just break yer legs and leave ya' fer dog meat.

CROW: That's about all you'll get outa' second. Better shift it now Leathers.

(HOSS *shifts to 1920s gangster style.*)

HOSS: You mugs expect to horn in on our district and not have to pay da' price? Da' bosses don't sell out dat cheap to small-time racketeers. You gotta tow da' line punk or you'll wind up just like Mugsy.

(CROW *begins to feel more confident now that he's got* HOSS *to switch.*)

CROW: Good undertow. A riptide invisible moon shot. Very nice slide Leathers.

(HOSS *goes back to his own style.*)

HOSS: Don't give me that. I had you hurtin'. You were down on one knee Crow Bait. I saw you shakin'.

CROW: Fuel injected. Sometimes the skin deceives. Shows a power ripple. Misconstrued Leathers.

(CROW *is into* HOSS'S *walk now and does it perfect.*)

HOSS: You were fish tailin' all over the track meathead! I had you tagged!

CROW: Posi-traction rear end. No pit stops the whole route. Maybe you got a warp in your mirror.

HOSS: There's no fuckin' warp. You were down!

CROW: Sounds like a bad condenser. Points and plugs.

HOSS: Suck ass! I had you clean! And stop walkin' like that! That's not the way you walk! That's the way I walk!

(CROW *stops still. They stare at each other for a second.* HOSS *rises slow.*)

All right. I can handle this action but we need a Ref. I ain't playin' unless we score.

CROW: It's your turf.

HOSS: Yeah, and it's stayin' that way. I'm gonna beat you Gypsy. I'm gonna whip you so bad you'll wish we *had* done the shivs. And then I'm gonna send you back with a mark on your forehead. Just a mark that won't never heal.

CROW: You're crossin' wires now Leathers. My send is to lay you cold. I'll play flat out to the myth but the blood runs when the time comes.

HOSS: We'll see. You're well padded Crow Bait but the layers'll peel like a skinned buck. I'm goin' to get a Ref now. You best use the time to work out. You ain't got your chops down. You're gonna need some sharpening up. When I get back it's head to head till one's dead.

(HOSS *exits. The band starts the music to* CROW'S *song. He sings.*)

"Crow's Song"

CROW: What he doesn't know—the four winds blow
Just the same for him as me
We're clutchin' at the straw and no one knows the law
That keeps us lost at sea

But I believe in my mask—The man I made up is me
And I believe in my dance—And my destiny

I coulda' gone the route—of beggin' for my life
Crawlin' on my hands and knees
But there ain't no Gods or saviors who'll give you flesh and
    blood
It's time to squeeze the trigger
But I believe in my mask—The man I made up is me

And I believe in my dance—And my destiny
The killer time—will leave us on the line
Before the cards are dealt
It's a blindman's bluff—without the stuff
To reason or to tell

But I believe in my mask—The man I made up is me
And I believe in my dance—And my destiny

(*The song ends.* HOSS *enters with the* REFEREE. *He's dressed just like an N.B.A. ref with black pants, striped shirt, sneakers, a whistle, baseball cap and a huge scoreboard which he sets up down right. He draws a big "H" on the top left side of the board and a big "C" on the other. He separates the letters with a line down the middle. As he goes about his business* HOSS *talks to* CROW.)

HOSS: I suppose you wouldn't know what's happened to my people? Becky. Cheyenne, Doc, Star-Man—they're all gone. So's my short.

CROW: Lotsa' force concentration in this spot Leathers. Could be they got bumped out to another sphere. They'll be back when the furnace cools.

HOSS: I don't fancy tap dancers Crow Bait. I like both feet on the ground. Nailed. Joe Frazier mode.

CROW: I vision you brought the rule, man.

HOSS: Yeah. He's gonna see that things stay clean. Points scored and lost on deviation from the neutral field state.

CROW: I'd say you already broke the mercury in round one.

HOSS: That don't count! We start when he's ready.

CROW: I can't cipher why you wanna play this course, Leathers. It's a long way from shivs.

HOSS: Just to prove I ain't outside.

CROW: To me or you?

(HOSS *considers for a second but shakes it off.*)

HOSS: I don't know how it is with you but for me it's like looking down a long pipe. All the time figurin' that to be the total picture. You take your eye away for a second and see you been gyped.

CROW: "Gyped"—coming from "Gypsy."

(*Through all this the* REF *puts himself through several yoga positions and regulated breathing exercises, cracks his knuckles, shakes his legs out like a track star and runs in place.*)

HOSS: I'm gonna have fun skinnin' you.

CROW: If narrow in the eye ball is your handicap then runnin' a gestalt match figures suicidal. Look, Leathers, may be best to run the blades and forget it.

HOSS: No! You ain't no better than me.

CROW: You smell loser, Leathers. This ain't your stompin' turf.

HOSS: We'll see.

CROW: It took me five seconds to suss your gait. I ran it down to Skip James via Ginger Baker. How long's it gonna take you to cop mine?

HOSS: I ain't a Warlock, I'm a Marker.

CROW: So stick to steel. Pistols. How 'bout the ancient chicken? Maserati against the Chevy. That's fair.

HOSS: I see you turnin' me in. I ain't stupid. I'm stickin' with this route Gypsy and that's what you want so can the horseshit. There's no Marker on the planet can out-kill me with no kinda' weapon or machine. You'd die with the flag still in the air. That's straight on. But too easy. I'm tired of easy marks. I'm drawin' to the flush. I'm gonna leave you paralyzed alive. Amputated from the neck down.

CROW: Just like you.

HOSS: We'll see.

(REF *wipes himself off with a towel and tests his whistle.*)

REF: All right. Let's get the show on the road. We all know the rules. When the bell rings, come out swingin'. When it rings again go to your corners. No bear hugs, rabbit punches, body pins or holdin' on. If a man goes down we give him five and that's it. After that you can kick the shit out of him. Ready? Let's have it!

(*An off-stage bell rings. The band starts slow, low-keyed lead guitar and bass music, it should be a lurking evil sound like the "Sister Morphine" cut on "Sticky Fingers." HOSS and CROW begin to move to the music, not really dancing but feeling the power in their movements through the music. They each pick up microphones. They begin their assaults just talking the words in rhythmic patterns, sometimes going with the music, sometimes counterpointing it. As the round progresses the music builds with drums and piano coming in, maybe a rhythm guitar too. Their voices build so that sometimes they sing the words or shout. The words remain as intelligible as possible like a sort of talking opera.*)

Round 1

CROW: Pants down. The moon show. Ass out the window. Belt lash. Whip lash. Side slash to the kid with a lisp. The dumb kid. The loser. The runt. The mutt. The shame kid. Kid on his belly. Belly to the blacktop. Slide on the rooftop. Slide through the parkin' lot. Slide kid. Shame kid. Slide. Slide.

HOSS: Never catch me with beer in my hand. Never caught me with my pecker out. Never get caught. Never once. Never, never. Fast on the hoof. Fast on the roof. Fast through the still night. Faster than the headlight. Fast to the move.

CROW: Catch ya' outa' breath by the railroad track.

HOSS: Never got caught!

CROW: Catch ya' with yer pants down. Whip ya' with a belt. Whup ya' up one side and down to the other. Whup ya' all night long. Whup ya' to the train time. Leave ya' bleedin' and cryin'. Leave ya' cryin' for Ma. All through the night. All through the night long. Shame on the kid. Little dumb kid with a lisp in his mouth. Bleedin' up one side and down to the other.

HOSS: No! Moved to a hard town. Moved in the midnight.

CROW: Comin' in a wet dream. Pissin' on the pillow. Naked on a pillow. Naked in a bedroom. Naked in a bathroom. Beatin' meat to the face in a mirror. Beatin' it raw. Beatin' till the blood come. Pissin' blood on the floor. Hidin' dirty pictures. Hide 'em from his Ma. Hide 'em from his Pa. Hide 'em from the teacher.

HOSS: Never did happen! You got a high heel. Step to the lisp. Counter you, never me. Back steppin' Crow Bait. History don't cut it. History's in the pocket.

CROW: The marks show clean through. Look to the guard. That's where it hides. Lurkin' like a wet hawk. Scuffle mark. Belt mark. Tune to the rumble. The first to run. The shame kid. The first on his heel. Shame on the shame kid. Never live it down. Never show his true face. Last in line. Never face a showdown. Never meet a face-off. Never make a clean break. Long line a' losers.

(*All the other characters from Act One come on dressed in purple cheerleader outfits. Each has a pom-pom in one hand and a big card with the word "Victory" printed on it. They do a silent routine, mouthing the word "Victory" over and over and shaking their*

pom-poms. They move around the stage doing a shuffle step and
stupid routines just like at the football games. CROW *and* HOSS *keep*
up the battle concentrating on each other. The REF *bobs in and out*
between them, watching their moves closely like a fight ref.)

HOSS: Missed the whole era. Never touched the back seat.
CROW: Coughin' in the corner. Dyin' from phenmonia. Can't
play after dinner. Lonely in a bedroom. Dyin' for attention.
Starts to hit the small time. Knockin' over pay phones.
Rollin' over Beethoven. Rockin' phenmonia. Beboppin' to
the Fat Man. Driving' to the small talk. Gotta make his big
mark. Take a crack at the teacher. Find him in the can can.
There he's doin' time time. Losin' like a wino. Got losin' on
his mind. Got losin' all the time.
HOSS: You can't do that!

(*At some point the cheerleaders all come downstage in a line, turn*
their backs on the audience, take their pants down and bend over
bare assed. When the bell rings marking the end of the round, they
all turn around and show the reverse side of their cards which has
the word "Fight" in big letters. Then they all hobble off with their
pants around their ankles giggling like school kids.)

CROW: In the slammer he's a useless. But he does his schoolin'.
Tries to keep a blind face. Storin' up his hate cells. Thinks
he's got it comin'. Bangin' out the street signs. Tryin' to do
his time time. Turns into a candy-cock just to get a reprieve.
Lost in the long sleeve. Couldn't get a back up. So he takes
his lock up. Calls it bitter medicine. Makes a sour face. Gotta
pay his dues back. Fakin' like a guru. Finally gets his big
chance and sucks the warden's dinger. Gotta be a good boy.
Put away the stinger. Put away the gun boy. I'll take away
your time. Just gimme some head boy. Just get down on your
knees. Gimme some blow boy. I'll give ya' back the key. I'll
give ya' back the key boy! Just get down on my thing boy!
Just get down! Get on down! Get on down! Get down! Get
down! Get down! Come on!

(*The bell rings. The music stops. The cheerleaders flash their*
cards and exit. REF *goes to the scoreboard and without hesitation*
chalks up a big mark for CROW. CROW *lies flat on his back and*
relaxes completely. He looks like he's dead. HOSS *paces around*
nervous.)

HOSS: What the fuck! What the fuck was that! (*to the* REF) You call that fair? You're chalkin' that round up to him! On what fucking grounds!

CROW: Good clean body punches. Nice left jab. Straight from the shoulder. Had you rocked on your heels two or three times. No doubt about it.

HOSS: Are you kiddin' me! If flash and intensity is what you want I can give you plenty a' that. I thought we were shootin' honest pool. This kid's a fuckin' fish man. Nothin' but flash. No heart. Look at him. Wasted on his back and I'm still smokin'.

CROW: (*looking at his watch*) Better get some rest. You got thirty seconds left.

HOSS: I don't need rest. I'm ready to rock. It's him that's stroked out on the fuckin' floor, not me. Look at him. How can you give him the round when he's in that kinda' shape.

REF: Good clean attack.

HOSS: Clean! You call that clean? He was pickin' at a past that ain't even there. Fantasy marks. Like a dog scratchin' on ice. I can play that way if I was a liar. The reason I brought you into this match was to keep everything above the table. How can you give points to a liar.

REF: I don't. I give 'em to the winner.

(*The bell rings.* CROW *jumps to his feet. The band strikes a note.* HOSS *steps in. He speaks to the band.*)

HOSS: All right look. Can the music. This ain't Broadway. Let's get this down to the skinny.

REF: What's going on! Play the round!

HOSS: What'sa matter, Crowbait? Afraid to do it naked? Drop the echo stick and square me off.

CROW: You should be past roots on this scale, Leathers. Very retrograde.

HOSS: Don't gimme that. I wanna strip this down to what's necessary.

CROW: (*laughing*) Necessity?

REF: This is against the code. Either play this round or it's no match.

CROW: We'll walk this dance so long as sounds can push round three. Certain muscles have gone green on me, Leathers. You can cipher.

(*The bell rings again.* HOSS *and* CROW *put down their mikes slowly and deliberately as though they both had knives and agreed instead to wrestle.* REF *moves around them. The band remains quiet.*)

Round Two

HOSS: (*talking like an ancient delta blues singer*) Chicago. Yeah, well I hear about all that kinda 'lectric machine gun music. All that kinda 'lectric shuffle, you dig? I hear you boys hook up in the toilet and play to da mirror all tru the night.

CROW: (*nervously*) Yeah. Well, you know, twelve bars goes a long way.

HOSS: (*growing physically older*) It come down a long way. It come down by every damn black back street you can move sideways through. 'Fore that even it was snakin' thru rubber plants. It had Cheetahs movin' to its rhythm. You dig?

CROW: Yeah. Sure. It's a matter a' course.

(CROW *moves to get away from him as* HOSS *becomes a menacing ancient spirit. Like a voodoo man.*)

HOSS: Yo' "yeah" is tryin' to shake a lie, boy. The radio's lost the jungle. You can't hear that space 'tween the radio and the jungle.

CROW: It's in my blood. I got genius.

HOSS: Fast fingers don't mean they hold magic. That's lost to you, dude. That's somethin' sunk on another continent and I don't mean Atlantis. You can dig where the true rhymes hold down. Yo' blood know that if nothin' else.

CROW: Blood. Well listen, I need some spray on my callouses now and then, but it's not about endurance.

HOSS: Ha! Yo lost dew claw. Extra weight. You ain't come inside the South. You ain't even opened the door. The brass band contain yo' world a million times over.

CROW: Electricity brought it home. Without juice you'd be long forgot.

HOSS: Who's doin' the rememberin'? The fields opened up red in Georgia, South Carolina. A moan lasted years back then. The grey and blue went down like a harvest and what was left?

CROW: That scale hung itself short.

HOSS: What was left was the clarinet, the bass drum, the trumpet. The fixin's for a salad. All hung gold and black in the pawnshop window. All them niggers with their hollers hangin' echoes from the fields. All the secret messages sent through a day a' blazin' work.

CROW: I can't do nothing about that. I'm in a different time.

HOSS: And what brought their heads up off the cement? Not no Abraham Lincoln. Not no Emancipation. Not no John Brown. It was the gold and black behind them windows. The music of somethin' inside that no boss man could touch.

CROW: I touch down here, Leathers. Bring it to now.

HOSS: You'd like a free ride on a black man's back.

CROW: I got no guilt to conjure! Fence me with the present.

HOSS: But you miss the origins, milk face. Little Brother Montegomery with the keyboard on his back. The turpintine circuit. Piano ringin' through the woods. Back then you get hung you couldn't play the blues. Back when the boogie wasn't named and every cat house had a professor. Hookers movin' to the ivory tinkle. Diplomats and sailors gettin' laid side by side to the blues. Gettin' laid so bad the U.S. Navy have to close down Storyville. That's how the move began. King Oliver got Chicago talkin' New Orleans, Ma Rainey, Blind Lemon Jefferson. They all come and got the gangsters hoppin'.

CROW: I'm a Rocker, not a hick!

HOSS: You could use a little cow flop on yer shoes, boy. Yo' music's in yo' head. You a blind minstrel with a phoney shuffle. You got a wound gapin' 'tween the chords and the pickin'. Chuck Berry can't even mend you up. You doin' a pantomime in the eye of a hurricane. Ain't even got the sense to signal for help. You lost the barrelhouse, you lost the honkey-tonk. You lost your feelings in a suburban country club the first time they ask you to play "Risin' River Blues" for the debutante ball. You ripped your own self off and now all you got is yo' poison to call yo' gift. You a punk chump with a sequin nose and you'll need more'n a Les Paul Gibson to bring you home.

(REF *blows his whistle.*)

REF: Hold it, hold it, hold it!

(HOSS *snaps back to himself.*)

HOSS: What's wrong?

REF: I don't know. Somethin's funny. Somethin's outa whack here. We'll call this one a draw.

HOSS: A draw!

REF: I can't make heads or tails outa this.

HOSS: I had him cut over both eyes!

REF: We leave it. Let's get on with round 3.

HOSS: Look at him! He's unconscious standin' up.

REF: Play the round!

(*The bell rings.* CROW *jumps into action, dancing like Muhammad Ali.* HOSS *moves flatfooted trying to avoid him.* CROW *is now on the offensive. The music starts again.*)

Round 3.

CROW: So ya' wanna be a rocker. Study the moves. Jerry Lee Lewis. Buy some blue suede shoes. Move yer head like Rod Stewart. Put yer ass in a grind. Talkin' sock it to it, get the image in line. Get the image in line boy. The fantasy rhyme. It's all over the streets and you can't buy the time. You can't buy the bebop. You can't buy the slide. Got the fantasy blues and no place to hide.

HOSS: O.K., this time I stay solid. You ain't suckin' me into jive rhythms. I got my own. I got my patterns. Original. I'm my own man. Original. I stand solid. It's just a matter of time. I'll wear you to the bone.

CROW: Collectin' the South. Collectin' the blues. Flat busted in Chicago and payin' yer dues.

HOSS: Kick it out fish face! This time you bleed!

(REF *blows his whistle. The music stops.*)

REF: (*to* HOSS) No clinches. This ain't a wrestlin' match.

HOSS: I was countering.

REF: Just keep daylight between ya'. Let's go.

(*The music starts again.* HOSS *goes back to the offense.*)

HOSS: (*to* REF) I was countering, man!

CROW: Ain't got his chops yet but listens to Hendrix. Ears in the stereo lappin' it up. Likes snortin' his horses too chicken to fix. Still gets a hard on but can't get it up.

HOSS: Backward tactics! I call a foul!

(REF *blows his whistle again.*)

REF: No stalls. Keep it movin'. Keep it movin'.
HOSS: I call a foul. He can't shift in midstream.
REF: Let's go, let's go.
HOSS: He can't do that!

(REF *blows his whistle again. The music comes up.*)

CROW: Can't get it sideways walkin' the dog. Tries trainin' his voice to sound like a frog. Sound like a Dylan, sound like a Jagger, sound like an earthquake all over the Fender. Wearin' a shag now, looks like a fag now. Can't get it together with chicks in the mag. Can't get it together for all of his tryin'. Can't get it together for fear that he's dyin'. Fear that he's crackin' busted in two. Busted in three parts. Busted in four. Busted and dyin' and cryin' for more. Busted and bleedin' all over the floor. All bleedin' and wasted and tryin' to score.

(REF *blows his whistle.*)

HOSS: What the fuck's wrong now?
REF: I'm gonna have to call that a T.K.O.
HOSS: Are you fuckin' crazy?
REF: That's the way I see it. The match is over.
HOSS: I ain't even started to make my move yet!
REF: Sorry.

(HOSS *lets loose a blood-curdling animal scream and runs to one of the pistols on the floor, picks it up and fires, emptying the gun into the* REF. REF *falls dead.* HOSS *should be out of control then snap himself back. He just stands there paralyzed and shaking.*)

CROW: Now the Keepers'll be knockin' down your hickory, Leathers.
HOSS: Fuck 'em. Let 'em come. I'm a Gypsy now. Just like you.
CROW: Just like me?
HOSS: Yeah. Outside the game.
CROW: And into a bigger one. You think you can cope?
HOSS: With the Gypsies? Why not. You could teach me. I could pick it up fast.
CROW: You wanna be like me now?
HOSS: Not exactly. Just help me into the style. I'll develop my own image. I'm an original man. A one and only. I just need some help.

CROW: But I beat you cold. I don't owe you nothin'.

HOSS: All right. Look. I'll set you up with a new short and some threads in exchange for some lessons.

CROW: No throw Leathers.

HOSS: I'll give ya' all my weapons and throw in some dope. How's that?

CROW: Can't hack it.

HOSS: All right, what do you want? Anything. It's all yours.

(CROW *pauses*)

CROW: O.K. This is what I want. All your turf from Phoenix to San Berdoo clear up to Napa Valley and back. The whole shot. That's what I want.

(HOSS *pauses for a while, stunned. Then a smile of recognition comes over him.*)

HOSS: Now I get it. I should cut you in half right now. I shoulda' slit yer throat soon's you came through the door. You must be outa' yer fuckin' cake man! All my turf?! You know how long it's taken me to collect that ground. You know how many kills it's taken! I'm a fuckin' champion man. Not an amateur. All my turf! That's all I got.

CROW: Yer throwin' away yer reputation, so why not give me yer turf. You got nothin' to lose. It won't do you no good once the Keepers suss this murder.

HOSS: I still got power. The turf is my power. Without that I'm nothin'. I can survive without the image, but a Marker without no turf is just out to lunch.

CROW: I thought you wanted to cop Gypsy style.

HOSS: I do but I need my turf!

CROW: The Gypsies float their ground, man. Nobody sets up colors.

HOSS: *You* want it bad enough. What's a' matter with you. You movin' outa' Gypsy ranks?

CROW: Razor Leathers.

HOSS: Wait a minute. You tricked me. You wanna trade places with me? You had this planned right from the start.

CROW: Very razor. An even trade. I give you my style and I take your turf.

HOSS: That's easy for you and hard for me.

CROW: You got no choice.

HOSS: I could just move out like I am and keep everything. I could make it like that.

CROW: Try it.

HOSS: You got it all worked out don't ya, fish face? You run me through a few tricks, take everything I got and send me out to die like a chump. Well I ain't fallin' for it.

CROW: Then what're you gonna do?

HOSS: I'll think a' somethin'. What if we teamed up? Yeah! That's it! You, me and Cheyenne. We start a Gypsy pack.

CROW: I'm a solo man. So are you. We'd do each other in. Who'd be the leader?

HOSS: We don't need a leader. Cheyenne could be the leader.

CROW: Not on my time. Rip that one up, Leathers.

HOSS: How did this happen? This ain't the way it's supposed to happen. Why do you wanna be like me anyway. Look at me. Everything was going so good. I had everything at my finger-tips. Now I'm outa' control. I'm pulled and pushed around from one image to another. Nothin' takes a solid form. Nothin' sure and final. Where do I stand! Where the fuck do I stand!

CROW: Alone, Leathers.

HOSS: Yeah, well I guess I don't got your smarts. That's for sure. You played me just right. Sucked me right into it. There's nothin' to do but call ya'. All right. The turf's yours. The whole shot. Now show me how to be a man.

CROW: A man's too hard, Leathers. Too many doors to that room. A Gypsy's easy. Here, chew on some sap.

(*He hands* HOSS *a stick of gum.* HOSS *chews it in a defeated way.*)

Bite down. Chew beyond yourself. That's what ya' wanna shoot for. Beyond. Walk like ya' got knives on ye heels. Talk like a fire. The eyes are important. First you gotta learn yer eyes. Now look here. Look in my eyes. Straight out.

(HOSS *stands close to* CROW'S *face and looks in his eyes.* CROW *stares back.*)

No! Yer lookin' in. Back at yourself. You gotta look out. Straight into me and out the back a' my head. Like my eyes were tunnels goin' straight through to daylight. That's better. More. Cut me in half. Get mean. There's too much pity, man. Too much empathy. That's not the target. Use yer eyes like a weapon. Not defensive. Offensive. Always on the offense. You gotta get this down. You can paralyze a mark with a good set of eyes.

HOSS: How's that?

CROW: Better. Get down to it. Too much searchin'. I got no answers. Go beyond confidence. Beyond loathing. Just kill with the eyes. That's it. That's better. Now. How do you feel?

HOSS: Paralyzed.

CROW: That'll change. The power'll shift to the other side. Feel it?

HOSS: No.

CROW: It'll come. Just hang in there. Feel it now?

HOSS: No. Can I blink now?

CROW: Yeah. Give 'em a rest.

(HOSS *blinks his eyes and moves away*.)

It'll come. You gotta practice like a musician. You don't learn all yer licks in one session. Now try out yer walk. Start movin' to a different drummer man. Ginger Baker's burned down. Get into Danny Richmond, Sonny Murray, Tony Williams. One a' them cats. More Jazz licks. Check out Mongo Santamaria, he might get yer heels burnin'.

(HOSS *starts moving awkwardly around the stage*.)

HOSS: I never heard a' them guys.

CROW: O.K. pick one. Any one. Pick one ya' like.

HOSS: Capaldi.

CROW: Too clean man. Try out Ainsley Dunbar. Nice hot licks. Anyone that gets the knife goin'. You gotta slice blacktop man. Melt asphalt.

HOSS: Keith Moon.

CROW: Too mush flash. Get off the cymbals. Stop flyin' around the kit. Get down to it. Get down.

HOSS: Buddy Miles.

CROW: Just loud, man. Blind strength but no touch.

HOSS: Let's go on to somethin' else.

CROW: O.K. Body moves. Do a few chick moves. Fluff up yer feathers. Side a' the head shots. Hand on the hip. Let the weight slide to one side. Straight leg and the opposite bent. Pull on yer basket.

(HOSS *tries to follow*. CROW *acts out all the gestures with a slick cool*.)

Spit out yer teeth. Ear pulls. Nose pulls. Pull out a booger. Slow scratches from shoulder to belly. Hitch up yer shirt. Sex man. Tighten your ass. Tighten one cheek and loosen the other. Play off yer thighs to yer calves. Get it all talkin' a language.

HOSS: Slow down! I ain't a fuckin' machine.

CROW: Yer gettin' it. Yer doin' O.K. It's comin'. Talk to yer blood. Get it together. Get it runnin' hot on the left side and cold on the right. Now split it. Now put it in halves. Get the top half churnin', the bottom relaxed. Control, Leathers. Ya' gotta learn control. Pull it together.

HOSS: I'm not prepared. I can't just plunge into this. I gotta have some preliminaries.

CROW: O.K. You're right. Tell ya' what. Sit down in the chair and relax. Just take it easy. Come on.

HOSS: Maybe I'm too old.

CROW: Come on, just sit yerself down.

(HOSS *sits in the chair*. CROW *paces around him*.)

We gotta break yer patterns down, Leathers. Too many bad habits. Re-program the tapes. Now just relax. Start breathin' deep and slow. Empty your head. Shift your attention to immediate sounds. The floor. The space around you. The sound of your heart. Keep away from fantasy. Shake off the image. No pictures just pure focus. How does it feel?

HOSS: I don't know. Different I guess.

CROW: Just ease down. Let everything go.

(BECKY *comes on down left facing the audience. She wears a black wig and is dressed like Anna Karina in* "Alphaville." *She caresses herself as though her hands were a man's, feeling her tits, her thighs, her waist. Sometimes when one hand seems to take too much advantage she seizes it with the other hand and pushes it away.* HOSS *seems to turn into a little boy*.)

HOSS: You won't let nobody hurt me will ya'?

CROW: Nobody's gonna hurt ya'.

HOSS: Where have I been. All this time. No memory. I was never there.

(BECKY *talks straight out to the audience. But directs it at* HOSS.)

BECKY: I never knew you were that kind of a guy. I thought you were nice. A nice guy. I never thought you'd be like the others. Why do you do that? You know I'm not that kind of a girl. Come on. I just wanna talk. I wanna have a conversation. Tell me about yourself. Come on. Don't do that. Can't we just talk or something. All right, I wanna go then. Take me home. Come on. Let's go get a Coke. Come on. I mean it. Don't do that! Don't!

(*Her hands pull off her sweater. The wig comes off with it. She's wearing a stiff white bra underneath. She struggles against her hands then lets them go then struggles again.*)

Can't we go back? I'm going to be late. Can't we just kiss? No! Don't! Come on. I don't wanna do this. I'm not that kind of a girl. Look, just keep your hands off! I mean it. I don't like it. I just wanna talk. Tell me something nice.

(*Her hands rip off her bra and feel her tits.*)

Just talk to me. Tell me about your car. What kind of an engine has it got? Come on. Don't! Do you go racing a lot? Don't you take it down to the strip. No! Don't do that! Has it got overhead lifters. I really like those fat tires. They're really boss. Cut it out! No! Stop it! Don't!

(*Her hands unzip her skirt and tear it off. One hand tries to get inside her panties while the other hand fights it off.*)

I don't go all the way. I can't. I've never ever gone this far before. I don't wanna go all the way. I'm not that kind of a girl. I'll get pregnant. Stop it! All right, just get away from me! Get away! I'm getting out. Let me outa' the car! Let me out! Don't! Let go of me! Let go! (*she starts screaming*) Let me out! Let me out! Let me out! Let me out!

(*She picks up her clothes and runs off.*)

CROW: How is it now?
HOSS: I don't know. Trapped. Defeated. Shot down.
CROW: Just a wave. Time to scoop a Gypsy shot. Start with a clean screen. Are you blank now?
HOSS: I guess.

CROW: Good. Now vision him comin'. Walking towards you from a distance. Can't make out the face yet. Just feel his form. Get down his animal. Like a cat. Lethal and silent. Comin' from far off. Takin' his time. Pull him to ya'. Can you feel him?

HOSS: I think so. It's me. He's just like me only younger. More dangerous. Takes bigger chances. No doubt. No fear.

CROW: Keep him comin'. Pull him into ya'. Put on his gestures. Wear him like a suit a' clothes.

HOSS: Yeah. It *is* me. Just like I always wanted to be.

(*The band starts playing the first two chords to "Slips Away."* CHEYENNE, STAR-MAN, DOC *and* GALACTIC JACK *come on dressed in white tuxedos with pink carnations in their lapels. They stand in a tight group and sing harmony notes to the music. They move in perfect choreographed movements like the old a capella bands. The music should build slowly with* HOSS'S *voice until he stops talking and the* SINGERS *go right into the song.*)

Mean and tough and cool. Untouchable. A true killer. Don't take no shit from nobody. True to his heart. True to his voice. Everything's whole and unshakeable. His eyes cut through the jive. He knows his own fate. Beyond doubt. True courage in every move. Trusts every action to be what it is. Knows where he stands. Lives by a code. His own code. Knows something timeless. Unending trust in himself. No hesitation. Beyond pride or modesty. Speaks the truth without trying. Can't do anything false. Lived out his fantasies. Plunged into fear and come out the other side. Died a million deaths. Tortured and pampered. Holds no grudge. No blame. No guilt. Laughs with his whole being. Passed beyond tears. Beyond ache for the world. Pitiless. Indifferent and riding a state of grace. It ain't me! IT AIN'T ME! IT AIN'T ME! IT AIN'T ME!!

(*He collapses in a ball and holds himself tight. The* FOUR GUYS *sing.*)

"Slips Away"

FOUR GUYS: I saw my face in yours—I took you for myself
I took you by mistake—for me
I learned your walk and talk—I learned your mouth
I learned the secrets in your eye

But now I find the feelin' slips away
What's with me night and day is gone

Where you left off and I begin
It took me time to break the line
And on your own is tough enough
Without the thread that we got broken

But now I find the feelin' slips away
What's with me night and day is gone

If we could signify from far away
Just close enough to get the touch
You'd find your face in mine
And all my faces tryin' to bring you back to me

But now I find the feelin' slips away
What's with me night and day is gone

(*repeat chorus*)

(*The song ends. The* FOUR GUYS *exit.*)

CROW: Hey, Leathers. Come on man it's time to cope. Get ready to bop. The world's waitin'.

(HOSS *doesn't move.*)

Leathers, you gotta move out to it now. I taught ya' all I know. Now it's up to you. You got the power.

(HOSS *rises holding the gun in his hand.*)

HOSS: In the palm a' my hand. I got the last say.
CROW: That's it. Get ready to roll. You're gonna knock 'em dead.
HOSS: Knock 'em dead.
CROW: Yeah. What about it.
HOSS: You know somethin' Crow? I really like you. I really have respect for you. You know who you are and you don't give a shit.
CROW: Thanks, Leathers.
HOSS: I just hope you never see yourself from the outside. Just a flash of what you're really like. A pitiful flash.
CROW: Like you?
HOSS: Like me.

CROW: No chance, Leathers. The image is my survival kit.

HOSS: Survival. Yeah. You'll last a long time Crow. A real long time. You're a master adapter. A visionary adapter.

CROW: Switch to suit, Leathers, and mark to kill.

HOSS: Tough as a blind man.

CROW: Tough enough to beat the champ.

HOSS: Yeah. You win all right. All this. Body and soul. All this invisible gold. All this collection of torture. It's all yours. You're the winner and I'm the loser. That's the way it stands. But I'm losin' big, Crow Bait. I'm losin' to the big power. All the way. I couldn't take my life in my hands while I was alive but now I can take it in death. I'm a born Marker Crow Bait. That's more than you'll ever be. Now stand back and watch some true style. The mark of a lifetime. A true gesture that won't never cheat on itself 'cause it's the last of its kind. It can't be taught or copied or stolen or sold. It's mine. An original. It's my life and my death in one clean shot.

(HOSS *turns his back to the audience. And puts the gun in his mouth. He raises one hand high in the air and pulls the trigger with the other. He falls in a heap. This gesture should not be in slow motion or use any jive theatrical gimmicks other than the actor's own courage on stage. To save the actor's face from powder burns an off-stage gun should be fired at the right moment.* CROW *stands silent for a while.*)

CROW: Perfect, Leathers. Perfect. A genius mark. I gotta hand it to ya'. It took ya' long enough but you slid right home. (*he calls off stage*) All right! Let's go!

(BECKY *and* CHEYENNE *enter, dressed like they were in Act One.*)

Becky, get some biceps to drag out these stiffs. Get the place lookin' a little decent. We're gonna have us a celebration.

BECKY: I had a feeling you'd take him. Was it hard?

CROW: Yeah. He was pretty tough. Went out in the old style. Clung right up to the drop.

BECKY: He was a good Marker man. One a' the great ones.

CROW: Not great enough.

BECKY: I guess not.

(*She exits.* CROW *talks to* CHEYENNE *who eyes him.*)

CROW: You eye me bitter wheel-boy. What's the skinny?

CHEYENNE: I guess you want me to drive for you now.

CROW: Maybe I hear you're the top handler in the gold circuit.

CHEYENNE: You hear good.

CROW: I cipher you turnin' sour through. Suicidal like the master. I don't fashion goin' down to a Kami-Kazi collision just after I knock the top.

CHEYENNE: You're cuttin' me loose?

CROW: That's it.

CHEYENNE: You got big shoes to fill Gypsy. They'll be comin' for you next.

CROW: Naw. That's fer lames. I'm throwin' the shoes away. I'm runnin' flat out to a new course.

CHEYENNE: (*looking at* HOSS'S *body*) He was knockin' at the door. He was right up there. He came the long route. Not like you. He earned his style. He was a Marker. A true Marker.

CROW: He was backed up by his own suction, man. Didn't answer to no name but loser. All that power goin' backwards. It's good he shut the oven. If he hadn't he'd be blowin' poison in non-directions. I did him a favor. Now the power shifts and sits till a bigger wind blows. Not in my life run but one to come. And all the ones after that. Changin' hands like a snake dance to heaven. This is my time Cowboy and I'm runnin' it up the middle. You best grab your ticket and leave the Maserati with the keys.

CHEYENNE: Sure.

(*He reaches in his pocket and pulls out the keys to the car.*)

Good luck.

(*He throws the keys at* CROW'S *feet and exits.* CROW *smiles, bends down slowly and picks up the keys. He tosses them in his hand. The band starts the music.* CROW *sings "Rollin' Down."*)

"Rollin' Down"

CROW: Keep me rollin' down
Keep me rollin' down
Keep me in my state a' grace
Just keep me rollin' down

I've fooled the Devil's hand
I've fooled the Ace of Spades

I've called the bluff in God's own face
Now keep me from my fate

If I'm a fool then keep me blind
I'd rather feel my way
If I'm a tool for a bigger game
You better get down—you better get down and pray

Just keep me rollin' down
Keep me rollin' down
Keep me in my state a' grace
Just keep me rollin' down.

(*The song ends. The lights go to black.*)

LA TURISTA

La Turista was first performed at the American Place Theater in New York City on March 4, 1967. The director was Jacques Levy, and the cast was as follows:

SALEM	Joyce Aaron
KENT	Sam Waterston
BOY	Lawrence Block
DOCTOR	Michael Lombard
SON	Joel Novack
DOC	Michael Lombard
SONNY	Lawrence Block

ACT ONE

SCENE: *Two single beds with clean white sheets and pillows upstage center. Between the beds is a small yellow desk with a telephone on it. The entire upstage wall is bright canary yellow. A bright orange door in the wall to stage right with the words "CUARTO DE BAÑO" printed on it in red letters. Another bright orange door, stage left, with a cardboard sign hanging by string from the doorknob. The sign reads: "NO MOLESTAR POR FAVOR" in red letters. At the foot of each bed, on the floor, are two huge overstuffed suitcases. A large fan hangs from the ceiling, center stage.* SALEM, *a woman in panties and bra, sits on the stage left bed propped up with a pillow, facing the audience and reading* Life *magazine.* KENT, *a man in underwear, sits in the same position on the stage right bed reading* Time *magazine. Both* SALEM *and* KENT *have bright red skin. The lights come up to bright yellow, the fan is on,* SALEM *and* KENT *sit reading for a while. They continue reading as they talk.*

SALEM: The woman in—where was it? Puerto Juarez or something. The very rich Spanish woman. Remember? The young woman with her mother who spoke such good English. Very rich.

KENT: What did she say?

SALEM: She said the white of an egg is what you use for second or third degree burns. The pain is eased right away. What happens when the skin is burned? I mean what actually happens?

KENT: Well, the epidermis is actually cooked, fried like a piece of meat over a charcoal fire. The molecular structure of the fatty tissue is partially destroyed by the sun rays, and so the blood rushes to the surface to repair the damage.

SALEM: So your skin doesn't really turn red like magic, it's just the blood rushing to the surface.

KENT: Right.

SALEM: So Mexicans aren't really tan, are they. They just have darker skin, tougher skin with a tighter fatty molecular structure.

KENT: I think that's an anthropological argument now, where some say the dark skinned people of the earth were born that way to begin with for camouflage reasons to protect them against death, and others say it was to protect them against the sun.

SALEM: It doesn't make much difference.

KENT: No. But the sun theory seems to make more sense. Well no, I guess the death theory makes more sense since Icelandic people, people who live in snowy places, have light skin to match the snow. So I guess it has to do with camouflage, since camouflage has to do with deceiving death.

SALEM: What about Eskimos.

KENT: Eskimos are more on the yellow side, aren't they. More Mongoloid. Eskimos aren't really dark.

SALEM: Well, Mexicans are more Mongoloid than Negroid and you call them dark.

KENT: That's true. (KENT *jumps to his feet and starts for the stage right door and then stops short.*)

SALEM: Que paso!

KENT: I started to feel it coming and then it stopped. I don't know whether it's coming or stopping.

SALEM: Que turista! No!

KENT: Speak English, will you. (*He starts again for the door and stops.*)

SALEM: Is it dysentery?

KENT: I don't know. It starts and stops.

SALEM: (*Like a nurse*) Cramps in the stomach?

KENT: Slight ones.

SALEM: Nausea?

KENT: Slight.

SALEM: Rumbling in the bowels?

KENT: A little.

SALEM: Esta turista? (KENT *starts to run for the door and stops again.*)

KENT: You sound glad or something.

SALEM: No. Yo es muy simpatico.

KENT: We both ate the same food, you know, so you'll be getting it soon too.

SALEM: My metabolism is very high.

(KENT *returns to the stage right bed, picks up the magazine, and continues to read.*)

KENT: Relaxation is the thing you seek. You spend thousands of hours and dollars and plane rides to get to a place for relaxation. To just disappear for a while. And you wind up like this. With diarrhea.

SALEM: You came here to disappear?

KENT: That's right. Didn't you? To relax and disappear.

SALEM: What would you do if you did disappear?

KENT: Nothing. I'd be gone.

SALEM: I ask you that face to face. It deserves to be answered.

KENT: Do you know how soon it is before you can start peeling it?

SALEM: Not before it's dead, I can tell you that much. Right now it stings. That means it's alive and hurting. Pretty soon it itches. Then you know it's dying. Then it stops itching and you know it's dead. Then you can start peeling. Not before.

KENT: You can start peeling as soon as it begins to itch. I know that much. That's when you itch so you scratch it and that gets you peeling.

SALEM: You can't start before the itching stops.

KENT: Why not? You could even start while it's still stinging if you wanted. You could even start before it starts stinging and get a head start.

SALEM: And then really get burned. You'd be in sad shape then, boy.

KENT: Then you start peeling again.

SALEM: There's only three layers, you know. It doesn't go on forever.

KENT: Obviously you've never heard of the fourth degree burn. A fourth degree burn is unheard of because it's never happened, but one day it will, and doctors will be dismayed from coast to coast, and a new word will be born into their language. *The Fourth Degree Burn!*

SALEM: What is it like! What is it like!

(KENT *rises on his bed and demonstrates for her*).

KENT: The fourth degree burn comes about after the most extreme and excruciating process has taken its course. The first degree has already occurred and a layer has dropped away almost of its own accord. Effortlessly it floats to the floor at your feet and piles around your ankles like sheets of Kleenex. The second degree comes with a little more shock and a little more pain. It scrapes off like dust and covers the sheets.

SALEM: And now for the third!

KENT: Yes! But the third takes time. The third begins slowly and creeps along the surface, grabbing hold and easing up. Biting down and relaxing away until the spaces get fewer and the biting gets harder. Everything burns and everything you touch is as hot as the sun. You stand away from everything else. You stand in midair with space all around you. The ground is on fire. The breeze feels like boiling-hot water. The moon is just like the sun. You become a flame and dance in mid-air. The bottom is blue. The middle is yellow and changes to green. The top is red and changes to orange. The breeze dances with you. The flame reaches up and then shrinks and bursts into sparks. The ground bursts into flame and circles the breeze. The sparks dart through the breeze and dash back and forth hitting up against the flames, and—

(*The stage left door opens, and a dark skinned boy, but not Negro, enters with bare feet and carrying a shoe shine kit. Both* SALEM *and* KENT *scream and pull the top sheet of their beds over their bodies so just their heads are sticking out. The boy crosses in between the beds and just stares at them with his hand out.*)

KENT: Basta!

SALEM: Vaya!

KENT: Give him some money.

SALEM: How do you say go away?

KENT: Just give him some money.

SALEM: I can't, it's in the suitcase.

KENT: Well get it.

SALEM: How do I get it?

KENT: Crawl down under the sheet and get it.

SALEM: Can't you get up?

KENT: Salem, you're the closest one to the money.

SALEM: Oh, all right.

(*She crawls underneath the sheet to the foot of the bed and sticks her hand out to reach the suitcase on the floor. As she does this,* KENT *speaks to the* BOY, *who just stares with his hand out.*)

KENT: She'll have it for you in just a second.

BOY: Lustre?

KENT: She'll be right with you. If you weren't so poor, I'd kick you out on your ass.

BOY: Lustre?

KENT: Just hold on. Are they taught by their mothers and fathers to look more despondent than they really are?

(SALEM *is still under the sheet and struggling to open the suitcase.*)

SALEM: Sometimes.

KENT: It works. All they have to do is stare. A blank stare does more than a grimace.

SALEM: Just stare back.

KENT: If I was that poor I'd kill myself. I wouldn't pretend I was sadder than I really was. I couldn't take it all the time, everywhere I went, every time I got up, knowing I was no better off and no worse than yesterday. Just the same all the time. Just poor.

BOY: Lustre?

KENT: To just go on and on, getting older and older, and staying just as poor, and maybe even getting poorer. And pretending all the time I was poorer than I was.

SALEM: That's why the mothers sometimes give their babies away to tourists, because they know there's a better chance of them getting rich.

KENT: Who'd want a poor kid?

SALEM: Some people who can't have a rich one.

BOY: Lustre?

KENT: What's he want?

SALEM: To shine your shoes.

KENT: No shine. Go away. Basta!

BOY: Lustre?

KENT: No! (*He puts his head under the sheet. The* BOY *just stands.*)

SALEM: Let him shine your shoes.

KENT: No! I can't even look at him. His hands are full of pork grease; his eyes are red; his breath smells. Get him away.

SALEM: Ah ha!

(*She opens the suitcase, and money pours out of it. She gestures with her hand for the* BOY *to come and take some money. Her hand is the only visible part of her.*)

SALEM: Aqui niño! Aqui! (*The* BOY *keeps staring at* KENT, *who remains under the sheet.*)

KENT: Is he gone?

SALEM: Chico. Aqui. Quiere diñero? Por favor. Aqui.

KENT: What's he doing?

SALEM: Will you be quiet. He won't even move. He doesn't even know there's free money to be had.

KENT: Great.

SALEM: Niño por favor. Aqui. Es muy bueno.

(*This speech should sound like an English safari hunter warning somebody about a man-eating lion. During this,* SALEM'S *hand can be seen waving money at the* BOY. KENT *stays under the sheet through the speech.*)

KENT: He'll never leave now. He's probably never seen a house like this in his life. He grew up in a village, in a hut. He nursed his mother's milk until he was four and a half and then almost died from dysentery at the time he was weaned. He's eaten nothing but rice and beans all his life and slept on the dirt and sold dirty Coca Cola to passing cars. He'll never leave now no matter how much you give him. The fan to him is like the finest air conditioning. The beds to him are like two Rolls Royces. He likes the sound of my voice because it's so strange and soothing and he knows I'm talking about him, and he likes that because, where he lives in the jungle, nobody talks about him, because he's nothing different to them. They're all the same and silent, and sleep and walk around each other like herds of wild boar getting ready to run or kill each other, depending upon the air and the wind and the sun.

SALEM: Well what shall we do about that.

KENT: Can you reach the phone?

SALEM: You're closer to it than me.

KENT: O.K. Maybe the manager will know what to do.

(KENT *starts to reach for the phone. The* BOY *rushes to the phone and pulls it out of the wall, then crosses downstage center with it and sets it on the floor. He sits down next to the phone and sets the shoe shine kit down and smiles at the audience. Throughout the following, the* BOY *makes different monster faces at the audience, from sticking his tongue out to giving them the finger.*)

SALEM: (*still under the sheet*) What happened?

KENT: (*Now visible*) The little prick pulled the phone out of the wall. (SALEM *laughs.*) All right!

(KENT *jumps out of bed and crosses down to the* BOY, *who just sits center stage facing the audience.*)

SALEM: (*Still under the sheets*) Are you out of bed, dear?

KENT: (*To the* BOY) You have to leave now. This is not your home. Go back from where you come from.

(*The* BOY *stands and spits in* KENT'S *face.* KENT *rushes back to the bed and wipes the spit off with the sheet. The* BOY *sits again and continues making faces to the audience.*)

KENT: OOOooooh! Oh my God! Aaaah! Spit! He spit on me! Oh no! Oh my God! Jesus! He spit on me!

SALEM: What's the matter?

KENT: He spit! He spit! He spit all over me. Oh my God!

(*He wipes himself frantically with the sheet. The* BOY *smiles at the audience.* SALEM *works her way under the sheets to the head of the bed and pokes her head out.*)

SALEM: What's going on?

KENT: Oh, I can't stand it. The little prick! Oh God! I'll have to take a shower! Aaah! Oh my God! What a rotten thing to do!

(*He rushes to the stage right door and goes inside, slamming the door behind him.* SALEM *speaks to the* BOY *from the bed. The* BOY *does not turn to her but continues making faces to the audience.* KENT *can be heard groaning behind the door.*)

SALEM: When I was about ten I think, little boy, I'd just returned home from a car trip to the county fair with my family. My father, my mother, my sisters and brothers. We'd just gotten home after driving for about two hours, and it had just gotten dark, but none of us had spoken for the whole trip. Are you listening. It was the same as though we'd all been asleep, and we drove in the driveway, and my father stopped the car. But instead of any of us getting out right away like we usually did we all just sat in the car staring ahead and not speaking for a very long time. I was the first to get out and start walking toward the cement steps that led to the porch and I could hear my family behind me. My father, my mother, my sisters and brothers. And I could hear all four doors of the car slam one after the other like gun shots from a rifle. And I could hear their feet following me up the stairs to the porch right behind me. Very silent. I was leading them sort of and I was only about ten years old. I got to the top of the stairs and I was standing on the porch. I was the first one there and I turned to see them and they all looked right at me. All staggered because of the steps, and all their eyes staring right at me. I saw them like that just for a second, and then do you know what I did little boy? I spit on the very top step just before my father stepped down. And just as he stepped on that little spot of spit that had nothing dirtier in it than cotton candy and caramel apple, my whole family burst into noise like you never ever heard. And my father took off his belt that he'd just bought at the county fair. A black leather belt with a silver buckle and a picture of Trigger engraved on the front. And my father took one more step to the top of the porch with the belt hanging down from his right hand and the buckle clinking on the cement. Then he swung his arm around slowly behind his back so that the belt dragged through the air following his wrist and came back so fast that all I could hear was a crack as it hit my ankles and knees and I fell. Then they were silent again and waited there on the steps until my father put the belt back through the loops and buckled the buckle and hitched his jeans up over his hips. Then they all went into the house in a line. My father first, my mother second, my sisters and brothers third. And I stayed there in a ball, all rolled up, with my knees next to my chin and my hands rubbing my ankles. And I felt very good that they'd left me there by myself.

(The telephone rings; the BOY *picks up the receiver and answers.)*

BOY: Hello. What? How did you know where I was?

SALEM: Who is it?

KENT: (*From behind the door, yelling*) Salem! I do have diarrhea after all!

BOY: (*To the telephone*) If I told you it wouldn't make any difference. What difference? I'm in a hotel somewhere. Why don't you leave me alone?

SALEM: Your papa?

BOY: Or else what. You threaten me with what. Warm Coca Cola? Refried beans? Wormy corn? A hammock at night?

SALEM: Your mama?

BOY: I have air conditioning and two Rolls Royces. Match that, baby.

SALEM: Your sisters and brothers.

KENT: Salem!

BOY: Later, man. Tell it to the old lady. I'm out here on my own. Adios. (*He hangs up the phone and stands; he turns to* SALEM.)

SALEM: Your papa, right? He wants to know where you are?

(*The* BOY *crosses up to the stage right bed and feels the mattress, then takes off his pants and climbs into the bed and gets under the sheets.*)

KENT: Salem! I won't be able to move!

SALEM: Now you're in muy mucho trouble, kid.

BOY: What do you know about trouble, mom?

SALEM: Mom?

BOY: You ever had Mexican ranchers ride into your village at two in the morning and kill your father and steal your sisters and brothers for working in the fields for twelve hours a day for a bowl of soup. Lord have mercy.

SALEM: That sounds like a movie.

BOY: I was in a movie once.

SALEM: Yeah?

BOY: I had to follow this cat around with a palm fan while he scored on all the native chicks.

SALEM: Did he ride a horse?

BOY: How do you score chicks on a horse?

SALEM: Well he could get off now and then.

BOY: You mean he rides from village to village and leaves the broads pregnant, and then the doctor comes around and asks them who the man was, and they all say: "I don't know. He never told me his name," and then you hear this, "Hi Yo Silver! Away!" in the distance?

SALEM: Maybe.

BOY: No, this guy was very cool. He wore linen shirts and

handmade Campeche boots and one of those straight brimmed Panamanian hats and a pistol with abalone plates on the handle. And nobody bugged him because they never knew what he was really like, you dig? Like a jaguar or an ocelot. They look very together and calm. Like you could walk up to one and just pet him gently on the nose and feel his silky fur, but you don't do that because they have something else going on that you're not sure about. Something hidden somewhere. Well this cat was like that and even moved like a jaguar. You know, sort of slinky. He hardly ever talked, and when he did it was like a rumble, like a purr.

KENT: (*Still behind the door*) Salem! It's getting worse! It's very, very loose!

SALEM: So what did he do?

BOY: Who?

SALEM: The guy with the linen shirts.

BOY: That's what I'm saying. He didn't have to *do* anything. He just sat around and did his stick and everything was taken care of. No worry about a place to sack out. No worry about food or booze. And when he felt like splitting he just took off. But the movie was a drag because they forced him to blow his cool at the end.

SALEM: How?

BOY: What difference. They just did. In real life he never would. I mean a cat like that doesn't get all turned around when some villager makes a wise crack about his hat.

SALEM: That's what happened?

BOY: Yeah. This fool walked up and told him his hat made him look like a clown or something like that and the cat fell right into a trap where the villagers tore him up and ate him alive. Like cannibalism or something.

SALEM: Then what happened?

BOY: All the women committed suicide.

SALEM: Really?

BOY: Yeah. But that's what I want to be like, mom. Except I wouldn't blow my cool. Not about a hat anyway. A hat's just something you wear to keep off the sun. One hat's as good as another. You blow your cool about other shit. Like when a man spits in your face.

(KENT *enters from the stage right door dressed in a straight brimmed*

Panamanian hat, a linen shirt, handmade boots, underwear, and a pistol around his waist. His skin is now pale white and should appear made up. He crosses center stage, strutting.)

KENT: Well! I feel like a new man after all that. I think I finally flushed that old amoeba right down the old drain.

(He struts up and down, hitching his pistol on his hips.)

BOY: Ole!

KENT: Yes, sir! Nothing like a little amoebic dysentery to build up a man's immunity to his environment. That's the trouble with the States you know. Everything's so clean and pure and immaculate up there that a man doesn't even have a chance to build up his own immunity. They're breeding a bunch of lily livered weaklings up there simply by not having a little dirty water around to toughen people up. Before you know it them people ain't going to be able to travel nowhere outside their own country on account of their low resistance. An isolated land of purification. That's what I'd call it. Now they got some minds, I'll grant you that. But the mind ain't nothing without the old body tagging along behind to follow things through. And the old body ain't nothing without a little amoeba.

SALEM: Bravo!

(SALEM and BOY hum, "When Johnny Comes Marching Home," as KENT struts more proudly up and down and takes out the pistol and starts twirling it on his trigger finger.)

KENT: Yes sir! That's always been true as long as man's been around on this earth and it ain't going to stop just on account of a few high falootin' ideas about comfort and leisure. No sirree! Why it'll get so bad up there that even foreigners won't be able to come in on account of they won't be able to take the cleanliness. Their systems will act the same way in reverse. Nobody can come in and nobody can get out. An isolated land. That's what I call it.

BOY: Bravo! Bravo!

(KENT gets more carried away with himself as they hum louder in the background.)

KENT: Then the next step is in-breeding in a culture like that

where there's no one coming in and no one getting out.
Incest! Yes sirree! The land will fall apart. Just take your
Indians for example. Look what's happened to them through
incest. Smaller and smaller! Shorter life span! Rotten teeth!
Low resistance! The population shrinks. The people die
away. Extinction! Destruction! Rot and ruin! I see it all now
clearly before me! The Greatest Society on its way downhill.

(SALEM *and* BOY *stop humming.* KENT *blows imaginary smoke out of
the pistol and puts it back in the holster, he sees the* BOY *in his bed
and screams.*)

KENT: What's he doing in my bed!

(*He faints on the floor.* SALEM *screams and jumps out of bed,
she rushes to* KENT *and feels his wrists and slaps his face, she
rushes to the telephone downstage and dials. The* BOY *just sits in bed
watching.*)

SALEM: He's fainted! He's completely out! All because of your
dirty water. Is there a doctor in this town?
BOY: I don't know. Isn't that what the big daddy bear said when
he saw Goldilocks? What's he doing in my bed, mothafucka?
SALEM: (*On the phone*) Hello. Can you get me a doctor right
away? Oh shit. Puede un doctor quiere muy- muy- (*To the*
BOY) Can you tell him? Please. Tell him I need a doctor. Tell
him it's dysentery. Please. I don't speak very well.
BOY: Pardon me no babla español.
SALEM: Thanks son. Hello. Puede quiere un doctor de medecina
muy pronto aqui! Comprende! No, no, no. Un doctor de
medecina. Si! Pronto por favor. Muchas gracias. No, no! Mi
esposo es muy enfermo para la turista. Sabe? Bueno. Muchas
gracias.

(*She hangs up the phone and rushes back to* KENT, *she slaps his face
again and feels his wrists.*)

BOY: (*Still sitting in bed*) They say the white of an egg is good for
poisoning.
SALEM: Just shut up. He's got the trots.
BOY: You force about half a dozen egg whites down the throat
and then they vomit up the poison. It's very easy. They use
it on dogs even.
SALEM: Look sonny, you just sit tight and don't say another

word, or I'll call the chief of police and have them take you
back to your mommy and daddy. What he needs is a wet
towel. A cold wet towel.

(*She crosses to the stage right door and goes inside, closing the door
behind her.*)

BOY: A wet towel is working from the outside in! With poison
you have to work from the inside out!

SALEM: (*Behind the door*) It's not poison!

(*A loud knock on the stage left door.*)

SALEM: (*Behind the door*) That must be the doctor! Would you
answer it please! I'll pay you for it!

BOY: I don't have any pants on!

SALEM: (*Behind the door*) Well put them on for Christ's sake!

BOY: Yes, mam. 'Scuse me, mam.

(*He jumps out of bed and puts his pants back on, another loud knock
at the stage left door.*)

Be right with you boss. Just as fast as I can. Yes sir. Just hold
tight for Jesus sake. We got a busy house here what with the
master sick and all.

SALEM: Hurry up!

BOY: Yes, mam. Right away, mam.

(*He goes to the stage left door and opens it. There are a witchdoctor
and his son standing in the door; they are both very dark skinned.
The* SON *looks exactly like the* BOY *and is dressed the same way.
The* WITCHDOCTOR *is dressed in sandals, short black pants, a
bright red shirt, a short black jacket with elaborate floral designs on
the sleeves and the back, a purple bandana wrapped around his
head like a turban with tassels hanging down the back. He has two
live chickens tied by the feet and hanging upside down from each of
his wrists; he carries a long rope whip in one hand, a long machete
hangs from his belt. The* SON *carries a burlap bag full of incense,
firecrackers, and candles in one hand, and in the other is a large
coffee can full of burning incense, strung with a long leather thong; he
swings the can back and forth by the thong so that the smoke from the
incense rises. They cross center stage. At all times they should behave
as though they have nothing to do with the play and just happen to be
there.*)

BOY: The doctor is here, mam! Shall I show him in?
SALEM: (*Behind the door*) Show him where Kent is and tell him
    I'll be right there!
BOY: (*Motioning to* KENT) Doctor, this is Kent. Kent is very sick
    from poisoning and needs your help.
DOCTOR: (*Crouching down next to* KENT) Pason!
BOY: Si.
SON: Pason!
DOCTOR: Pason! Aeey!
BOY: Si.

(*The* WITCHDOCTOR *rises slowly and motions to his* SON *to set down
the bag and the incense can, then he motions to the two suitcases on
the floor. The* SON *goes to each suitcase and carries them over to*
KENT, *who remains limp on the floor through all this. The* SON *then
opens each suitcase and dumps the contents all over* KENT; *these
should be money and various tourist items. The* WITCHDOCTOR, *at
the same time, crosses center stage and sets the chickens on the floor;
he then picks up the incense can and waves it several times over the
chickens, crossing himself as he does this; he crosses to* KENT *and
does the same thing with him and then whips* KENT *across the back
several times with the rope. He goes through the same actions over
and over again, crossing from the chickens to* KENT, *and then back
to the chickens, while the* SON *takes out incense from the burlap bag
and places it in small metal bowls, also from the bag, in a circle all
around* KENT. *Then he lights each bowl of incense very methodically
and crosses himself as he does this; then he goes to the bag again
and takes out candles; he places the candles also in a circle around*
KENT *and lights each one as he did with the incense; after this is
finished he goes to the bag and takes out a string of firecrackers and
lights it at* KENT'S *feet. All during this, they chant these words over
and over in any order they want to: "Quetzal, Totzal, Copal,
Pason." They can repeat each word several times or say them in
series; the whole thing should be very habitual and appear as though
they'd done it a thousand times before. They should now and then
look at the audience and wonder why it's there, as they go through the
motions. Meanwhile, the* BOY *crosses to the downstage apron and
talks directly to the audience, as a tourist guide speaking to tourists.
He crosses casually back and forth.* SALEM *remains behind the stage
right door.*)

BOY: The people in this area speak the purest Mayan existing today. The language has changed only slightly since the days of the great Mayan civilization before the time of the conquest. It's even more pure than the Mayan spoken by the primitive Lacandones, who live in the state of Chiapas. It's even purer by far than the Mayan spoken in the Yucatan, where much Spanish and Ladino admixtures have been added. In short, it's very pure and nearly impossible for an outsider to learn, although many have tried.

SALEM: (*Still behind the door*) Tell him to do whatever he has to! Don't worry about the money!

BOY: The man here is the most respected of all, or I should say, his profession is. But then, we can't separate a man from his profession, can we? Anyway, there are several witchdoctors for each tribe and they become this through inheritance only. In other words, no one is elected to be a witchdoctor. This would be impossible since there is so very much to learn and the only way to learn it is to be around a witchdoctor all the time. Therefore the witchdoctor's oldest son, whom you see here, will fall heir to his father's position. He listens carefully and watches closely to everything his father does and even helps out in part of the ceremony as you see here. A great kid.

SALEM: Tell him that I'm sick too and may need some help!

BOY: The people of the village are very superstitious and still believe in spirits possessing the body. They believe that in some way the evil spirits must be driven from the body in order for the body to become well again. This is why you see the witchdoctor beating the man. This is to drive the evil spirits out. The firecrackers are to scare them away. The incense smoke, or copal, as it's called here, is to send the prayers up to the god. They believe the smoke will carry the prayers to heaven. The candles are so that the god will look down and see the light and know that there's somebody praying down here, since the god only looks when something attracts his attention.

SALEM: I think I've got the same thing!

BOY: Although there are several European doctors in town, the people will not go to them for help. Instead they call for the witchdoctor who comes to their home and prays for them and beats them up and then goes to the top of the mountain where the god of health is supposed to be. There is an idol there that the witchdoctor prays to in much the same way as

you see here. Please don't try to go to the top of the mountain alone though, without a guide, because it can be very
dangerous. Last year a group of students from an American
university went up there and tried to steal the idol for an
anthropological study and they were almost killed. It's perfectly safe with a guide though, and you can always find me
in front of the pharmacy. Or just ask someone for Sebastian
Smith.

SALEM: It's getting worse now! It's very, very loose!

BOY: Of course, in the days before Christ, they used to sacrifice
young girls to the gods. But now that's been made illegal by
the government so the people use chickens instead. That's
what the two chickens are for. They usually give the poor
chicken a little drink of cane liquor to deaden the pain but
sometimes they don't even bother. You'll notice a slight
mixture of Catholic ritual incorporated into the pagan rites.
This has become more and more apparent within the last
century but the people still hold firmly to their primitive
beliefs.

SALEM: Ask him if he can come in here as soon as he's done
with Kent!

BOY: The marriage is fixed by the family, and the partners have
nothing to say in this matter. The girls begin having babies at
the age of fourteen and usually have about fifteen children
before they die. The average life expectancy is thirty-eight
for women and forty-two for men. The women hold equal
property rights as the men and get paid a salary by the men
for each baby they have. The eldest son in each family
always falls heir to the father's property. The puberty rites
for boys are very stringent here and vary all the way from
having the thumbnail on the right hand peeled away to
having three small incisions made with a razor on the end of
the penis. By the time the penis has healed they believe the
boy has become a man.

SALEM: Tell him to hurry! It's getting much worse!

(*At this time, the* SON *takes all of* KENT'S *clothes off except his
underwear, and piles them neatly at his feet, while the* WITCHDOCTOR
*takes out his machete and waves it over the chicken. He also swings
the coffee can back and forth and chants more intensely.*)

BOY: At this time the clothes are removed from the man in

preparation for the sacrifice. The chickens will be decapi-
tated and their bodies held over the man to allow the blood to
drop onto his back. This will allow the good spirits to enter
his body and make him well again. The clothes will be
burned since it is believed that the evil spirits still reside in
his clothes. And if anyone should put them on they would
have bad health for the rest of their days and die within two
years.

SALEM: I can't stand it anymore!

BOY: After this, the witchdoctor will pray over the heads of the
chickens and then take them to the top of the mountain,
where he will throw them into the fire and then do some
more praying. Now is the time for the sacrifice. For those of
you who aren't used to this sort of thing you may close your
eyes and just listen, or else you could keep in mind that it's
not a young girl but a dumb chicken.

(*The* SON *goes to the chickens and stretches their necks out on the
floor. The* WITCHDOCTOR *cuts off both their heads with one stroke of
his machete.* SALEM *screams from the bathroom.*)

SALEM: Oh my God!

(*The* WITCHDOCTOR *takes both the chicken bodies and holds
them over* KENT *so that they bleed on his back. The* SON *chants
over the heads and crosses himself; the* WITCHDOCTOR *also chants.*
SALEM *enters from the bathroom; her skin is pale white now; she
clutches her stomach and goes in circles around the stage in great
pain.*)

BOY: Why madame, your sunburn is gone.

SALEM: I'm sick and pale, and dying from the same thing as
Kent. What's happened to Kent? How is my Kent? How is
my boy?

BOY: He's dead.

SALEM: No he's not dead. I'm not dead and I have the same
thing. The same rotten thing.

BOY: You're both dead.

(*The* SON *and the* WITCHDOCTOR *continue to chant and stay in
their positions watching* SALEM *and the* BOY, *but remaining unin-
volved.* SALEM *goes in circles and paces back and forth clutching her
stomach.*)

SALEM: Don't tell me that. I wish I was dead but I'm not. Don't tell me that now when I need comfort and soothing. When I need an alcohol rub down and some hot lemonade. How can you speak to me in this way. I'm having cold chills. My body is burning alive. How will I make it back to my home?

BOY: Plane or train or bus or car.

SALEM: Don't tell me that now. Look at me sweat. Who's around who knows what to do? Who is there?

BOY: The doctor's right here.

(SALEM *becomes more and more delirious, clutching her stomach and head.*)

SALEM: I'm seeing things in front of my eyes. I'm shaking all over. Look at me shaking. What's going on! My eyes are popping out of my head.

BOY: You could lie down. Kent's lying down.

SALEM: Kent's faking. Kent's playing dead while I'm the one who needs attention. Look at me now. Just look. Don't look at him.

BOY: I see.

SALEM: No you don't. You said I was dead so you must see a corpse. Now I'm getting scared, you know.

BOY: How come?

SALEM: You wouldn't understand. Look at me. I'm not even dressed.

(*The* BOY *crosses and picks up off the floor a Mexican poncho that was one of the items in the suitcase and hands it to* SALEM, *who keeps pacing up and down.*)

BOY: You can wear this.

SALEM: No, no. I need something like a nice wool sweater and some nice cotton slacks and a nice big bracelet and some jade earrings and some nice warm shoes. And I need to have my hair all done and my nails fixed up and someone to take me out to dinner.

BOY: Well wear this, mom, and as soon as daddy's well, we'll all go out to dinner.

SALEM: All right. All right. But don't call me names.

(*She puts on the poncho and then continues to pace as the* BOY *crosses to* KENT *and feels his head. The* WITCHDOCTOR *and his* SON *continue to chant.*)

SALEM: I feel so silly.

BOY: Don't feel silly. They keep you very warm. It's what the natives wear.

SALEM: Not about that. I feel silly because I'm sick and cold, and Kent's very sick, and I'm not sure at all about what I should do, about who I should ask about what I should do. I don't speak and I'm not from here.

BOY: Ask me. I've been around.

SALEM: Around where, for instance? Around what? You've got built-in immunity. Just look at me. I'm almost naked.

(*The* BOY *begins to put on each item of* KENT'S *costume as they continue.*)

BOY: Better than being too weighted down with extra junk you don't need. Just take a canteen, some sandwiches.

SALEM: Take them where? I'm staying here. You're the one who's got to leave. We rented this room, Kent and me. *We're* on vacation, *you're* not.

BOY: Good. I hope you have a nice trip back.

SALEM: Not back! Here! We've just come here! We're not going back now! You can see Kent lying there dead and at the same time tell me I should have a nice trip back? I can tell you it won't be so nice!

BOY: Well, I hope you have a nice time here then.

SALEM: Put down those clothes! Get out of this room before I call the police.

BOY: Someone pulled out the phone.

SALEM: I don't care! I want you to leave.

BOY: You'll need me around to translate. To run downstairs to the pharmacy and get what you need.

SALEM: What will I need?

BOY: Well, you'll need sterile white gauze and tubes of green ointment and different kinds of hot and cold salve. And you'll need ice packs and pain killers and iodine and stimulants and penicillin pills.

SALEM: I haven't been gored by a bull. I've been screwed by amoeba and I don't even know what they look like. They probably have little white heads and red eyes and two legs, but I know they don't go on forever.

BOY: They'll follow you around wherever you go.

SALEM: Don't try to scare me, sonny. I've been around. You don't know the first thing about amoeba. You could eat chile right off the street and not catch a thing. It's me who's in danger, not you. So don't give me advice. Look how strong you are. Just look. Now look at me.

BOY: Well, how do I look?

SALEM: Come up here, boy, and stand straight. Come on up here! Come on! Come on! Come up here with me and let's see what you look like now that you've grown.

(*The* BOY *crosses up to her, now fully dressed in* KENT'S *costume.* SALEM *takes him by the hand and leads him downstage center; she leads him back and forth by the hand downstage and speaks to the audience as though it were a market place full of villagers. The chanting gets louder in the background.*)

Mira! Mira! Mira! Look what is here! Look what I have for you! For any of you who has the right price! Quantos pesos por el niño! El niño es muy bravo no! Si! He has come to me from the hills with his father's clothes and his mother's eyes! Look at his hands! How strong! How brave! His father says he is old enough now to work for himself! To work for one of you! To work hard and long! His father has given him over to me for the price of six hogs! I give him to you now for the price of twelve! Doce paygar por el niño aqui! Come on! Come on! No?

(*She drags the* BOY *by the hand, down off the edge of the stage into the audience, and walks up and down the aisles showing the* BOY *to the people and yelling loudly. The* WITCHDOCTOR *and his* SON *watch* SALEM *and the* BOY *in the same way the audience does, and in some way reflect the audience's reaction back to them, but go on with their chanting.* KENT *remains limp.*)

Quantos pesos por el niño! Quantos! Quantos! What more could you want? At this time in his life, he is worth more to you than all the ponchos you could make in three months. In four months! He'll bring in your sheep at night! He'll take them out in the morning! He'll scare away dogs and crows and cut up your corn! Feel his calves and thighs! Look at his eyes and his mouth! He's honest too! He'll never steal or lie or cheat! He also sings songs from his native tribe and carves wooden animals in his spare time! He'll speak to you only when he's spoken to and he'll never ever laugh behind your back! He's trained to haul wood and carry water up to thirty miles without resting once! What more could you want? What more could you ask? You can always re-sell him, you know. And you'll never get less than six hogs! His skin is clean! He has no scars! Probably cleaner skin than any of yours! His hair is free of lice and ticks! He has all his teeth! What are you waiting for? How much will you pay? Cuantos! Cuantos! You'll never get another chance! How much will you pay for this boy?

(*The phone suddenly begins to ring.* SALEM *and the* BOY *stop immediately and turn to the stage; they are in the center aisle at the back of the theater. The* SON *and the* WITCHDOCTOR *stop chanting and just stare at the phone as it rings; the* SON *slowly crosses up to the phone and answers it.*)

SON: Hello. What? (*He holds one hand over the receiver and yells to the* BOY.) It's for you! (*The* BOY *crosses down the aisle toward the phone.* SALEM *remains where she is.*)

SALEM: Tell them you're going away on a trip. Tell them you're going to the U.S.A.! Tell them whatever they want to hear!

(*The* BOY *takes the phone from the* SON *and answers it. The* SON *goes back to the* WITCHDOCTOR *and they both begin chanting quietly over* KENT'S *body again. The lights slowly begin to fade at this point; also the fan begins to die down.*)

BOY: (*On the phone*) Bueno. Si. Si. Esta bien. No. Si. Volver a la casa. Si. Si. En esta noche. No. No me gusto. Si. Esta bien. No. Esta mejor.

SALEM: What do they want! Tell them you're going with me!

(*She begins to slowly cross down the aisle toward the stage now.*)

BOY: Estoy muy triste aqui. Si. Bueno. Tu tambien? Bueno. Hasta luego. Si. Buena noche papa. Adios.

(*He hangs up the phone and stares at* SALEM, *who crosses slowly toward him up the aisle. The* WITCHDOCTOR *and his* SON *just stand staring at* KENT *and chanting softly. The lights keep fading.* KENT *remains on the floor.*)

BOY: That's my father.

SALEM: Your father is dead. You're going with me. We have more things to do.

BOY: That's the first time he ever speaks on a phone in his life. He says to start walking down the road toward my home and he'll start walking toward me, and we'll meet halfway and embrace.

SALEM: How will you meet in the dark? You can't even see the road.

BOY: We'll meet in the light. My home is far from here. We'll meet as the sun come up. We'll see each other from very far off and we'll look to each other like dwarfs. He'll see me, and I'll see him, and we'll get bigger and bigger as we approach.

SALEM: You and your father will die in your hut. You could come with me. I could teach you how to drive a car. We could go everywhere together.

BOY: Then we'll tell about where we've been, and I'll sing songs that he's never heard.

SALEM: Your father is deaf!

(*She gets closer to the* BOY *as the lights get dimmer.*)

BOY: And we'll sit together and smoke by the side of the road, until a truck come by heading toward my home. And my father will kiss me good-bye and climb on the back and drive off, and I'll wait for another truck going the other way. A pale blue truck with a canvas back, carrying chickens and goats, and a small picture of the Madonna on the dashboard, and green plastic flowers hanging from the rear view mirror, and golden tassels and fringe around the window, and striped tape wrapped around the gear shift and the steering wheel, and a drunk driver with a long black beard, and the radio turned up as loud as it goes and singing Spanish as we drive out into the Gulf of Mexico and float to the other side.

SALEM: You'll never make it alive!

(*The lights dim out and the fan stops as* SALEM *reaches the* BOY.)

ACT TWO

SCENE: *The set is organized exactly the same as Act One except the impression this time is that of an American hotel room. All the color is gone from Act One and replaced by different shades of shiny tan and gray. The signs on each door are in English and read "BATHROOM" and "PLEASE DO NOT DISTURB" in black and white. The telephone is plastic. The fan is gone. The suitcases at the foot of each bed are matching plastic.* KENT *is in the stage right bed propped up by pillows and sleeping with a thermometer hanging out his mouth. He wears long underwear.* SALEM *is in the bathroom. She wears American plastic clothes. The lights come up fast. Loud knocks on the stage left door.* KENT *remains asleep.* SALEM *comes out of the bathroom and crosses to the door. She opens it and* DOC, *played by the actor who played* WITCHDOCTOR, *is standing in the doorway with his son,* SONNY, *played by the actor who played* BOY. DOC *is dressed like a country doctor from Civil War times, with boots, a coat with tails, string tie, suspenders, a pistol carried in a shoulder holster, wide brimmed black hat, and a large black satchel with supplies.* SONNY *is dressed exactly the same as* DOC *but without the satchel and pistol.*

SALEM: Oh good. Finally. Come in. You *are* the ones from the clinic?

(*They both enter.*)

DOC: Yes, ma'am. (*Takes off his hat.* SONNY *follows suit.*)
SALEM: You brought help? You didn't have to bring help. It's nothing serious.
DOC: No, ma'am. This here's my boy, Sonny.
SALEM: How do you do?

277

SONNY: All right.

DOC: He's tagging along. Learning the trade. Apprenticeship, you know.

SALEM: Well there he is.

DOC: Let's have a look.

(*He crosses to* KENT *and sits beside him, checking his eyes, forehead, etc., as he talks.* KENT *appears to sleep through this.* SONNY *and* SALEM *stand by.*)

SALEM: I don't know what to tell you more than what I told you over the phone.

DOC: Well you ain't told me nothing. Was my secretary or something you must a' spoke to. You ain't told me.

SALEM: Oh.

DOC: So tell me somethin'.

SALEM: Well. You mean symptoms?

DOC: Somethin'. Gotta go on somethin' when you're treatin' illness. Otherwise you might as well be treatin' health.

SALEM: Well. He goes in cycles.

DOC: Cycles?

SALEM: Yes. One thing and then another.

(*Through this,* DOC *motions to* SONNY *to open up his satchel and hand him different instruments for checking the heart, eyes, ears, mouth, etc.* DOC *goes through these procedures, while* SALEM *paces around.*)

DOC: From what to what?

SALEM: From sleep to being awake.

DOC: Me too.

SONNY: Same here.

SALEM: No. No. Not like him. It's not the same. We're talking about something. We'll be talking back and forth and we'll be not necessarily deeply involved in what we're saying, but nevertheless talking. And he'll gradually begin to go away.

DOC: How do you mean?

SALEM: You'll see a person. Like you're seeing me now, and I'm talking to you, and you're talking to me, and gradually something happens to me while we're talking, until I disappear.

DOC: He leaves the room?

SALEM: No, he falls asleep. Like now. He's sleeping. But
before you came, he was talking to me. Now he's asleep.

DOC: Now look here, ma'am. I need things like runny nose,
aching back, itchy skin, bloody urine, runny bowels. Things
like that.

SALEM: They aren't there. What's there is what you see. Sleeping.
I thought it was just fatigue, so we came here to rest and get
strong. But it's worse than that. I can tell.

DOC: How?

SALEM: By the way you look.

SONNY: (*Spoken in one breath*) You shouldn't worry, ma'am. Pa
looks like that always when he's checking to see what's
wrong. Honest. All the time. And I should know, since I'm
always around when he's checking to see what's wrong, and
you're not always around. In fact this is the first time ever
you've been able to see Pa in action. So you should trust me
and him and not yourself.

SALEM: I know doctors. I've been around doctors and they
change faces. They have different faces that tell you what's
what. And I can tell what's what from the face he has on. So
don't tell me.

DOC: You'll have to tell me somethin' more, ma'am, to speed
things up.

SONNY: The more we know the faster we can get to work.

SALEM: What do you mean? Do you help? You're not a doctor.

DOC: Look lady, no more dilly dally.

SALEM: I'm trying to concentrate.

SONNY: Don't try. You can't concentrate if you try.

SALEM: Boy! You should be a doctor, Sonny. You have all this
valuable information up your sleeve.

SONNY: I do my best.

DOC: Symptoms, ma'am, symptoms.

SALEM: Symptoms!

SONNY: Things that show on the outside what the inside might
be up to.

SALEM: I know, I know. Yawning. A lot of yawning, and then a
lot of talking, then more yawning and talking, and finally
sleep, and then waking and talking and yawning and sleep
again. Over and over.

(DOC *stands abruptly.*)

DOC: I have it! Of course!

SALEM: What?

DOC: We must wake him up immediately. Right now, before it's too late. Help me.

(*He and* SONNY *pull* KENT *out of bed and stand him up.* KENT *remains asleep.*)

SALEM: What is it?

DOC: Your husband, ma'am, is subject to what we call chronic Encephalitis Lethargica, also known as sleepy sickness and as Epidemic Encephalitis, von Economo's Disease. A disease that appears from time to time, especially in spring, in the form of epidemics.

SONNY: See there. I told ya'.

(SONNY *and* DOC *slap* KENT'S *face and begin pacing him around the room as they talk to* SALEM. KENT *slowly comes out of sleep into a groggy stupor.* DOC *crosses to his satchel and leaves* SONNY *pacing with* KENT. *He pulls out a medical chart from his satchel and unrolls it; the chart is a nude photograph of* KENT, *with labels and diagrams illustrating encephalitis. He hangs it on the upstage wall as he continues to talk. He points to different sections of the chart with a marker as he gives the speech, like an aging college professor who can't remember his lecture.*)

DOC: It is a virus infection, attacking chiefly the basal ganglia, the cerebrum, and the brain stem. These undergo dropsical swelling, hemorrhages, and, ultimately, destruction of areas of tissue involving both nerve-cells and fibres. The process may involve other parts of the brain, the spinal cord, and even other organs.

SALEM: Oh no.

DOC: The illness begins, usually, with rise of temperature and increasing drowsiness or lethargy, which may gradually proceed to a state of complete unconsciousness. In some cases, however, the patient, instead of being drowsy, passes at first through a stage of restlessness, which may amount to maniacal excitement. As a rule, the drowsiness deepens gradually over a period of a week or more, and accompanying it there appear various forms of paralysis, shown by drooping of the eyelids, squint, and weakness of one or both sides of the face. The nerves controlling the muscles of the throat are also sometimes paralyzed, causing changes in the voice and difficulty in swallowing. In some cases the disease affects the spinal cord, producing severe pain in one or more of the limbs, and it is frequently followed by partial paralysis. Signs of inflammation are not infrequently found in other organs, and hemorrhages may be visible beneath the skin and in the muscles, or blood may be vomited up or passed in the stools. The effects last usually for many months; the patient remains easily tired and somnolent, or frequently showing rigidity of muscle, masklike faces, festinant gait, and rhythmical coarse tremors, resembling the clinical picture of paralysis agitans and known in epidemic encephalitis as Parkinsonism. Other cases show a considerable resemblance in symptoms to chorea, and still others to the disease known as general paralysis; and many cases which result in physical recovery are left with profoundly deteriorated mental powers.

SALEM: I knew he was sick. What'll we do? We were on our way to Mexico, doctor. To give him a rest.

SONNY: A rest?

SALEM: Yes. I mean to get him better.

DOC: There is no specific treatment for the disease, but he must be kept in motion and, if possible, induced to talk. The more motion the better, lest it prove fatal. Benzedrine sulphate is also useful in some patients at this stage.

SALEM: Do you have some?

DOC: Sure do. You take his arm, ma'am, with Sonny, and walk him up and down while I get the pills. Keep him moving at all cost.

(*She follows his instructions while* DOC *gets a bottle of pills out of his satchel.* KENT *is yawning.*)

SALEM: What a thing to have. It sounds just terrible. And we were on our way for a vacation.

(*When* KENT *speaks he is in a world unrelated to anything on stage, even when he talks to the other actors and even when his dialogue seems coherent to the action around him.*)

KENT: Haa! Your hands are something, boy. Fast hands.

SONNY: He talks.

DOC: Good, good. Keep him going. Keep him talking.

KENT: Don't have screwy knuckles like that just playing hand

ball or something. Hand ball you use the palm. But bloody
knuckles. Wowee.

SALEM: What?

DOC: Don't worry. Give him these when you get a chance, but
let him talk.

SALEM: What are they?

DOC: Benzedrine. Just keep him going.

(*He hands* SALEM *the pills, then crosses to the stage left bed and
takes off his coat and sits on the bed with his hands clasped behind
his head, and watches.* KENT *paces, with* SONNY *and* SALEM *holding
onto his arms.*)

KENT: Just don't worry. It carries me through.

SALEM: Shouldn't you be doing something else for him, doctor?
What are you doing now?

SONNY: You should let Pa alone now, ma'am. It's up to us to
carry through with what he says.

DOC: Just keep him movin'.

SALEM: What are *you* doing?

DOC: Thought I'd take a snooze here for a bit. It's been a long
ride out.

(*He closes his eyes begins to sleep, as* SONNY *and* SALEM *keep* KENT
pacing.)

SALEM: Great. You're doing nothing.

SONNY: It *was* quite a ride, ma'am.

SALEM: What do I care about your ride. You're *supposed* to ride
when you have a sick patient. Doctors have been riding
for years. Back and forth. Wherever they're needed, they
go. They even have to swear that they'll do it before they
can—

KENT: How should anyone know. They get thrown into it.

SALEM: (*To* DOC) Listen, is he eventually supposed to come out
of it, or do we just keep this up forever? Hey!

SONNY: Shh! He's asleep, ma'am.

SALEM: Well how are we going to tell when he's all right?

SONNY: Pa will give the sign.

SALEM: But he's asleep.

SONNY: He wakes up every half hour on the hour, then goes
back to sleep.

SALEM: How come?

SONNY: He used to raise puppies. They have to be fed once every half hour until they're at least nine weeks old.

KENT: A doctor shouldn't fall asleep on the job.

SALEM: That's right. What is he, a veterinarian?

SONNY: If he's on the job and he's too tired to do the job justice, then he should fall asleep and wake up rested to do a good job.

SALEM: Do you want some uppies, Kent?

SONNY: Not yet.

(*They keep pacing with* KENT, *while* DOC *sleeps. The pacing should change back and forth, from* KENT *pulling them along, to them pulling* KENT *along; it should cover the entire stage and continually change speed and quality. At no time do* SONNY *and* SALEM *let go of his arms.*)

KENT: I know that type. That sneaky type. That member of the horror show who disappears into it when he doesn't want to be seen, and then pops out when he does.

SALEM: I don't know how to talk to him.

SONNY: Just relax. Let him do the talking.

KENT: That type came to our door once, with my family inside, where they always were. Watching horror shows on —— The monster's always a nice guy. Notice that. Always nice.

SALEM: Kent! Wake up.

SONNY: Shh. Let him go.

SALEM: But we were going to Mexico.

KENT: So he knocks on the door, and Pa answers it, and the guy comes in with a briefcase. Right into the house. And the house is in the middle of the prairie, with nothing around but prairie and one huge factory where they make something inside that you never see outside. All you can see is smoke coming out. And he comes in, with Ma and brothers and sisters all around chewing on the furniture, and Pa dying for a smoke.

(DOC *yawns, then begins snoring loudly.*)

SALEM: Doctor! Do something!

KENT: Shh! And Pa can hardly walk from lack of everything he needs. So the guy from the factory sits down next to Pa, who's dying, and says to him, I see you've got all these lovely sons and daughters, and Pa nods. Then the guy from the horror show says, and I see they're all dying, and Ma nods. And the guy says, I know you never get a chance to see inside our factory, to see what exactly it is that we make, and they shake their heads. So right now I'm going to give you a chance, and he opens up the briefcase which is loaded with different packs of cigarettes. Pa smiles and licks his nose. The kids gather around. Ma faints. The guy says, I'm going to make you a little offer, my friend.

SONNY: Pa!

KENT: If you change each one of the stupid names you gave your eight kids, from whatever it is now, to one of the eight brand names of our cigarettes, I'll set you up in your own little business, and give you all the smokes you need. So don't go shoving benzedrine in my face.

SALEM: It's for your own good, Kent.

SONNY: Pa! I think we need help.

KENT: You're doing fine. You don't even have to hold on. The pace is great.

SONNY: Don't believe him, ma'am. They all say that. And just at the point when they say that, you know that the last thing in the world you should do is to do what they say.

SALEM: But maybe he means it. Kent? Are you O.K.?

SONNY: Just keep hold a' that arm, lady. Do exactly the opposite of whatever he wants. Believe me. I've learned.

KENT: You're no doctor.

SONNY: Last week Pa and I were out at the Tuttle farm, out past Lansingville, to see old lady Tuttle, since her neighbors called us up and asked us to go give her a look-see, since she was doing a lot of fiddle playin' late at night and they was all worried. So we rode out there about 3 A.M. one mornin' last week, thinkin' we'd catch her at it if she was really doin' what they said she was doin', and she was all right. She was doin' it.

SALEM: Look, we have to get him well so we can get started on our trip.

SONNY: Sittin' out there on her front porch just as plain as day. Tappin' her foot and rockin' to the tune she was doin'. Think it was, "Hang Toad's Got No Stock In My Mind." Somethin' like that.

SALEM: Doctor!

SONNY: So we sneak up on her through the shrub pine and sit

there in the dark for a spell just listenin' to that fine old fiddle a' Mrs. Tuttle's.

(DOC *wakes up suddenly and sits up on the bed; he stands abruptly and puts on his coat; he checks his watch. The rest keep pacing.*)

DOC: What!

SONNY: Just tellin' the lady here about old lady Tuttle, Pa.

(DOC *gets involved in the story and wanders downstage.*)

DOC: Oh yes. Well it was a strange night. A night the likes a' which could make you figure old lady Tuttle was the only one in the world to speak of, and we two, my boy and I, we was like shrub pine. Just lookin' on. Growin' slowly. Rooted in one place. Lettin' seasons change us. And Mrs. Tuttle was playin' for us like she was playin' for the world of bushes and plants and insect life.

KENT: So Pa was set up in business at last.

DOC: Shut up! Keep him still!

(*They keep pacing* KENT, *while* DOC *comes down and speaks to the audience while walking around.*)

SALEM: Doctor.

DOC: So there we was. My boy and I, hidden from view. Invisible to old lady Tuttle. And we noticed after a bit how we was gettin' entranced by that darn fiddle a' hers. That old lady had us hypnotized there for a while, until my boy here realized it and snapped us both out of it.

SALEM: Doctor! Pay attention to your patient.

DOC: Well we figured it out between the two of us but only after it was too late. Instead we fell right into her trap and walked right up to her porch just as plain as you please and—

SONNY: That's not exactly how it went, Pa.

DOC: You shut up! How it went is no concern of mine or yours. All I want to do is finish up and go home.

KENT: And leave me stranded.

SALEM: How can a doctor leave you stranded, Kent?

DOC: By ridin' out, lady.

SALEM: I'll call the clinic.

DOC: Try it!

SONNY: Pa cut the wires on the way in, ma'am.

SALEM: You what! That's rotten.

DOC: (*To audience*) So we walk right up to old lady Tuttle, who doesn't even see us. Like we're not there, even.

KENT: That means that I'll fall asleep and never wake up.

SALEM: Don't be silly. We'll keep you going all night if we have to.

KENT: What about tomorrow?

SALEM: And tomorrow we'll go to Mexico.

DOC: And the closer we get the better we see that she could be anywhere. She couldn't care less.

KENT: Let go of me. I want to check the phone.

DOC: Don't let him go at any cost!

KENT: I want to check on the phone!

(*They keep* KENT *pacing.*)

DOC: (*To audience*) There's one thing I could never stand in all those years ridin' back and forth treatin' sores and wounds and shrunken hands.

SONNY: What's that, Pa?

DOC: That's the absolute unwillingness that all them sickly, misfit imbeciles had for going along with what I'd prescribe. You say one thing and they do the exact opposite right off the bat. Soon as you turn your back off they'd go in the wrong direction. Straight into what I was tryin' to lead them out of.

SALEM: Doctor! He seems to be all right now.

SONNY: Ya' gotta watch the tricks, ma'am. Ya' gotta develop an eye for the tricks so you can tell one kind from another kind.

DOC: It got to a point there, in my traipsin' around, where I felt like a doctor was the last thing needed. Just let the fools work it out for themselves.

SALEM: He's moving and everything. He's talking and walking. That's what you wanted. Can't we let him go now? Doctor.

DOC: Sure! Sure enough! Let him go!

(*They all stop still.*)

SALEM: Kent?

(*They let go of* KENT'S *arms and back away.* KENT *remains standing still. Doc crosses up to him and checks his eyelids, then steps back.*)

DOC: All right.

SALEM: What? He's all right now, isn't he?

DOC: Sure. Fit as a fiddle.

(KENT *rushes to the phone and picks it up; he tries to dial with no success; he freezes as he hangs up the phone.*)

KENT: They cut the wires. The juice.

SALEM: Kent. We can take off tomorrow if you want.

SONNY: Why Mexico? Why not Canada, where you'd be less noticeable?

SALEM: That's right, Kent. In Mexico they're all dark. They'd notice us right off the bat.

DOC: Especially with a corpse.

SONNY: They'd notice a corpse anywhere.

SALEM: What do you mean?

KENT: Not here. In Lansingville. Get a T.V. in here. Some sandwiches.

SALEM: No. That's silly. We want to get out, not in.

DOC: I could stop by once a week.

SALEM: Here's some pills, Kent. Take some pills. You'll be all right.

(*She hands* KENT *the pills. He holds them in his hand and remains frozen.*)

I'll get you a glass of water.

(*She exits into the bathroom.* DOC *and* SONNY *move in on* KENT, *who stays frozen.*)

SONNY: Unless ya' want to follow Pa's directions, fool, you'll never get out a' this hole.

DOC: That's right. Listen to the boy.

SONNY: He knows what he's sayin', Pa does.

DOC: Ain't been travelin' through hick town after town, tearin' the scabs off a' infection that otherwise would a' made a corpse out of a live man if the pus wasn't allowed to draw off. Ain't been doin' that and not comin' back with some savvy.

SONNY: They do it with trees too, so don't feel bad.

DOC: Just keep yourself movin', son. It's the only way out.

(SALEM *enters with a glass of water and hands it to* KENT.)

SALEM: Here, Kent.

DOC: See here, your woman's right behind ya', boy.

(KENT *takes the pills and a gulp of water; he hands the glass back to* SALEM, *then stands.*)

KENT: Well. Thanks, Doc. Hope you have a nice trip back.

DOC: Oh. Well. Nice? Sure. It won't be so nice. I mean it won't be any nicer than it was coming out.

KENT: How nice was that?

DOC: So, so.

KENT: Well I hope it's nicer than that.

(KENT *begins wandering around freely, looking at the walls of the room.*)

SONNY: That can't be. It's always the same. Dusty, hot. Ya' get tired and rest at the same places along the road, under the same trees.

KENT: Why's that?

DOC: Well, that's where the wells are, ya' see. Ya' have to get tired where the water is so's you don't pass 'em by. Otherwise, you're just out a' luck.

KENT: Don't you carry a canteen or something?

SALEM: We can take off tomorrow then, Kent. If you feel all right.

KENT: How will you reserve tickets? The wires are cut. The juice is off.

SONNY: That's right.

DOC: Anyway we gotta hang around for a bit to check you out. Make sure ya' don't have a relapse.

KENT: A what?

DOC: A relapse. To make sure the same business doesn't start all over again.

SONNY: You need your bag, Pa?

SALEM: I could walk down the road and make a call from the pay phone.

DOC: Ya' see ya' could easily fall back into it if ya' don't watch your step. It depends on a very fragile margin in the basal ganglia. One little jar, and poof. You have to keep the opposite pole in motion in order not to activate the opposite one.

SONNY: He's right.

SALEM: Shall I go make reservations, Kent?

DOC: Not yet! He's in no shape to be wanderin' into the freezin' night the way he is. Out there with the crickets.

KENT: I think I'll stay.

SALEM: Well then I'll go.

DOC: No. You should stay too, lady.

KENT: Why should she?

DOC: Well, I mean we'll need somebody to mix up some jasmine tea with honey, and—

KENT: Sonny can do that.

SONNY: It needs a woman.

SALEM: Look. Kent's all right now, so why don't the two of you go back and leave me with him alone.

SONNY: You're no doctor.

DOC: Right. Your husband should get some rest now and special tea. Only a doctor with many years experience and——

SALEM: Just what is your experience?

SONNY: Don't talk to Pa like that.

SALEM: And what's this business about cutting wires.

DOC: We never cut your wires, lady.

(KENT *advances on* DOC *as* DOC *backs up.*)

KENT: I thought you said before that you cut our wires.

DOC: Naw. Never did.

KENT: I was under the impression we were juiceless here. Out of touch. No way of reaching the outside.

DOC: Try it then. Pick up the phone and try it.

KENT: Try it, Salem.

(SALEM *goes to the phone and picks up the receiver, as* KENT *backs* DOC *around the stage.* SONNY *looks on.*)

DOC: You could call Berlin if you wanted.

KENT: Why would we call Berlin if we wanted?

SALEM: No juice. (*She hangs up.*)

DOC: Now that's downright silly. Sonny, you give it a try.

KENT: Don't move, Sonny, or I'll gun you down. (SONNY *freezes.*)

DOC: Now go ahead, son. I have a gun. He don't. I'm the one that's armed. Go on now. Let's settle this once and for all.

KENT: Don't make a move.

DOC: You got a lot a' gall, bucko. Just 'cause you're feelin' your oats and all, now that you're cured. You're forgettin' pretty fast who got ya' out a' your dilemma. Remember? Your old Doc got ya' out a' what looked to me like suicide. Plain and simple.

(SONNY *stays frozen.*)

SALEM: Don't say that. Kent, let's just leave.

KENT: He'll die if he makes a move.

DOC: Now that's pushin' it right to the edge, mister. You gotta have a full house to be callin' bluffs like that.

(KENT *draws an imaginary pistol and points it at* DOC, *as he moves him around the stage faster.* SONNY *stays frozen.*)

KENT: It's been proven that the wires are cut. Salem proved it.

DOC: Now Sonny you just go and give it a check, and then we can leave. Sonny! (*He stays frozen.*)

SALEM: Kent, let him check the phone if he wants. Then we'll go.

DOC: Who are you foolin' with a finger. I ain't from Egypt, ya' know.

SALEM: Look, I'll phone the operator and show you both.

(*She moves toward the phone and freezes when* DOC *speaks.*)

DOC: Don't make a move!

(*He draws his pistol and aims it at* KENT. *Now* DOC *begins backing* KENT *around the stage.* KENT *keeps his finger pointed at* DOC. SA-LEM *and* SONNY *remain frozen in their places.*)

KENT: Now why in the world—I ask myself why in the world would a doctor from a respectable clinic want to disconnect the phone of a dying man. A man he's supposed to cure. A man who's prepared to pay him two suitcases full of money in exchange for his good health. I ask myself why and come up with only one answer.

DOC: Now what would that be?

KENT: That this doctor is up to no good. That this doctor, in cahoots with his fishy son, is planning to perform some strange experiment on this dying man that he don't want to leak out to the outside world. So if this experiment fails no one will be the wiser, and the only one to have lost anything will be the dying man who's dying anyway.

(*They change directions again with* KENT *advancing and* DOC *retreating.*)

DOC: And I ask myself something too. I ask myself why this dying man who's got nothing to lose but his life accuses the one and only person who could possibly save it of such a silly thing as cutting the wires to his telephone. I ask myself that and come up with only one answer.

KENT: Yes?

DOC: That this dying man isn't dying at all. That this here man is aching all over for only one thing. And he cunningly puts the idea into the mind of the doctor, and the doctor then acts it out. The doctor performs the experiment with his faithful son at his side and transforms the dying man into a thing of beauty.

KENT: How?

(DOC *advances on* KENT.)

DOC: By beginning slow. From the hair down. Piece by piece. Peeling the scalp away neatly. Carving out the stickiness and placing cool summer breezes inside. In place of the hair goes a grassy field with a few dandelions falling toward the back.

KENT: And the eyes?

DOC: Wet spongy moss covers each one and opens into long tunnel caves that go like spirals to the back where the light pours in. The nose swoops down and has crows and chickadees roosting all day on its tip. The doctor's scalpel moves quickly over the mouth.

(KENT *advances on* DOC.)

KENT: Oh no. The mouth hangs in strips for lips that droop all the way down to the chin. And underneath are thick round teeth with edges sharper than diamonds, so they flash at night when he's eating. The flashes warn everything living within twenty miles, and they stay inside until morning comes.

DOC: The chin—

KENT: I told you! You can't see the chin because of the lips. They hang down. And so does the hair. Long sheets of black hair that hang down past its waist and rustle like paper when it runs.

(DOC *advances on* KENT.)

DOC: Doc and his faithful son stay up through the night thinking of shoulders and arms and a chest for the beast.

(SONNY *makes a sudden move for the phone but freezes when* KENT
yells.)

KENT: Hold it! I'll blow you to bits!

DOC: At 3 A.M., they get down to work. Moving fast and
patiently over the torso. The arms dangle down past its hair
and gently flow into beautiful womanly hands that look like
they've never been outside of goatskin gloves until this very
moment.

KENT: When it jerks up its head and bursts from the leather
strap across its thin chest.

DOC: No! (KENT *advances on* DOC.)

KENT: But then it's too late. The moment has come for its
birth, and nothing can stop it from coming.

(KENT *stalks* DOC *with his finger pointed at him; he manipulates*
DOC *all over the stage while the others stay frozen in place.*)

DOC: Not yet! There's the legs and the feet left to do!

KENT: It opens its arms and its mouth and tests everything out.
It feels how the juices drain from its brain, down through the
nose and into the mouth where it tastes like honey. He licks.
He kicks off the sheets. He rolls off the edge of the stainless
steel table that rolls on its tiny rubber wheels straight for the
wall.

DOC: You can't start before—

KENT: The fall from the table to the floor starts other juices
going. He feels the stream of fluid pulling him off the ground
and onto his feet.

DOC: He can't even walk! He doesn't have feet!

(KENT *changes his finger from a gun to a knife and begins making
quick lunges toward* DOC, *who jumps back.*)

KENT: He finds the fluid pounds through his legs and his waist.
It catches hold and loosens up. It draws back and snaps out
like a snake. He moves across the room in two steps and
flattens out against the wall. He disappears and becomes the
wall. He reappears on the opposite wall. He clings to the

floor and slithers along. Underneath cages of rats and rabbits and monkeys and squirrels. He becomes a mouse and changes into a cobra and then back on the floor. Then onto the roof.

DOC: Stop it!

(DOC *fires the pistol.* KENT *keeps advancing; his gestures and movements become wildly extravagant, like an African dance.* DOC *retreats to every corner of the room, running away, while* SALEM *and* SONNY *stay frozen.*)

KENT: Then jumping from roof to roof with his paper hair flying behind and his lips curling back from the wind and tasting the juice that's pouring down from his nose and his ears.

(DOC *fires again.*)

He zigzags sharply around T.V. antennas and his ears catch the sound of the dogs panting as they rush up the steps to the top of the roof. He can hear barking and screaming and whistles. Beams of white light cut through the night and follow his trail. Sirens sound through the streets.

(DOC *fires.*)

He keeps jumping space after space and roof after roof. And each jump he makes he looks down right in mid-air between the roof he left behind and the roof he's jumping to. He looks down and he sees a miniature world where things move like bedbugs and ticks. And then he looks up and he sees miniature lights that flick on and off.

(KENT *leaps off the stage and onto the ramp; he runs up the ramp and behind the audience, where he speaks.* DOC *intercedes with his lines from the stage.*)

DOC:
Now come back down here and stop playin' around!

KENT:
The Doctor is torn by desires that cut through his brain as he leads the hysterical mob on the trail of the beast he once loved.

DOC:
I ain't playin' around anymore!

KENT:
Now it must be destroyed. If he could somehow get to the beast ahead of the mob. Trap it somehow in a quiet place between smooth wet boulders, and talk to it calmly.

DOC:
I'll walk right out on ya', boy!

KENT:
Perhaps even stroke its long hair and wipe off its chin. To find some way of telling the beast that the mob will calm down if *he* only does.

DOC:
I'd just a' soon let ya' rot away! There ain't nothin' keeping me here.

KENT:
The Doctor makes a dash away from the mob and ducks into a dark stand of sycamore trees. The mob is confused and frightened without the Doctor. They become enraged and set the forest on fire.

DOC:
Now ya' gotta be fair about this!

KENT:
Doc moves away from the flames easily, since he's passed through this section of land many times before on his calls.

DOC:
I done all I could. I diagnosed the disease. I treated what ails ya'! I can't do no more! What more can I do?

KENT:
He finds a narrow stream, where he usually drinks on his way back and forth, and slowly submerges under the surface. He swims along easily and lets the current propel him downstream. Moving through flowing green plants and yellow goldfish, and surfacing once in a while to check where he is.

The monster has a complete view now, from his perch.

DOC:
I got'ta keep my distance, boy!
A doctor has got to keep a
distance! I mean I can't go falling asleep on the job!

Look what would happen if
that were to happen!

(DOC'S *"look"* sequence during this;
DOC *goes through different gestures
that were* KENT'S *in the first Act:
running to the bathroom, swagger-
ing, fainting, etc.*)

I gotta keep strong!

That's my job!

To keep strong and quick and
alert!

KENT:
He sees the stream cutting the
land in half, with one half on
fire, and the other half dark
and quiet. He's calmer now
and sits on a rock, catching up
with his breath.

The Doctor comes up onto the
shore panting for breath and
clutching at long clumps of
grass.

He drags himself up on dry
land and staggers on through
the night. Afraid if he stops for
a rest that the beast will be
lost forever.

Now the beast begins to even
enjoy being up so high. Above
everything else but the sky and
watching the golden fire move
down one side of the stream
and consuming everything dark.

Doc begins to feel lost now in
the trees with no living thing
around him but leaves that
whistle and hum as though
sensing the fire's approach. He
must find the beast. He begins to think if I were him
how would I hide and how
would I run? Which way would
I go and how would I choose?

The beast even likes the idea
of not having to move. To sit
in one place on a smooth shiny
rock and just swivel to different positions and face in different directions.

DOC:
I mean what earthly good would I be to you or to anyone else if I was walkin' around just as sick as my patients? No good at all. Now you can see that as plain as I can. That's why I make a point to keep fit.

That's why I'm always in shape.

Notice that! My eyes are clear! My skin is smooth! My hair is free of lice and ticks! My muscles are well tuned up for any situation! Just watch me! Look at the way I can move if I want! You should trust me, boy! I'll get ya' through! Just let me show ya' the way! You'll have to go with me though! I can't go with you! I'll show ya' how! Step by step. One foot in front of the other foot. Let your arms swing free at the sides. Let the words come.

KENT:
Doc bends slowly downward and finds he moves faster with his head pushing him on. He seeks out the shadowy places, always staying upwind and straining his eyes to find a higher place.

Gently, the monster pulls the moss flaps back from his eyes and lets the wind fill them up.

His beautiful hands stroke the smooth rock.

He chuckles at the spits that the fire makes as it reaches the stream and goes out. Doc's feet slip and clutch the shale rock and sand and his hands grasp for vines and stumps and roots and anything strong enough to hoist his aching body up to the top. The beast stretches and yawns and smiles. He misses only one thing: the face of the Doc the way it used to be, looking down and smiling with his big dark eyes and his scalpel in hand.

(DOC *goes to* SONNY *and* SALEM *and shakes them out of their freeze as he continues to talk to* KENT. *Slowly he gets them to move, he points to* KENT *and persuades them to try to bring him back on the stage. They slowly move downstage, like somnambulists. As* DOC *remains on stage talking to* KENT *they move off the stage and onto the ramp toward* KENT. SALEM *and* SONNY *hum,* "When Johnny Comes Marching Home Again," *as they close in on* KENT.)

DOC:
Yes sir, ya' won't have no trouble at all if ya' go along with
the cure. We'll be unbeatable,
the two of us.

KENT:
Doc almost forgets why he's
climbing so fast and so hard
until he hears shouts from
the dark side of the forest at
the base of the hill. They've
crossed the river and picked
up his trail. Doc pries loose a
boulder and lets it crash down
the side.

I'll get ya' one a' them pinto
stallions with a silver saddle
and a golden bit.

His beautiful hands are bleeding from clawing. His feet feel
like they're not even there.

And hand tooled Indian boots.
I'll show ya' how to use a thirty
odd six and a forty odd eight.
You don't have to worry your
head about nothin', boy! We'll
walk into each town like they
was puddles a' water waiting
around for a boot to come by
and splash them out a' their
hole. We'll always be taken
care of, you and me. Always!
Just wait and see.

He lunges and pulls toward
the top. He twists in and out
of small thorny bushes. He
squeezes in between cracks in
the rock as bullets ring out and
torches flare in the sides of his
eyes. He uses his mouth to
pull himself up, and his dia-
mond teeth blind the mob with
their flash. Doc must get there
first and escape with the beast.

Get him! Grab ahold of his
arms! Get him back down here!
Don't let him get away!

His arms rip from the shoulders and chest, and juices gush
out down his sides. He must
find him there and hide in a
cave. His hair tears and floats
away, flapping in air like an
owl at night looking for mice
in the field far below. He must
meet him alone for one final
time. His teeth drag him up.
Dragging the body along. Pulling and chomping down on the
earth. Pulling up and chomping
down.

SALEM *and* SONNY *make a lunge for* KENT, *who grabs onto a rope and swings over their heads. He lands on the ramp behind* DOC *and runs straight toward the upstage wall of the set and leaps right through it, leaving a cut-out silhouette of his body in the wall. The lights dim out as the other three stare at the wall.*

TONGUES

A piece for voice and percussion
by Sam Shepard and Joseph Chaikin

NOTE: *This piece was first performed in 1978 at the Magic Theatre, San Francisco, for a limited run. It began from almost nothing but a desire to work together. Joe Chaikin and I agreed to meet on a regular basis over a period of about three weeks, each time changing the location—a restaurant, a beach, a park, hotel rooms, a truck— then, toward the very end, a theatre. We agreed on a piece to do with the voice. Voices. Voices travelling. Voices becoming other voices. Voices from the dead and living. Hypnotized voices. Sober voices. Working voices. Voices in anguish, etc. Sometimes we would just talk without trying to push the content into the structure of the piece. Other times the talk would be translated verbatim, written down on the spot, turned into monologue or dialogue, trance poem, or whatever. As the piece neared completion on paper, the concept of performance leaned toward some kind of musical accompaniment. I brought some percussion instruments into the theatre and we started to jam and experiment with various possible sounds. Soon a form began to take shape. Joe sat in a straight-backed chair, facing the audience, with a Mexican blanket draped over his lap. I sat directly behind him on a low platform, my back to his, with the instruments in front of me. His position was static except for the face. The gestures of my arms playing the different instruments were seen as extensions of Joe's static body. The choices we made in performance were very personal and almost impossible to repeat on paper. These notes are only an indication of how we arrived at a means of collaboration. Actors wishing to perform this piece would necessarily have to develop their own means and experiment according to their given situation. The various voices are not so much intended to be caricatures as they are attitudes or impulses, constantly shifting and sliding into each other, sometimes abruptly, sometimes slowly, seem-*

ingly out of nowhere. Likewise, the music is not intended to make comments on the voice but to support these changing impulses, to make temporary environments for the voice to live in. The choices of instrumentation can be very open but I feel they should stay within the realm of percussion.

September 29, 1978   SAM SHEPARD

SCENE: *Bare stage. Black backdrop in semicircle upstage. Downstage center at the extreme edge, a straight-backed chair draped in a bright Mexican blanket (simple, traditional design). The blanket provides the only color. Directly behind the chair is a low platform raised about a foot off the stage floor, measuring about four feet square. On the platform are the various percussion instruments arranged in a semicircle, visible to the audience from the sides. The lighting is very simple, essentially white, and lit with a maximum of three instruments. Lights to black. Percussionist and speaker enter in dark. Lights up to reveal speaker sitting in chair, blanket covering his lap, white shirt with no collar. The percussionist, dressed in all black, in unseen for the moment. SPEAKER remains motionless. The right arm of percussionist appears to the left side of the speaker holding two maracas and in a slow, rolling motion sets a four/four hypnotic tempo. The sound is heard for a while alone and then continues as the SPEAKER begins.*

SPEAKER:

He was born in the middle of a story which he had nothing to
   do with.
In the middle of a people.
In the middle of a people he stays.

All his fights.	*Percussion accent within 4/4*
All his suffering.	*accent*
All his hope.	*accent*
Are with the people.	*no accent, continues 4/4*
All his joy	*accent*
All his hate	*accent*
All his labors	*accent*
Are with the people.	*no accent, continues 4/4*

302

SPEAKER:

All the air	*accent*
All the food	*accent*
All the trees	*accent*
All colors	*accent*
All sound	*accent*
And smell.	*accent, continues 4/4*

All the dreams	*accent*
All the demons	*accent*
All the saints	*accent*
All taboos	*accent*
All rewards	*accent*
Are with the people.	*no accent, continues*

The people named	*no accent*
All the stones	*accent*
All the birds	*accent*
All the fish	*accent*
All the plants.	*sudden stop, no sound, percussionists's arm frozen straight out, holding maracas through* SPEAKER'S *next stanza.*

He was honored.	*slight spasm of percussionist's wrist after each line*
He was dishonored.	
He was married.	
He became old.	
He became older.	*sudden drop of arm to floor with maracas, arm disappears behind* SPEAKER

This night.	*unseen, low tense pulsing sound of tapping on bongo, stretching head to achieve high and low tones.*
He goes to sleep in his same bed.	
This night.	
He falls to sleep in his same way.	
This night.	
This dream he dreams he's dreaming.	
This night.	

SPEAKER:
    A voice.   *continues bongo, mounting slightly*

    A voice comes.
    A voice speaks.
    A voice he's never heard.

                                  stops dead, no sound

(short staccato speech)
    You are entirely dead.   *no sound throughout stanza*
    What is unfinished is for-
       ever unfinished.
    What happened has hap-
       pened.
    You are entirely gone from
       the people.

    In a second he mourns for   *low roll on bongo, unseen*
       himself.
    For his whole life he mourns.

    In the next second he's en- *roll continues, stops abruptly on*
       tirely dead.   *the word "next," rests*

    In a second he mourns for   *roll starts up again*
       the others.
    For all the others he mourns.

    In the next second he's en- *stops again on "next," rests*
       tirely dead.

    In a second he forgets.   *roll starts again*
    All life with the people he
       forgets.

    In the next second he leaves. *deep resounding boom from Doum-*
                                bak, moves into tense, pulsing 6/8
                                time stretching skin

SPEAKER: *(short staccato speech continued)*
    His whole body he leaves.
    He leaves his whole body
       behind.   *abrupt stop with boom on Doum-*
                                  bak, silence, long rest as SPEAKER
                                breathes, the breathing leads him
                                into next voice

SPEAKER: (*worker's voice*)
   If I get this job. I hope I get this job. The other job I had I
just quit.

> *left hand of percussionist, visible
> to* SPEAKER'S *right, comes crash-
> ing down with small pipe striking
> a cast iron object, hand remains
> in place after striking*

You couldn't hear anybody talk. Soon as you walked into the
building.
You couldn't hear anybody. There was all this heat.

> *left hand of percussionist quickly
> disappears, sound of metallic rat-
> tling, pipe striking rim of tam-
> bourine, glass clinking, all unseen*

Noise. You had to get up just before the light. Everything dark in
the house. But this other job—this job I can sleep late. No noise.

> *again left hand of percussionist
> strikes down with pipe on* SPEAK-
> ER'S *right*

You get up in the light. You come home in the light. Not the
same risks. No danger of getting your hand crushed.

> *hand quickly disappears, sound of
> clacking wood and metal, unseen*

Pay's just as good. Get the same insurance. This new job I can
make something out of. I can move. Maybe work my way up
a little.

> *again left hand appears, crashes
> down, strikes iron object, then quick-
> ly snatches up a small African "Talk-
> ing Drum" with seeds inside, in
> quick, sweeping motion the arm holds
> the drum vertically, very straight so
> it's visible above* SPEAKER'S *head,
> freezes in that position*

SPEAKER: (*new mother's voice*)
   Everybody tried to prepare me. They told me how to breathe.
   How to relax. How to think about something else

They told me what kind of pain I'd have. How the spasms would come. How to deal with the pain. How to push. Nothing they told me was like this. I don't know whose skin this is. I touch the skin. Soft head. Is my hand the same skin. My fingers. I touch the head. Soft head. Just washed. Nothing they told me. This blood. This blood from me. Just washed. Nothing they told me was like this. Just born. My arm is his bed.

very slowly the percussionist's arm starts to describe a downward arc with the "Talking Drum" causing the seeds inside the drum to fall from one skin to the other, the sound is very light and soft like sand falling on dry leaves, the arm is kept straight throughout. when the arm reaches the very bottom of the arc, it fluidly reverses the action, again causing the seeds to make sound

arm comes down suddenly from vertical position, places drum down with a thud, arm disappears—unseen—free tempo is set up on several drums, voice joins, voice and percussion jam for short time evolving tempo of next voice which is very broken, stuttering, almost frantic feel to it. As soon as voice begins to manifest in words, the percussion shifts emphasis leaving gaps for the words to appear in and exchanging as though in conversation

SPEAKER: (*calling*)

Where— Let's see— Is this— Wait— Now— Listen— Now— No— Wait— Let's see— Is this— Is this the one? No— Just a minute. Wait just a minute. Just let me catch my breath. Now! No, just a minute. Just a minute more. Just wait. It'll come. Don't— Don't try to— It's not that it's lost. Not that it won't come back. It's just a temporary thing. Something— Something must have— It's not that I can't hear myself. I can hear myself. I CAN HEAR MYSELF NOW! There.

There it was. That was it. That was it just then. Just then. Just came out. Just like that. How could that be. How come it happened then and not now? WHY NOT NOW! Nothing to worry about. Sometimes these things just happen. Something loses something. Temporarily. It's not that big a deal. It's not like I'm not ever going to find my voice again. Ever again. Nothing as final as that. It's like a lapse. That's it. A little lapse. It's already coming back. I can feel a certain familiarity.

> *percussion shifts into very constant tapping meter, under voice, almost metronome feel*

Something in the tone. The patter. The turn of phrase. Before long I'll be recognizable to all those around me. I'll be heard in my familiar way. Even in the dark the others will know it's me. They'll call me by my name. I'll call them. They'll hear me saying their name. They'll say they know me. By my sound. Soon everything will be just like it always has been.

> *percussion continues tapping, fades slowly into silence, rest, no sound, next voice begins with no percussion*

SPEAKER: (*voice to a Blind One*)
In front of you is a window. About chest level. It's night out. In the window, in the glass, is your reflection. There's a small table to your right. About the height of your knees. On the table is a blue cup. The same cup you just drank from. On the wall are pictures from your past. One is a photograph. You as a boy. You standing in front of a cactus. You're wearing a red plaid shirt.

> *soft tone of a gong, one stroke, then a very faint high droning sound begins and builds slowly throughout speech but never dominates* SPEAKER'S *voice*

The walls around you are green. The paint is old. In places the paint is peeled away. Underneath it's white. There's a bed in the corner, with a Mexican blanket. A calendar hangs on the wall by the window. A lamp made from an Olive Oil can. Now there's the light of an airplane passing outside

the window. The night is absolutely black. The light of the
plane keeps passing slowly. Blinking. Red and blue. Yellow
and blue. Now it disappears. A star is blinking in its place.
You can't see the moon from here. Now, even the star disappears. A car goes by. Moths are plunging into the glass.
Tiny bugs crawl. Electricity fades then comes back. Everything else is still. Absolutely still. Nothing is moving now
except for your breath. Your chest. The shirt on your chest.
Your shirt is blue. Your glasses are black. A mosquito races
around your ear. The same mosquito you're hearing.

>   *the droning tone rings out into
>   silence, rest*

SPEAKER:

(*Hunger Dialogue—these next two voices are made very distinct from
each other in tone; for instance, sounding one voice in a high register
and the other low, almost dividing the* SPEAKER'S *voice in half, no
percussion to open*)

Would you like to go eat? Isn't it time to eat?

I don't mind.

We don't have to. It's up to you.

Didn't we eat already?

Did we?

I thought we did.

That was before. Wasn't it?

Yes. I think so. It must've been.

Well, we don't have to.

No. I don't mind.

Only if you're hungry. Are you hungry?

I must be.

I'm not all that hungry myself.

You're not?

SPEAKER:

No, not really. I mean I'd have something if you wanted something.

But you wouldn't eat if you were on your own?

No, I don't think so.

You'd just be eating for my sake?

Well, I'd have something with you. A little something.

Well I don't want to force you to have something if you're not hungry.

I'm a little bit hungry. Not enough for a full meal.

I'm famished!

> *very softly, sound of wood scraper, constant gnawing rhythm under voice*

You are?

Absolutely. Starved! I'm so hungry I could eat a house!

Well, why didn't you say something?

Because I thought you weren't hungry.

I'm always hungry. I was just being polite.

I'm so hungry I could eat a horse!

Well then we should eat!

Nothing I ate could satisfy this hunger I'm having right now!

Well let's find a place then.

This hunger knows no bounds! This hunger is eating me alive it's so hungry!

Just hang on! We'll find something.

> *gnawing rhythm picks up tempo and volume through next passage, both hands and arms of percussionist appear on right and left sides of* SPEAKER *playing wood*

*scraper gourd, this motion is a
large sweeping half circle so that
percussionist's arms appear to one
side, disappear behind* SPEAKER,
*then reappear on the other side
continuously.*

SPEAKER:

Nothing we find will satisfy it. Absolutely nothing. Whatever we find won't be enough. It will only subside. For
a little while. It won't disappear. It will come back. It
will be stronger when it comes back. It will devour everything in sight when it comes back. It will eat me alive
when it comes back. It will be ravenous when it comes
back. It will devour me whole when it comes back. It will
go through all the food in the world when it comes back.
It will go through all the possessions in the world when
it comes back. It will go through all the sex in the world
when it comes back. It will go through all the power in the
world when it comes back. It will go through all the ideas
in the world when it comes back. It will go through all
the goods in the world when it comes back. When it comes
back there'll be no stopping it when it comes back. When
it comes back there'll be no appeasing it when it comes
back. When it comes back there'll be nothing left but
the hunger itself when it comes back. Nothing left but the
hunger eating the hunger when it comes back. Nothing
left but the hunger eating itself. Nothing left but the
hunger.

*abrupt stop of voice and sound,
pause, sudden movement of percussionist's right arm jabbing out
horizontally, holding a string of
small, brass prayer bells which
dangle down, pause, wrist of percussionist makes a downward spasm
causing bells to jingle, arm remains horizontal, pause, again
spasm of wrist and bells jingle,
voice comes*

SPEAKER: (*Invocation*)
  Between the breath I'm breathing
    and the one that's coming

  Something tells me now

                percussion—spasm of wrist, bells jingle

  Between the space I'm leaving
    and the space I'm joining

  The dead one tells me now

                percussion—wrist repeats

  Between the shape I'm leaving
    and the one I'm becoming

  The departed tells me now

                percussion—wrist repeats

  Between the ear
    and the sound it hears

  A ghost one tells me now

                percussion—wrist repeats

  Between the face I'm making
    and the face that's coming

  A spirit tells me now

                percussion—wrist repeats

  Behind the voice that's speaking
    and the one that's thinking

  A dead one tells me now

                percussionist's arm crashes directly to floor as though suddenly released by voice, bells hit floor, hand releases bells and disappears behind SPEAKER

                immediate metronome cadence on wood block, unseen, constant underlying tempo

SPEAKER: (*Voice from Dead*)
There was this moment. This moment taking place. I tried to stop this moment. This can't happen now. I thought. This can't be going to happen. I thought. Not now. I thought. It's still possible to avoid it. I thought. It's not that this won't pass. I thought. Not that I won't still be here tomorrow. I thought. I will still be here tomorrow. I thought. It's inconceivable that I won't be. I thought.

> *full stop, short silence, then tempo resumes*

There was this moment. This moment where I vanished. This moment, where the whole of me vanished. The whole of my thoughts. Vanished. The whole of my feelings. Vanished. The whole of my self. Vanished. The whole of what I call my self. Vanished. The whole of my body was left.

> *percussion stops, pause, voice finishes without percussion*

SPEAKER:
There was this moment that passed. Taking me with it.

> *Pause—sudden rattle of mallet stick in cowbell, then silence, continuous single pulse on bongo sets in, broken intermittently by sudden urgent rattle of cowbell, then returns to single pulse on bongo under voice of* SPEAKER

SPEAKER: (*Inquiry to Dead One*)
Is this you in death?
If you are dead
why isn't there candles?

Is it you, dead?
If you are
then why isn't there tears?

Is it you posing as dead?
Where are the mourners?
The grief?

Is this really you appearing?
Again appearing?

SPEAKER:
    Are you asking me to believe it?
    What are you asking?

    Is this really you in death?
    Not as you were?
    Not as you once were?

    Am I knowing you differently now?
    Am I making you up?
    Conjuring up this shape of you?
    As I remember you once?
    Putting you back together.

    Is this me calling you up
    or are you appearing?
    Volunteering yourself?
    Beckoning?

    What are you asking?
    Can you tell me?
    Can you say that you know you're not here
    in this world
    in this world I'm speaking from?

> *voice stops, cowbell "talks" con-*
> *stantly now building into almost*
> *frantic persistence, as though trying*
> *to break through to the world of*
> *the voice*—SPEAKER'S *voice cuts the*
> *cowbell off as it breaks in, then*
> *percussion picks up quick, jagged*
> *rhythm of the voice, playing off*
> *different combinations of instru-*
> *ments*

SPEAKER: (*quick, halting rhythm*)
    I— There— I. Me. Me saying "I" to myself. That was me.
    Just then. That was it. Me. I speak. Me. No one else. That
    was me just then. Must've been. Who else? Why should I
    doubt it? Not me? Who else could it have been?

> *stop, short pause, percussion goes*
> *into 4/4 stop time on cymbal,*

*like Glenn Miller "Big Band"
sound, as voice sings in accompaniment*

SPEAKER: (*sings first verse straight*)
"From this moment on
you and me dear
only two for tea dear
from this moment on"

(*sings second verse in prolonged, exaggerated tones*)
"From this lucky day
I'll be flyin' high babe
from this moment on."

cymbal fades, short pause

SPEAKER: (*flat, monotonous tone*)
I'm writing you this today from a very great distance. Everything here is fine. I'm hoping everything there is fine with
you. I'm hoping you still miss me as much as you once did. I
know that I miss you as much as ever. I'm also hoping this
reaches you as soon as possible.

Something happened today which you might find amusing. I
know I found it amusing at the time. A dog came into the
hotel and ran around the lobby. Nobody knew what to do.
Everyone was in a stew.

Here's hoping this finds you in good health.

All my love,
Larry

sharp accent on cymbal

All the best,
Stuart

sharp accent on cymbal

Warm Regards,
Mel

ring on bell of cymbal

SPEAKER: (*flat, monotonous tone continued*)
                            Yours,

                                            Nat

                            flat punch, edge of cymbal

                            With fond wishes,
                                        Randy

                            let cymbal ring out

                            Sincerely,
                                        Mathew

                            flat accent, cymbal

                            Cordially,
                                            Josh

                            bright ring, cymbal

                            Your loving husband,
                                        Stanley

                            sharp splash, cymbal

                            Your oldest son,
                                        Tom

                            sharp accent, cymbal

                            Your faithful servant,
                                        Daniel Eric

                            sharp crash, cymbal

                            Respectfully,
                                        Mitchell Lewis Scott

                            very sharp accent, cymbal

                            Yours as always,
                                        Rebecca

                            cymbal rings out

                            Lovingly,
                                        Andrew

                            soft, bell tone, cymbal

SPEAKER:

>With all my heart,
>   Jacob
>
>*soft, short tone*
>
>Forever,
>   Lucille
>
>*loud crash, cymbal, silence—per-*
>*cussion begins deep, driving 6/8*
>*rhythm on hand drums (Conga,*
>*Doumbak), rhythm leads voice*
>*then fades and swells back again*
>*to foreground as voice continues*

SPEAKER: (*pompous voice*)

It's not often, actually, that I find myself at a loss for words. But in this particular instance I was left speechless. Absolutely numb. No words could even begin to describe the impact of it.

>   *drumming gains force but remains*
>   *in same tempo*

SPEAKER: (*public voice*)

I'm not here today to lay down the law to you people. On the contrary. I'm here so that you can openly voice your opinions. I'm here so that you can see that those opinions are not falling on deaf ears. I'm here so that we can join together in this struggle. So that we can unite. So that together we can bring about a resolution to this problem which has haunted us for more than a decade.

>   *percussion abruptly fades but con-*
>   *tinues a faint, pulsing rhythm be-*
>   *hind voice*

SPEAKER: (*to One about to Die*)

I don't know what to tell you exactly. I don't want to lie to you. I don't want to just make something up. I don't really know where you'll be going. That's the truth. I don't have any idea. It's all right to be afraid I guess. You don't have to be brave. Who says you have to be brave? I just wish I knew what to tell you. I could make something up. Should I make something up? All right. I might as well.

*percussion stops pulsing rhythm,
hands move quickly and snatch up
large sleigh bells, held in both
hands, the bells are shook in con-
stant arcing motion exactly the
same as the movement with the
scraping gourd accompanying the
"voices of hunger," bells continue
through next section*

SPEAKER:
   When you die
      you go straight to Heaven or Hell.
   When you die
      you disintegrate into energy.
   When you die
      you're re-born into another body.
   When you die
      you turn to shit.
   When you die
      you travel to other planets.
   When you die
      you get to start all over.
   When you die
      you get marked in the book.
   When you die
      you're re-joined with your ancestors.
   When you die
      all your dreams will come true.
   When you die
      you'll speak to the Angels.
   When you die
      you'll get what you deserve.
   When you die
      it's absolutely final.
   When you die
      you never come back.
   When you die
      you die forever.
   When you die
      it's the end of your life.

*bells stop, percussionist's right arm
is extended vertically to the left of
SPEAKER, holding a tambourine,
very slowly the arm describes an
arc to the right side of the SPEAKER,
as it drops the tambourine makes
a slight tinkle, simultaneously with
his left hand the percussionist softly
strikes a cymbal, this action is
continuous but timed so that the
sound of the tambourine and cymbal occur between the lines of the
SPEAKER*

SPEAKER: (*talk song, simple voice, direct*)
Today the wind roared through the center of town.
   Tonight I hear its voice.

percussion—soft

Today the river lay wide open to the sun.
   Tonight I hear it speaking.

percussion—soft

Today the moon remained in the sky.
   Tonight I feel it moving.

percussion—soft

Today the people talked without speaking.
   Tonight I can hear what they're saying.

percussion—soft

Today the tree bloomed without a word.
   Tonight I'm learning its language.

*no percussion, arms stay frozen,
silence, blackout*

SAVAGE-LOVE

by Sam Shepard and Joseph Chaikin

NOTE: *When Sam Shepard and I decided to work in close collabora-*
tion on a new theater piece, we wrote one another and talked on the
telephone between New York and California to make plans and express
first thoughts. Before meeting, we decided that our piece should be about
romantic love and about the closeness and distance between lovers. Our
agreement at the outset was to meet for three weeks to compose the piece.
At the end of the three weeks, we would perform both the new piece and
"Tongues" for a public audience in San Francisco.

We each felt that we wanted the piece to be easily and readily
identifiable, not esoteric. We felt it should be made up of love moments
which were as immediately familiar to most people in the audience as
they were to Sam and me. Although we had known each other for many
years, we had never talked about this subject. When we began to talk
and work, even though we each had very different stories, we found that
we shared many thoughts about the human experience of love. We talked
especially about the difficulty of expressing tenderness, and the dread of
being replaced.

The first step was to choose the moments, and then to speak from
within those moments. A "moment" could be the first instant of meeting
the lover, or it could be the experience of lovers sleeping next to one
another, with one a little bit awake watching the other one sleep.
Unlike our approach to "Tongues," I would improvise around or
inside a moment; Sam would write. We would later discuss and try
things.

During the last days of our work together, Harry Mann, who played
various horns, Skip LaPlante, who played home-made instruments as
well as a bass fiddle, and Ruth Kreshka, a stage manager, joined us.
Their presence, sounds and responses affected and changed the final
form of the piece.

As we moved toward performance, I became the actor looking for the body and gesture for each of the different movements.

We argued about the title. Sam continually defended "Savage/Love." I found something wrong with it each time I spoke and heard it. But by the second or third public performance, I felt the power and appropriateness of these two words.

"Savage/Love": common poems of real and imagined moments in the spell of love.

March 16, 1981   JOSEPH CHAIKIN

FIRST MOMENT

The first moment
I saw you in the Post Office
You saw me
And I didn't know.

The first moment
I saw you
I knew I could love you
If you could love me

You had sort of a flavor
The way you looked
And you looked at me
And I didn't know if you saw me
And there wasn't any question to ask

I was standing with some papers
I started shuffling the papers
But I didn't know what order to put them in

But I figured I wanted to do it in such a way
That it looked like I had some purpose

But I really just wanted to look at your eyes all the time

And you said
Look at me with your eyes
Look at me with your eyes

In that first moment
Your face burned into my dream
And right away I had this feeling
Maybe you're lost
Until now

Maybe I'm lost
Until now

And I thought
Maybe I'm just making this up

But your eyes
Looked like they were saying
Look at me more

I would shuffle the papers
Look at you
My breathing changed

Then I felt something dissolve
I felt there might be a danger
That anything could happen in the next moment
Maybe you would turn away from me

Or you could say
Let's go together
Forever

LISTENING FACES

When we sat across from each other
In the place where we met
You talked about your days by the water

                    face listens

You talked about yourself as a child

                    face listens

When we were lying next to each other
You told me your fear of the night
Of every night

face listens

You imagined moving to your ideal country

face listens

You told me secrets about people in your life
Strangers

face listens

You showed me their pictures

face

You played me your favorite music
I couldn't hear the music in it

TANGLED UP

When we're tangled up in love
Is it me you're whispering to
Or some other

When we're tangled up in sleep
Is it my leg you feel your leg against
Or is it Paul Newman's leg.

When I move my eyes like this
Is it causing you to think of Marlon Brando

When we're tangled up in meeting other people
Is it me you're introducing
Or is it Warren Beatty

When I stand with my body facing in one direction
And my head in the other
Do you think of Mick Jagger

If you could only give me a few clues
I could invent the one you'd have me be

BABBLE (ONE)

I
Uh
I wanna' show
Um
Some thing
SSSomething
That uh
Some
Something tender
That
Comes from you
Uh
I
Can't
My words
Won't
Find
I wanna'
Bring something out
That
Some
But
Uh
It doesn't fit this time

TERMS OF ENDEARMENT

What can I call you
Can I call you "Honey"
Or "Sweetie Pie"

Can I call you "My Treasure"
Or "Precious One"

Or can I call you "Babe"
  Or maybe I could call you "Darling"
Can I call you "Darling"

I heard someone else call someone "Angel" once
Can I try "Angel"

Can I call you "Sweetheart"
Or "Sugar"

Or maybe I could call you "Love"
Just "Love"

KILLING

It was in one moment
When we looked
When we saw each other
That I killed you

I saw you lying there
Unmourned

You didn't know
I didn't say I saw you dead

I saw you thinking of something else
You couldn't see
The thing I'd done to you

HOW I LOOK TO YOU

When I sit like this
Do you see me brave

Do I make a mystery for you
When I put on a gaze

When I stretch my arms like this
Do you see me sensual

When I look relaxed
Do you believe me

When I'm acting interested in your words
Do you believe I'm completely interested

Which presentation of myself
Would make you want to touch
What would make you cross the border

BEGGAR

Could you give me a small part of yourself
I'm only asking for the tiniest part
Just enough to get me from here to there

Could you give me something
Anything at all
I'll accept whatever it is

Could you just put your hand on my head
Could you brush against my arm
Could you just come near enough
So I could feel as though you might be able to hold me

Could you touch me with your voice
Blow your breath in my direction

Is it all right if I look straight into your face

Could I just walk behind you for a little while
Would you let me follow you at a distance

If I had anything of value I'd gladly give it to you
If there's anything of me you want just take it

But don't think I'm this way with everybody
I almost never come to this
In fact usually it's the other way around

There's lots of people
Who would love to even have a conversation with me
Who even ask me if they can walk behind me

So don't get any ideas that I'm completely alone
Because I'm not

In fact you're the one who looks like you could use a little
  company

Where do you get off thinking you have anything to give me
  anyway

I have everything I need
And what I don't have I know where to get it
Any time I want

In the middle of the night
In the middle of the afternoon
Five o'clock in the morning

In fact I'm wasting my time right now
Just talking to you

> *Hums*
> *A capella, melody line only*
> *no words*

"I'm in the mood for love"

HAUNTED

I'm haunted by your scent
When I'm talking to someone else

I'm haunted by your eyes
In the middle of brushing my teeth

I'm haunted by your hair
By your skin
When you're not around

Are you visiting me

Am I dreaming you up

SAVAGE

YOU
Who makes me believe that we're lovers
YOU
Who lets me pretend
YOU
Who reminds me of myself
YOU
Who controls me
YOU
My accomplice
YOU
Who tells me to lie
YOU
Who is acting as though we're still in the first moment
YOU
Who leads me to believe we're forever in love
Forever in love

ACTING

Now we're acting the partners in love
Now we're acting the estrangement
Now we're acting the reconciliation
Now we're acting that the reconciliation was a success
Now we're acting that our love has been deepened by the crisis
Now we're acting that we're both in endless harmony
Now we're acting that one of us has been injured
But we're not saying which one
Now one of us is acting the pain of premonition
Now we are acting the leaving
Now I see you in anguish
Now I watch you leaving
Now I feel nothing

Sings:

"The thrill is gone
 The thrill is gone
 I can see it in your eyes
 I can hear it in your sighs
 Feel your touch and realize
 The thrill is gone"

ABSENCE

You who are not here
You who are missing in my body
Holes in my body
Places like holes
Like bullets made
Patches of agony
Swimming
From my feet
To my hands

You who are gone
Missing from the place you lived in me
Instead of blood
Hollow veins
The groin is locked
You
The missing part of me
You
That disappeared

THE HUNT

I've lost 15 pounds for you
I've dyed my hair brown for you
I've designed a special smile for you
But I haven't met you yet

I've bought a flashy shirt for you
I've plucked my eyebrows out for you
I've covered myself in Musk Oil for you
I'm still hunting around for you

I've changed my walk for you
I've even changed my talk for you
I've changed my entire point of view for you
I hope we'll find each other soon

KILLING

It was in a moment we were together
The murder took place
Without any weapon
It took place
Between two moments
In no time

It was in a moment
Between two thoughts
When the murder took place
Without any weapons

I wasn't sure which one of us was killed

WATCHING THE SLEEPING LOVER

I wake up
Only a little ways
Out of sleep

You look like my child
Breathe
Helpless sleeper
Frightened of your dreams
Separation of sleep

I breathe with you
Breathe the same way
See how it is to be you
Sleeping

I feel like a detective
Spying
Your sleeping body

I'm not very far from sleep
Your dream changes
Your lips move

Talking to it
In words I've never heard

Then comes a longing
That I don't understand
Because it feels like it's towards you
But here you are
So I don't understand
What this longing's for

I embrace you in sleep
My arm moves with your breathing
Your breath makes my arm rise and fall

For one moment I think of the killing
Still
Frozen

I'm confused by the yearning
I want to have your dreams inside me
I want to strangle your dreams
Inside me

As the light comes through
And the night is turning into day
I want to know I'll die before you
I want to know I'll die before
We aren't lovers anymore

SALVATION

Now that I'm with you I'm saved
From all grief

Now that I'm with you I'm saved
From being in parts

Now that I'm with you I'm saved
From hoping for anything else

Now that I'm with you I'm saved
From all other wanting

BABBLE (TWO)

I
Can't
Uh
What
I want
What
The
The thing of it is
I
Some
Kind
Some kind of
Something
Won't
Come
Out
The
Way
I
Uh

Nothing
Seems
To
Uh
Fit
The
Expression
That
I
Uh
Um
Want
Won't
Uh
Come

HOAX

Even though you see it's a hoax
We continue as though it isn't

Even though we're duped
We agree to continue

OPENING

Sometimes I would want to reach
My arm would start
Something in my arm would start

Sometimes I would almost reach
Something near my neck would move
And then come back

I wanted something on my face to show
Some sign

Unlock my face
Instead I lock my arms

The head would nod
While you spoke
I wasn't sure about the head
Wasn't sure what it was saying
While I listened
Wasn't sure what you saw it saying
Agreeing or denying

I wanted my mouth to move
To carry something across
Some sign
One eye was going with it

Is this the face that shows me

It was a moment I wanted to be strong
Through the chest
It fell
You saw it falling
I went on as though you didn't
I brought it back

I was wanting to be clear through the hands
While the voice kept talking
I held my face together
My mouth on my hand
Then it dropped
My hands held each other

All the time you saw me

My whole body began to shudder
Everything began to shudder
Nothing would hold still

You tried to show me you didn't see me shaking

You took my hand away from me
And everything stopped

From your fingers I returned
You
You
You
You
repeats

(*Light fades to black*)

—END—